THE COMMON LAW LIBRARY

CHITTY
ON
CONTRACTS

Second Cumulative Supplement
to the
Twenty-Ninth Edition

Up-to-date to July 31, 2005

LONDON
SWEET & MAXWELL
2005

Published in 2005 by
Sweet & Maxwell Limited of
100 Avenue Road
http://www.sweet██████████.uk
Typeset by Interactive Sciences Limited, Gloucester
Printed in Great Britain by MPG Books Limited, Cornwall

A CIP catalogue record for this book is available from the British Library

ISBN Main Work (full set)   0 421 842601
ISBN Supplement   0 421 912308

No natural forests were destroyed to make this product,
only farmed timber was used and re-planted.

[iii]

C. G. J. MORSE, B.C.L., M.A.
of the Middle Temple, Barrister; Professor of Law,
King's College London

D. D. PRENTICE, LL.B., J.D., M.A.
of Lincoln's Inn, Barrister; Fellow of Pembroke College and Allen & Overy
Professor of Corporate Law in the University of Oxford

F. M. B. REYNOLDS, Q.C. (Hon.), D.C.L., F.B.A.
Honorary Bencher of the Inner Temple; Emeritus Fellow of Worcester College
and Professor of Law Emeritus in the University of Oxford

SIR GUENTER TREITEL, Q.C., D.C.L., F.B.A.
Honorary Bencher of Gray's Inn; Formerly Vinerian Professor of English Law
in the University of Oxford

JOHN UFF, C.B.E., Q.C., Ph.D., B.Sc., F.I.C.E., F.C.I.Arb., F.R.Eng.
Bencher of Gray's Inn; Recorder; Emeritus Professor of Engineering Law, King's
College, London

G. J. VIRGO, M.A. (Cantab.), B.C.L. (Oxon)
of Lincoln's Inn, Barrister; Reader in English Law in the University of
Cambridge and Fellow of Downing College Cambridge

R. P. WHISH, B.A., B.C.L. (Oxon)
Solicitor of the Supreme Court of Judicature; Professor of Law,
King's College, London

S. J. WHITTAKER, B.C.L., M.A., D.PHIL.
of Lincoln's Inn, Barrister; Fellow of St John's College and Reader in
European Comparative Law in the University of Oxford

HOW TO USE THIS SUPPLEMENT

This is the Second Cumulative Supplement to the Twenty-Ninth Edition of *Chitty on Contracts*, and has been compiled according to the structure of the two main work volumes.

At the beginning of each chapter of this Supplement the mini table of contents from the main volume has been included. Where a heading in this table of contents has been marked with a square pointer, this indicates that there is relevant information in the Supplement to which the reader should refer. Material that is new to the Cumulative Supplement is indicated by the symbol □. Material that has been included from the previous Supplement is indicated by the symbol ■.

Within each chapter, updating information is referenced to the relevant paragraph in the main volume.

It should be noted, however, that for this Supplement there is no material for chapters 17 and 20.

TABLE OF CONTENTS

VOLUME I

PART SIX—JOINT OBLIGATIONS, THIRD PARTIES AND ASSIGNMENT

PART SEVEN—PERFORMANCE AND DISCHARGE

PART EIGHT—REMEDIES FOR BREACH OF CONTRACT

PART NINE—RESTITUTION

PART TEN—CONFLICT OF LAWS

VOLUME II

TABLE OF STATUTES

Where a reference indicates significant discussion of the statute in the text, it is in **bold**. Where a reference is to a footnote, it is *italic*.

TABLE OF STATUTORY INSTRUMENTS

Where a reference indicates significant discussion of the statutory instrument in the text, it is in **bold**. Where a reference is to a footnote, it is *italic*.

TABLE OF NON-UK STATUTORY MATERIAL

Where a reference indicates significant discussion of the legislation in the text, it is in **bold**.
Where a reference is to a footnote, it is *italic*.

TABLE OF CASES

Where a reference indicates significant discussion of the case in the text, it is in **bold**. Where a reference is to a footnote, it is *italic*.

TABLE OF EUROPEAN CASES

Where a reference indicates significant discussion of the case in the text, it is in **bold**. Where a reference is to a footnote, it is *italic*.

[xlix]

VOLUME I

GENERAL PRINCIPLES

Part One

INTRODUCTION

CHAPTER 1

INTRODUCTORY

2. CENTRAL PRINCIPLES OF CONTRACT LAW

(c) *A principle of good faith or of contractual fairness?*

No general principle of good faith

1–020   [*Add new text to note 152: page* [19]]
See similarly *Bernhard Schulte GHBH & Co KG v Nile Holdings Ltd* [2004]
EWHC 977; [2005] 1 A.C. 503 at [113].

Fairness relevant: (2) Implied terms

1–026   [*Add to note 178: page* [23]]
Eastwood v Magnox Electric plc [2004] UKHL 35; [2005] 1 A.C. 503 at
[4]–[6].

3. THE HUMAN RIGHTS ACT 1998 AND CONTRACTS

(a) *Contracts made before October 2, 2000*

(i) *The construction and review of legislation governing contracts*

The impact of sections 3 and 4 of the 1998 Act on accrued contractual rights

1–032   [*Add to text at end of paragraph: page* [27]]
On the other hand, in *PW & Co v Milton Gate Investments Ltd*[215a] Neuberger
J. was prepared to accept that s.3 of the Human Rights Act could apply to an
issue arising from a lease made before its coming into force. There, the learned
judge had held that, apart from the operation of s.3, the exercise of a "break
clause" in a head tenancy did not determine the sub-tenancies entered into by the
tenant as permitted under the head-lease even though the head-landlord was
unable to recover rent under the sub-tenancy covenants.[215b] Having referred to a
number of passages in the speeches of their lordships in *Wilson v First County
Trust (No.2)*,[215c] Neuberger J. concluded that their reasoning did not preclude the
application of ss.3 or 4 of the 1998 Act to issues arising out of contracts made
before its coming into force as long as this did not impair "vested rights" or
otherwise create unfairness.[215d] In particular, he noted as "very much in point"
Lord Scott of Foscote's reference in *Wilson's* case to the example of the impact
of legislation intervening between the creation of a lease and its expiry where the
legislation could affect the rights and obligations arising under the transaction.[215e] On the facts before him, Neuberger J. considered that 'the earliest that
any "vested rights" could be said to have arisen under [the break clause in the
head-lease], was the date of the service of the Notice under that clause. Unless
and until [the break clause] was operated, the rights and obligations of any of the
parties as a result of the exercise were merely contingent and not vested.'[215f]

Since this notice had been served after the coming into force of section 3 of the 1998 Act there were no vested rights at the relevant time so as to prevent its operation on the legislative provisions whose application allegedly prejudiced the head-landlord's right to property under article 1 of the First Protocol of the European Convention. Moreover, in the learned judge's view, it was not more generally unfair to apply section 3 in this way even though the notice had been served only four days after its coming into force given, in particular, that the 1998 Act had been on the Statute Book for around two years before it came into force.[215g]

[215a] [2003] EWHC 1994 (Ch); [2003] All E.R. (D) 58 (Aug).
[215b] *ibid.*, at [103]–[104].
[215c] [2003] UKHL 40; [2004] 1 A.C. 816.
[215d] *ibid.*, at [107]–[115].
[215e] [2003] UKHL 40 at [161]; [2003] EWHC 1994 (Ch) at [110] and [114].
[215f] [2003] EWHC 1994 (Ch) at [114].
[215g] *ibid.*, at [115].

(b) *Contracts made on or after October 2, 2000*

(i) *The construction and review of legislation governing contracts*

Other examples

[*Add to text at end of paragraph*: page [32]]   **1–041**

Moreover, in *PW & Co v Milton Gate Investments Ltd*[255a] Neuberger J. accepted the argument of a head-landlord that the effect of ss.139 or 141 of the Law of Property Act 1925 should and could be interpreted so as to prevent the head-landlord from being deprived of rent under the covenants of sub-tenancies which had not determined by the exercise of a "break clause" by the head-tenant. In these circumstances, Art.1 of the First Protocol to the European Convention was engaged: if the underleases would survive the determination of the headlease without the tenant's covenants being enforceable, the head-landlord would be kept out of the premises in question for the remainder of the sub-leases without being able to recover any rent whatever. "That is scarcely 'peaceful enjoyment of [its] possessions.' "[255b]

In *Ghaidan v Godin Mendoza*[255c] a majority of the House of Lords relied on s.3 of the Human Rights Act 1998 to "read and give effect" to the provisions of the Rent Act 1977[255d] which grants a statutory tenancy to "[t]he surviving spouse (if any) of the original tenant if residing in the dwelling-house immediately before the death of the original tenant" so as to include homosexual cohabitees so as to give effect to their Convention right not to be discriminated against on the ground of sexual orientation in respect of their right to respect for a person's home.[255e] In doing so, their Lordships made a number of important observations on the ambit of the obligation imposed by s.3 of the 1998 Act.[255f]

[255a] [2003] EWHC 1994 (Ch); [2004] Ch. 142.
[255b] *ibid.*, at [126] *per* Neuberger J.
[255c] [2004] UKHL 30; [2004] 2 A.C. 557.
[255d] Rent Act 1977, Sch.I, paras 2 and 3 (as amended).
[255e] European Convention on Human Rights Arts.8 and 14.

²⁵⁵ᶠ [2004] UKHL 30 esp. [25]–[35] *per* Lord Nicholls of Birkenhead; [38]–[51] *per* Lord Steyn; [104]–[124] *per* Lord Rodger of Earlsferry; *cf.* [57]–[72] *per* Lord Millett (dissenting).

(ii) *Contracts made by "public authorities"*

"Public authorities" within the meaning of section 6 of the 1998 Act

1–042   In *Aston Cantlow and Wilmcote with Billesley Parochial Church Council v Wallbank* [2003] UKHL 37; [2004] 1 A.C. 546 the House of Lords considered what is meant by "public authority" and "functions of a public nature" within the meaning of s.6(1) and 6(3) of the Human Rights Act 1998 respectively. It held that the purpose of s.6(1) is that those bodies for whose acts the state is answerable before the European Court of Human Rights shall in future be subject to a domestic law obligation not to act incompatibly with Convention rights ([2003] UKHL 37 at [6], [7], [52], [88]) and that the phrase "a public authority" for the purpose of s.6(1) is therefore "essentially a reference to a body whose nature is governmental in the broad sense of the expression:" *ibid.*, at [7], [88], [171]. The House of Lords futhermore accepted the distinction between " 'core' or 'standard' public authorities" and " 'hybrid' public authorities" for the purposes of s.6: [2003] UKHL 37 at [8]–[11], [35], [85]. " 'Core' public authorities" were persons all of whose functions are of a public character, it being important to recall for this purpose that such persons are not themselves able to *claim* the benefit of Convention rights: *ibid.*, at [85] and [8] respectively. As regards " 'hybrid' public authorities", which exercise both public functions and non-public functions, there is no single test as to determining whether or not a particular function is "public" within the meaning of s.6(3)(b), though factors to be taken into account include "the extent to which in carrying out the relevant function the body is publicly funded, or is exercising statutory powers, or is taking the place of central government or local authorities, or is providing a public service": *ibid.*, at [12]. In this respect, although the domestic case law on judicial review may provide some assistance as to what does and does not constitute a "function of a public nature" within the meaning of s.6(3)(b), this case law must be examined in the light of the jurisprudence of the European Court of Human Rights as to those bodies which engage the responsibility of the state for the purposes of the Convention: *ibid.*, at [52].

In *R. (West) v Lloyd's of London* [2004] EWCA Civ 506; [2004] 3 All E.R. 251, the Court of Appeal held that decisions by Lloyd's of London under powers contained in its byelaws to approve minority buy-outs of four syndicates of which the applicant was a member (and which he complained were prejudicial to his rights of due process and of possession of this property under Art.6 of the Convention and under Art.1 to its First Protocol) were not subject to challenge by way of judicial review, whether by virtue of s.6 of the 1998 Act or more generally. In the view of the Court of Appeal, the relationship between Lloyd's and its members was entirely voluntary and contractual and their rights to participate in a syndicate governed exclusively by the terms of their contracts with their managing agents: [2004] EWCA Civ 506 at [8]–[9]. As regards judicial review generally, the decisions were solely concerned with the commercial relationship between the applicant and the relevant managing agents and were therefore of a private and not of a public nature, a position not affected by the fact that Lloyd's was constituted by private Act of Parliament: *ibid.*, at

[30]–[31]. And applying the approach of the House of Lords in *Wallbank*, the Court of Appeal held for the purposes of s.6 of the 1998 Act that the objectives of Lloyd's were "wholly commercial" and "not governmental even in the broad sense of that expression": it was rather the Financial Services Authority acting under the Financial Services and Markets Act 2000 "which is the governmental organisation which will be answerable to the Strasbourg court": *ibid.*, at [38] *per* Brooke L.J.

(iv) *Contractual confidentiality and section 12 of the 1998 Act*

Its impact on duties of confidentiality

[*note 307: page* [40]]   **1–056**
    Lady Archer v Williams [2003] EWHC 1670 is reported at [2003] E.M.L.R. 38.

5. Contracts Contained In Deeds

(a) *Form and Delivery*

Legislative reform of the requirements for the due execution and delivery of deeds

The legislative provisions described in the Main Work at paras 1–077–1–082   **1–077–** relating to contracts contained in deeds were themselves reformed by the Reg-   **1–082** ulatory Reform (Execution of Deeds and Documents) Order 2005 ((SI 2005/1906), made under the Regulatory Reform Act 2001, s.1, "the 2005 Order") so as to give effect to the principal recommendations of the Law Commission in its report *The Execution of Deeds and Documents by or on behalf of Bodies Corporate*, Law Com. No. 253 (1998). These amendments came into force as regards instruments executed on or after September 15, 2005, but leave unaffected any instrument executed before this date: 2005 Order, art.1(2). As a result, the law described in the Main Work still applies to contracts contained in deeds made up to and including September 14, 2005, but applies only as amended by the 2005 Order as regards contracts contained in deeds made on or after September 15, 2005. For this reason, this Supplement will first set out any amendments made to the existing paragraphs of the Main Text which govern instruments made on or before September 14, 2005, and then in the following paragraphs (which will be numbered as 1–082A *et seq.*) will describe the amended law in the present tense, this law governing instruments made on or after September 15, 2005.

The general abolition of the requirement of sealing

[*Delete paragraph 1–077 and replace with new paragraphs 1–077 and 1–077A: pages* [49]–[50]]
    Recent legislative history. In 1989, legislation was introduced which abol-   **1–077** ished the ancient requirement of sealing for the execution of the deeds in many situations.[397] As regards deeds executed by an individual, the requirement of

sealing was replaced with requirements that the intention of the party making a deed should make this intention clear on its face, of signature[398] by that party and of attestation.[399] As regards companies incorporated under the Companies Acts, the requirement of sealing for the execution of *documents*[400] was supplemented by an alternative method of execution of a document which required signature by a director and the secretary of the company or by two directors and the expression "in whatever form of words" that it was executed by the company; and it was further provided that where a document made clear on its face that it was intended to be a *deed* it should take effect on delivery as a deed, delivery being rebuttably presumed where it was so executed.[401] In the case of deeds executed by other persons (including other corporations aggregate and corporations sole), the common law requirement of sealing was left unaffected. However, in 2005 further (prospective) amendments were made to this position by an order ("the 2005 Order") made under the Regulatory Reform Act 2001.[401a] The main changes concern: (i) the creation of standard requirements for companies incorporated under the Companies Act 1985 (companies) and corporations aggregate[401b] (but not corporations sole[401c]) for the due execution of instruments in general and of deeds in particular[401d]; (ii) the making of specific provision for the execution of documents by persons (including companies and corporations aggregate) by or on behalf of another person (whether the latter is an individual, a company within the meaning of the Companies Act or a corporation)[401e]; and (iii) the clarification that the mere sealing of a document by a person (whether an individual or another corporate body) does not in itself satisfy the so-called "face-value requirement" that "an instrument shall not be a deed unless . . . it makes clear on its face that it is intended to be a deed by the person making it".[401f]

[397] On the ancient requirement see Sheppard's *Touchstone of Common Assurances* (7th ed., 1820), p.56.

[398] This requirement had been imposed by the Law of Property Act 1925, s.73.

[399] Law of Property (Miscellaneous Provisions) Act 1989, s.1.

[400] Companies Act 1985, s.36A(2).

[401] Companies Act 1985, s.36A(4) and (5).

[401a] Regulatory Reform (Execution of Deeds and Documents) Order 2005 (SI 2005/1906).

[401b] A corporation aggregate may be defined as consisting of "a body of persons which is recognised by the law as having a personality which is distinct from the separate personalities of the members of the body or the personality of the individual holder of the office in question for the time being": Law Com. No.253 para.4.1 n.1 referring to *Halsbury's Laws of England* (4th ed., reissue, 1998) Vol.9(2), para.1005.

[401c] A corporation sole may be defined as consisting of "one person and his or her successors in some particular office or status, who are incorporated in law in order to give them certain legal capacities and advantages which they would not have in their natural person": Law Com. No.253 para.4.23 referring to *Halsbury's Laws of England* (4th ed., reissue, 1998) Vol.9(2), para.1007.

[401d] Below, para.1–082E.

[401e] Below, para.1–082C.

[401f] Law of Property (Miscellaneous Provisions) Act 1989, s.1(2)(a) and see below, para. 1–082B.

1–077A   **The prospective effect of the 2005 changes.** The 2005 Order provides that it shall come into force on September 15, 2005.[401g] The Order further provides that its provisions "shall not apply to any *instrument executed* before the date on which this Order comes into force."[401h] This raises the question as to how this provision applies to changes contained in the Order to the law governing the making of *deeds*.[401i] It could be thought that a deed (the "instrument") is "executed" only after its delivery and not merely after the making of the document as only on delivery is the deed a valid instrument. However, it is submitted that the Order (following the Law Commission's recommendation[401j]) distinguishes clearly between the formal requirements required for the execution of an instrument (or document) and the further requirement for the execution of an instrument *as a deed* of delivery[401k] and that this argues for the temporal application of the new amendments contained in the Order to apply only to *documents executed* on or after September 15, 2005, and not also to documents executed as deeds on or before September 14, 2005, but delivered as deeds only after this date. This interpretation also has the practical advantage of not applying the amendments contained in the Order governing the execution of documents retrospectively to this albeit limited category of case.

[401g] The 2005 Order, art.1(1) (this being 12 weeks from June 23, 2005, the day on which the Order was made).

[401h] *ibid.*, art.1(2) (emphasis added).

[401i] *cf.* the discussion in Law Com. No.253, paras 3.6–3.12 as to the confusion over whether the term "executed" in the Companies Act 1985, s.36A, the Law of Property Act 1925, s.74 and the Law of Property (Miscellaneous Provisions) Act 1989, s.1 included "delivery".

[401j] Law Com. No.253, para.3.12.

[401k] See notably, the 2005 Order, arts 4, 6 and below, para.1–082E.

[Insert new heading before paragraph 1–080: page [51]]

(i) *Deeds executed on or before September 14, 2005*

Deeds executed by companies incorporated under the Companies Acts

[Delete first sentence and replace text at the beginning of the paragraph: page [51]]   **1–080**
In 1989, the law governing the execution of documents and deeds by companies incorporated under the Companies Acts was amended so as to create a "dual system".[410a] So, while it preserved the possibility for a company to execute a document (including a deed) by the affixing of its common seal,[411] it also provided that a document signed by a director and secretary, or by two directors, of a company incorporated under the Act and expressed to be executed by the company has the same effect as if executed under the common seal of the company and notwithstanding that the company has no common seal.[412] In either case, it is provided that a "document executed by a company which makes clear on its face that it is intended by the person or persons making it to be a deed has effect, upon delivery, as a deed."[413]

[410a] Law Commission, *The Execution of Deeds and Documents by or on behalf of Bodies Corporate*, Law Com. No.253 (1998), para.3.3.

[411] Companies Act 1985, s.36A(4) as inserted by Companies Act 1989, s.130(2).

[412] Companies Act 1985, s.36A(3) as inserted by Companies Act 1989, s.130(2).

[413] *ibid.*, s.36A(5).

Delivery

1–082   [*Delete text of note 430 from "Once a document" to the end: page* [52] *and insert new text*]

In *Bolton Metropolitan B.C. v Torkington* [2003] EWCA Civ 1634; [2004] Ch. 66 the Court of Appeal held that while s.74(1) of the Law of Property Act 1925 deemed a deed "duly executed" where a corporation's seal is affixed in the presence of and attested by its designated officers, it created no presumption as to its delivery: *ibid.* at [22], [45]. Moreover, while it was not necessary on the facts to decide the point, in Peter Gibson L.J.'s view, at common law "to describe the sealing by a corporation as giving rise to a rebuttable presumption may go too far, implying, as that does, that the burden is on the corporation affixing the seal": *ibid.* at [46]. Where, as on the facts before the court, negotiations were undertaken towards a lease expressly subject to contract, a court should not infer an intention to be bound from the mere sealing of a deed of execution of a lease: *ibid.*, at [53]. On the other hand, in the case of a company incorporated under the Companies Act 1985, where a document makes it clear on its face that "it is intended by the person or persons making it to be a deed . . . it shall be presumed, unless a contrary intention is proved, to be delivered upon its being so executed": Companies Act 1985 s.36A(5) as inserted by the Companies Act 1989, s.130(2).

[*Insert new heading after paragraph 1–082, and new paragraphs 1–082A–1–082H: page* [52]]

(ii) *Deeds executed on or after September 15, 2005*

1–082A   **The new general requirements for all deeds after the 2005 Order.** Under s.1(2) of the Law of Property (Miscellaneous Provisions) Act 1989 (as amended by the 2005 Order[431a]), an instrument shall not be a deed unless —

(a) it makes clear on its face that it is intended to be a deed by the person making it or, as the case may be, by the parties to it (whether by describing itself as a deed or expressing itself to be executed to be signed as a deed or otherwise); and

(b) it is validly executed as a deed

   (i) by that person or a person authorised to execute it in the name or on behalf of that person, or

   (ii) by one or more of those parties or a person authorised to execute it in the name or on behalf of one or more of those parties.

These requirements apply to *all* instruments whether executed by an individual, by a company incorporated under the Companies Act 1985, by a corporation aggregate, or by a corporate sole. However, even after the reforms of 2005, the significance and impact of these provisions differ somewhat according to these different categories of person. In this respect, a distinction is to be drawn between the condition contained in s.1(2)(a) (the so-called "face value requirement") and the condition in s.1(2)(b) of "valid execution".

^{431a} Regulatory Reform (Execution of Deeds and Documents) Order 2005 (SI 2005/1906), art.7(3).

The "face value requirement" for deeds. The reforms of 1989 introduced **1–082B** the idea that an instrument should qualify as a deed by reference to the intention of the party or parties to it as made clear on its face.^{431b} This change itself reflected earlier developments in judicial attitudes to the common law requirement of sealing, the courts adopting an approach which saw this requirement as satisfied where any evidence on the face of an instrument showed that it was intended to be executed as a deed.^{431c} Following the Law Commission's recommendations,^{431d} this face-value requirement was retained in 2005, though its formulation was clarified and standardised for instruments executed by individuals and companies.^{431e} In particular, it is now expressly provided that "an instrument shall not be taken to make it clear on its face that it is intended to be a deed merely because it is executed under seal."^{431f}

^{431b} Law of Property (Miscellaneous Provisions) Act 1989, s.1(2) (as enacted); Companies Act 1985, s.36A(5).
^{431c} *First National Securities v Jones* [1978] Ch. 109 and *Chitty on Contracts* (26th ed., 1989) para.23.
^{431d} Law Com. No.253, paras 2.29–2.34.
^{431e} 2005 Order, art.7(3) (individuals); Sch.2, repealing Companies Act 1985, s.36A(5) (companies); Law Com. No.253, paras 2.50, 2.54.
^{431f} Law of Property (Miscellaneous Provisions) Act 1989, s.1(2A) as inserted by the 2005 Order, art.8. This statutory clarification also casts doubt on the contrary approach taken by the unreported decision at first instance in *Johnsey Estates (1900) Ltd v Newport Marketworld Ltd*, unreported, May 10, 1996, Judge Moseley Q.C.), noted and criticised by Law Com. No.253, paras 2.17–2.18.

Execution on behalf of one or more of the parties to the instrument. **1–082C** Following the Law Commission's recommendations,^{431g} the 2005 Order introduced new clarifying provisions so as to provide expressly for execution in the name or on behalf of another person. So, it is provided that as regards individuals, a document may be executed by a person on behalf of another, and that it is the person who executes the document (whether or not on behalf of the other) who must comply with the formalities^{431h}; as regards companies, the provisions of the Companies Act 1985 which state how a company may execute a document and provide for deemed execution in favour of a purchaser, apply where a company executes a document on behalf of another person⁴³¹ⁱ; and as regards corporations aggregate, the Law of Property Act 1925 is amended so as to provide that deemed execution in favour of a purchaser applies where the corporation executes an instrument on behalf of another person.^{431j}

^{431g} Law Com. No.253, Pt 7.
^{431h} Law of Property (Miscellaneous Provisions) Act 1989, s.1(2)(b) and (4A), as amended and inserted by the 2005 Order, art.7(3) and 7(4) respectively.
⁴³¹ⁱ Companies Act 1985 s.36A(7) as inserted by the 2005 Order, art.7(2).
^{431j} Law of Property Act 1925 s.74(1A) as inserted by the 2005 Order, art.7(1).

"Valid execution": individuals. By s.1(3) of the Law of Property (Miscella- **1–082D** neous Provisions) Act 1989, for an instrument to be validly executed as a deed by an individual, it must be "signed (i) by him in the presence of a witness who attests the signature; or (ii) at his direction and in his presence and the presence of two witnesses who each attest the signature." "Signature" is defined later in the section to include making one's mark.[431k] The Act specifically preserved the further common law requirement that for an instrument to be validly executed as a deed it must be "delivered" as a deed.[431l]

[431k] Law of Property (Miscellaneous Provisions) Act 1989, s.1(4)(b) as amended by the 2005 Order, Sch.1, para.14.
[431l] Law of Property (Miscellaneous Provisions) Act 1989, s.1(3)(b) as amended by the 2005 Order, Sch.2 and see below, para.1–082D.

1–082E   **Delivery.** At common law, "[w]here a contract is to be by deed, there must be a delivery to perfect it."[431m] "Delivered", however, in this connection does not mean "handed over" to the other party. It means delivered in the old legal sense,[431n] namely, an act done so as to evince an intention to be bound.[431o] Any act of the party which shows that he intended to deliver the deed as an instrument binding on him is enough. He must make it his deed[431p] and recognise it as presently binding on him.[431q] Delivery is effective even though the grantor retains the deed in his own possession: there need be no actual transfer of possession to the other party.[431r] Moreover, where a solicitor, duly certified notary public or licensed conveyancer (or their agent) in the course of a transaction purports to deliver an instrument as a deed on behalf of a party to the instrument, it shall be conclusively presumed in favour of a purchaser that he is authorised so to deliver the instrument.[431s] Unlike the position as regards corporations,[431t] the execution of a document intended to be executed as a deed by an individual does not give rise to a presumption of delivery either at common law or by statute.

[431m] *Xenos v Wickham* (1863) 14 C.B.(N.S.) 435, 473; *Termes de la Ley*, s.v. Fait; Co.Litt. 171b.
[431n] But see *Yale* [1970] C.L.J. 52.
[431o] *Vincent v Premo Enterprises Ltd* [1969] 2 Q.B. 609, 619.
[431p] *Tupper v Foulkes* (1861) 9 C.B.(N.S.) 797; *Xenos v Wickham* (1867) L.R. 2 H.L. 296, 312; *Re Seymour* [1913] 1 Ch. 475.
[431q] *Xenos v Wickham*, above.
[431r] *Xenos v Wickham*, above, *per* Lord Cranworth at 323; *cf. per* Pigott B. at 309; *Doe d. Garnons v Knight* (1826) 5 B. & C. 671; *Macedo v Stroud* [1922] 2 A.C. 330; *Beesly v Hallwood Estates Ltd* [1960] 1 W.L.R. 549, affd. [1961] Ch. 105; *Vincent v Premo Enterprises Ltd* [1969] 2 Q.B. 609.
[431s] Law of Property (Miscellaneous Provisions) Act 1989, s.1(5) as amended by the 2005 Order, art.9 which therefore extended the presumption beyond its earlier restriction to transactions involving the disposition or creation of an interest in land.
[431t] Below, para.1–082F.

1–082F   **"Valid execution": companies and corporations aggregate.** One of the purpose of the 2005 Order was to harmonise the law governing the execution of instruments as deeds by corporate bodies.[431u] So, it is now provided that a document is validly executed *as a deed* by both companies and corporations aggregate so as to satisfy the general requirements imposed by the 1989 Act[431v] "if and only if" it is "duly executed" by the corporate body *and* if it is delivered as a deed.[431w] As regards delivery, it is provided for both types of corporate body that an instrument shall be presumed to be delivered for these purposes "upon its being executed, unless a contrary intention is proved."[431x] As regards companies, this provision marked a change from the previous law where the presumption of delivery was irrebuttable in these circumstances[431y]; as regards corporations aggregate, it clarified the position given that the existence of a rebuttable presumption at common law had been recently judicially doubted.[431z]

[431u] Law Com. No.153, Pt 4.
[431v] Law of Property (Miscellaneous Provisions) Act 1989, s.1(2)(b), para.1–082A, above.
[431w] Law of Property Act 1925, s.74A(1) as inserted by the 2005 Order, art.4 (corporations aggregate); Companies Act 1985, s.36AA(1) as inserted by the 2005 Order, art.6.
[431x] Law of Property Act 1925, s.74A(2) as inserted by the 2005 Order, art.4 (corporations aggregate); Companies Act 1985, s.36AA(2) (companies) as inserted by 2005 Order, art.6.
[431y] As a result, the 2005 Order, art.5 amended the Companies Act 1985, s.36A(6) and see Law Com. No.253, paras 6.37–6.43.
[431z] *Bolton Metropolitan B.C. v Torkington* [2003] EWCA Civ 1634; [2004] Ch. 66 at [46], above para.1–082, differing from the position taken by the Law Commission, which took the view that at common law, the sealing of a deed raises a rebuttable presumption of delivery: Law Com. No.253, para.6.1.

However, the conditions for "due execution" of a document still differ some-   **1–082G**
what as between companies and corporations aggregate. In the case of com-panies, there are alternative requirements: a document may be executed either by the affixing of its common seal[431aa] or by being signed "by a director and the secretary of the company, or by two directors of a company, and expressed (in whatever form of words) to be executed by the company."[431ab] Where a docu-ment is to be signed by a person as a director or the secretary of more than one company, it shall not be taken to be duly signed by that person for these purposes unless the person signs it separately in each capacity.[431ac] In the case of corpora-tions aggregate, the common law requirement of affixing the corporation's seal still applies in principle,[431ad] but it is provided that "in favour of a purchaser an instrument shall be deemed to have been duly executed . . . if a seal purporting to be the corporation's seal purports to be affixed to the instrument in the presence of and attested by (a) two members of the board of directors, council or other governing body of the corporation, or (b) one such member and the clerk, secretary or other permanent officer of the corporation or his deputy."[431ae]

[431aa] Companies Act 1985, s.36A(1) as inserted by the Companies Act 1989, s.130(2).
[431ab] Companies Act 1985, s.36A(4) as inserted by the Companies Act 1989, s.130(2).
[431ac] Companies Act 1985, s.36A(4A) as inserted by 2005 Order, art.10(1), Sch.1, para.10.
[431ad] Law Com. No.253, para.4.5.
[431ae] Law of Property Act 1925, s.74(1) as substituted by the 2005 Order, art.3. s.74(1B) of the 1925 Act as inserted by the 2005 Order, art.10(1), Sch.1, para.2 provides that for these purposes "a seal purports to be affixed in the presence of and attested by an officer of the corporation, in the case of an officer which is not an individual, if it is affixed in the presence of and attested by an individual authorised by the officer to attest on its behalf." And see Law Com. No.253, paras 4.6–4.9.

"Valid execution": corporations sole. Where a deed is executed by a cor-   **1–082H**
poration sole (such as a government minister or Church of England bishop[431af]), the common law requirement of sealing still applies.[431ag] However, as has been noted,[431ah] this requirement has been interpreted by the courts very liberally: "to constitute a sealing neither wax nor wafer nor a piece of paper nor even an impression is necessary."[431ai] Pieces of green ribbon[431aj] or a circle printed on the document containing the letters "L.S." (*locus sigilli*)[431ak] or even a document

bearing no indication of a seal at all[431al] will suffice, if there is evidence (*e.g.* attestation) that the document was intended to be executed as a deed.[431am] In the absence of such evidence, a signatory of a document expressed to have been "signed, sealed and delivered" by him may be estopped from denying that it was sealed.[431an]

[431af] Law. Com. No.253, para.4.23 and see above, for a definition of corporations sole.

[431ag] Law of Property (Miscellaneous Provisions) Act 1989, s.1(10) specifically provides that s.1's provisions governing "individuals" do not apply to corporations sole. Note also that s.1(9) specifically reserves the requirement of sealing at common law in relation to deeds required or authorised to be made under the seals of the county palatine of Lancaster, the Duchy of Lancaster or the Duchy of Cornwall.

[431ah] Above, para.1–082B.

[431ai] *Ex p. Sandilands* (1871) L.R. 6 C.P. 411, 413.

[431aj] *Ex p. Sandilands*, above, see also *Stromdale & Ball Ltd v Burden* [1952] Ch. 233, 230.

[431ak] *First National Securities Ltd v Jones* [1978] Ch. 109.

[431al] *First National Securities Ltd v Jones*, above; *Commercial Credit Services v Knowles* [1978] 6 C.L. 64.

[431am] *cf. National Provincial Bank v Jackson* (1886) 33 Ch.D. 1; *Re Balkis Consolidated Ltd* (1888) 58 L.T. 300; *Re Smith* (1892) 67 L.T. 64 (these cases were explained in *First National Securities Ltd v Jones*, above): *cf. TCB v Gray* [1986] 1 Ch. 621, 633.

[431an] *TCB v Gray*, above, *cf. Rushingdale Ltd v Byblos Bank* (1985) P.C.C. 342, 346–347.

6. The Relationship Between Contract And Tort

(c) *Concurrence of Actions in Contract and Tort*

(ii) *Torts Committed in the Course of Performance of a Contract*

Assumption of responsibility

1–120   [*Add new note 659a at end of paragraph: page* [75]]
[659a] *cf. Lennon v Metropolitan Police Commissioner* [2004] EWCA Civ 130; [2004] 2 All E.R. 266 where the principle in *Henderson v Merrett Syndicates* was applied so as to impose liability on a police authority vicariously in respect of its agent's express assumption of responsibility towards one of its constables (technically not being a contractual employee) in respect of the task of transferring him without loss of allowance to another police force.

(d) *The Influence of Contract on Tort beyond Privity*

1–157   [*Add new text to note 899: page* [103]]
Customs and Excise Commissioners v Barclays Bank plc [2004] EWCA Civ 1555; [2005] 1 W.L.R. 2082 at [23].

Subsequent cases

1–162   [*Add at end of note 925: page* [108]]
European International Reinsurance Co Ltd v Curzon Insurance Ltd [2003] EWCA Civ 1074; [2003] Lloyd's Rep. I.R. 793. *cf. Commissioners of Customs & Excise v Barclays Bank plc* [2004] EWHC 122; [2004] 1 Lloyd's Rep. 572 where Colman J. held that the principle of assumption of responsibility was not

always a helpful approach to deciding whether a duty of care arose in respect of pure economic loss. He further held that where a freezing injunction has been obtained, the defendant against whom the order has been made does not thereby occupy a relationship of proximity vis-à-vis the claimant, unless there is super-added to the relationship conduct amounting to an assumption of responsibility by that party. Given this, it would be inconsistent to hold that a bank holding the defendant's assets upon being given notice of a freezing injunction thereby owed the claimant a duty of care: *ibid.*, at [73].

Part Two

FORMATION OF CONTRACT

Chapter 2

THE AGREEMENT

2. The Offer

Conduct as offer

2–004   [*Add to note 21: page* [124]]

For further amendments of the Unsolicited Goods and Services Act 1971, see Regulatory Reform (Unsolicited Goods and Services Act 1971) (Directory Entries and Demands for Payment) Order 2005 (SI 2005/55) and Unsolicited Goods and Services Act 1971 (Electronic Commerce) (Amendment) Regulations 2005 (SI 2005/148).

Inactivity as offer

2–005   [*Add to note 30: page* [125]]

cf. Indescon Ltd v Ogden [2004] EWHC 2326 (TCC); [2005] 1 Lloyd's Rep. 31 (right to appoint arbitrator not lost by lapse of time).

Offer and invitation to treat

[*Add new text at end: page* [126]]

It has been held that a draft document sent in the course of contractual negotiations with the clear intention of inviting further comment from the recipient was not an offer.[35a]

2–006

[35a] *McNicholas Construction Holdings v Endemol UK plc* [2003] EWHC 2472; [2003] E.G.C.S. 136.

Other displays

[*Add to note 59: page* [129]]

See also *University of Edinburgh v Onifade* 2005 S.L.T. (Sh Ct) 63 where landowners displayed a notice on the land to the effect that persons parking their cars there without permit would be subject to a "fine" of £30 per day. It was held that a person who had so parked his car was liable for the specified amount. The judgment is mainly concerned with the question whether the motorist's conduct could be regarded as an acceptance (see below, para.2–025); but to reach this question the court must have made the assumption that the notice amounted to an offer. This is perhaps a questionable interpretation of the landowners' intention (even objectively ascertained) in putting up the notice. This could be said to have been rather to deter unauthorised parking than to invite it with a view to earning the specified amount.

2–014

3. THE ACCEPTANCE

(a) *Definition*

Acceptance defined

[*Add to note 100: page* [134]]

For the application of the objective test to an acceptance, see also *University of Edinburgh v Onifade* 2005 S.L.T. (Sh Ct) 63, where landowners displayed a notice on the land stating that persons who parked their car there without a permit would be liable to a "fine" of £30 per day. The defender, who was aware of the notice, repeatedly parked on the land without permit and was held liable for the stipulated amount on the ground that a contract had arisen between him and the owner. It was "nothing to the purpose that he did not intend to pay" as the landowners were "entitled to conclude that the defender, by parking without permit with knowledge of the notice, had accepted liability for the payment to them of £30" (at [6]).

2–025

Negotiation after apparent agreement

[*Add to note 109: page* [135]]

For an application of the principle of looking at the whole correspondence in order to determine whether a contract has been rescinded, see *Drake Insurance*

2–027

plc v Provident Insurance plc [2003] EWCA Civ 1834; [2004] Q.B. 601 at [100].

Acceptance by conduct

2–028   *[Add to note 115: page* [135]]

By reason of the objective principle, the offeree could not escape liability merely on the ground that he had no subjective intention to accept: see *University of Edinburgh v Onifade* 2005 S.L.T. (Sh Ct) 63, above, para.2–014 of this Supplement.

(c) *Posted Acceptance*

Dictated telegrams, faxes, emails and web-site trading

2–049   *[Add new footnote 209a at "circumstances": page* [147]*, line 8].*

[209a] In *JSC Zestafoni Nikoladze Ferroalloy Plant v Ronly Holdings Ltd* [2004] EWHC 245 (Comm) [2004] 2 Lloyd's Rep. 335 an acceptance by fax was classified as an "instantaneous communication" [at 75] and to take effect on receipt as the sender's machine would generally indicate whether the message had been received "effectively" (as distinct from having been received only in part). The further possibility of the message's having been wholly received, but of its being wholly or partly illegible, is not discussed.

Consumer's right to cancel distance contracts

2–062   *[Add to note 246: page* [152]]

For amendment of the Consumer Protection (Distance Selling) Regulations 2000, affecting the consumer's right to cancel distance contracts, see Financial Services (Distance Marketing) Regulations 2004 (SI 2004/2095); Consumer Protection (Distance Selling) (Amendment) Regulations 2005 (SI 2005/689).

(e) *Silence*

Silence and conduct

2–074   *[Add to note 296: page* [158]]

See also *Westminster Building Co Ltd v Beckingham* [2004] EWHC 138; [2004] B.L.R. 163 (terms of building contractor's offer to refurbish property accepted by owner's conduct in allowing the stipulated work to proceed); contrast *Mirant Asia-Pacific Construction (Hong Kong) Ltd v Ove Arup & Partners International OAPIL (No.2)* [2004] EWHC 1750; 97 Con. L.R. 1, where on the facts no inference of the owner's assent to the terms of a draft contract which had not been signed by the owner could be drawn merely from his allowing the work to proceed. In both cases the point at issue related to the terms, rather than to the existence, of the contract.

4. Termination of the Offer

(a) *Withdrawal*

General rule

[Add to note 335, line 4 after "Pt 36": page [163]]   **2–086**
For further proceedings in *Scammel v Dicker* see [2005] EWCA Civ 405;
[2005] 3 All E.R. 838, below paras 2–113, 2–126, 2–136, 2–137, 2–139 and
2–141 of this Supplement.

(f) *Supervening Personal Incapacity*

Mental patients

[Page [169]]   **2–100**
References in this paragraph to "mental patients" should now be to persons
who lack mental capacity as defined in ss.1 and 2 of the Mental Capacity Act
2005. The substantive rules stated in Main Work, para.2–100 are not affected by
this change in terminology.

6. Incomplete Agreement

Agreement required for continued operation of contract

[Add to note 425: page [175]]   **2–113**
See also *Scammell v Dicker* [2005] EWCA Civ 405; [2005] 3 All E.R. 838 at
[40] *per* Rix L.J. ("The world is full of perfectly sound contracts which require
further agreement for the purpose of their implementation").

Stipulation for the execution of a formal document

[Add to note 428: page [175]]   **2–114**
Thoresen & Co (Bangkok) Ltd v Fathom Marine Co [2004] EWHC 167
(Comm); [2004] 1 All E.R. (Comm.) 935 (agreement for the sale of a ship "sub
details" held not to be a binding contract).

[Add to note 429, line 9 after reference to The Kurnia Dewi: page [176]]
Harvey Shopfitters Ltd v ADI Ltd [2003] EWCA Civ 1752; [2004] 2 All E.R.
982.

General requirement of "exchange of contracts"

[Add to note 444: page [177]]   **2–117**
Secretary of State for Transport v Christos [2003] EWCA Civ 1073 is reported
in [2004] 1 P.&C.R. 17; *Bolton MBC v Torkington* [2003] EWCA Civ 1634;
[2004] Ch. 66 at [53], where the mere sealing (without delivery) of a counterpart

lease by a local authority was held not to give rise to a contract binding the authority: see above, para.1–082 of this Supplement.

Terms "to be agreed"

2–124   [*Add to note 477: page* [181]]
Minter v Julius Baer Investments Ltd [2004] EWHC 2472; [2005] Pens. L.R. 73 (letter stating that "the remaining terms of service shall be worked out" held to be no more than an agreement to agree and therefore to have no contractual force).

Options and rights of pre-emption

2–125   [*Add to note 485: page* [182]]
And see *Re Gray* [2004] EWHC 1538 (Ch); [2005] 1 W.L.R. 815 at [25]. On the exercise of a right of pre-emption, the right may acquire the characteristics of an option: see *Cottrell v King* [2004] EWHC 397; [2004] B.C.C. 307.

[*Add to note 486*]
For the distinction between options and rights of pre-emption, see also *Tiffany Investments Ltd v Bircham & Co Nominees (No.2) Ltd* [2003] EWCA Civ 1759; [2004] 2 P.&C.R. 10.

Agreement not incomplete merely because further agreement is required

2–126   [*Add to note 490: page* [182]]
See also *Scammell v Dicker* [2005] EWCA Civ 405; [2005] 3 All E.R. 838 at [31], [40].

Machinery laid down in the agreement

2–129   [*Add to note 511: page* [185]]
See also *Horkulak v Cantor Fitzgerald International* [2004] EWCA Civ 1287; [2005] I.C.R. 402 at [48], below, para.2–169 of this Supplement.

7. CERTAINTY OF TERMS

Requirement of certainty

2–136   [*Add to note 554: page* [190]]
See also *Scammell v Dicker* [2005] EWCA Civ 405; [2005] 3 All E.R. 838 at [41], describing *Scammell v Ouston* as "a rare case of uncertainty".

Qualification of the requirement of certainty

2–137   [*Add to note 557: page* [190]]
See also *Scammell v Dicker* [2005] EWCA Civ 405; [2005] 3 All E.R. 838, *per* Rix L.J. ("the courts should strain to be the preserver and not the destroyer of bargains").

Reasonableness

[Add to note 563: page [191]]   **2–139**
See also *Scammell v Dicker* [2005] EWCA Civ 405; [2005] 3 All E.R. 838 at [42], below para.2–141 of this Supplement where the agreement (in a consent order settling a boundary dispute) was "capable of being made definite without further agreement. It was reasonably certain."

Meaningless or self contradictory phrases

[Add new text: page [192]]   **2–141**
An agreement is not too uncertain to amount to a contract merely because of a conflict between two of its terms if, as is often the case, the conflict can be resolved by the court in the course of the normal adjudication of a contractual dispute. In *Scammell v Dicker*[569a] a consent order relating to a boundary dispute was alleged to be ineffective by reason of an alleged conflict between the terms of the order and a plan annexed to it. The Court of Appeal held that the order was not vitiated by uncertainty since it was "for the parties to resolve any disagreement as to interpretation" and if they failed to do so they would "go to tribunals to find the answer."[569b] The ordinary processes of construction can in such cases resolve the uncertainty.

[569a] [2005] EWCA Civ 405; [2005] 3 All E.R. 838.
[569b] *ibid.*, at [31].

8. CONDITIONAL AGREEMENTS

(b) *Degrees of Obligation*

Duty not to prevent occurrence of the event

[Add to note 584: page [195]]   **2–148**
cf. CEL Group Ltd v Nedlloyd Lines UK Ltd [2003] EWCA Civ 1716; [2004] 1 All E.R. (Comm) 689 at [11] (where the contract was not in terms conditional but the court applied a similar principle to that stated in Main Work, para.2–148 by virtue of the rule stated in Main Work para.13–012.)

9. CONTRACTUAL INTENTION

Agreements giving discretion to one party whether to perform

[Add to note 697: page [208]]   **2–169**
See also *Horkulak v Cantor Fitzgerald International* [2004] EWCA Civ 1287; [2005] I.C.R. 402 where a "discretionary bonus on dismissal" clause in a

contract of employment was held not to give the employer an unfettered discretion but one which had to be exercised "rationally and in good faith" (at [48]); *cf. ibid.*, at [46]: "bona fide and rationally".

Collective agreements

2–171   *[Add to note 699: page [208]]*
See also *Kaur v MG Rover Group Ltd* [2004] EWCA Civ 1507; [2005] I.R.L.R. 40, where a term of a collective agreement to the effect that there would be no compulsory redundancies was held not to have been incorporated in individual employment contracts as it was merely of an "aspirational nature" (at [33]) and not intended to constitute a binding contractual commitment.

Nature of relationship between the parties

2–175   *[Add to note 719: page [210]]*
cf. Essex Strategic Health Authority v David-John [2003] Lloyd's Rep. Med. 586 (relationship between general practitioner and Health Authority not contractual).

Vague agreements

2–176   *[Add at end: page [211]]*
The fact that some terms of an agreement are too vague to have contractual force does not preclude the enforcement of other terms which are, in themselves, sufficiently certain. This is, in particular, the case where the parties have acted in reliance on the latter term.[731a]

[731a] *Pena v Dale* [2003] EWHC 1065; [2004] 2 B.C.L.C. 508 at [95].

Other cases

2–178   *[Add to note 735: page [212]]*
cf. Sutton v Mishcon Reya [2003] EWHC 3166 (Ch); [2004] F.L.R. 837: cohabitation agreement by which one man was to be "slave" to another arguably "just an act or a role-play" (at [26]).

CONSIDERATION

2. DEFINITIONS

Performances and promises as consideration

[*Add to note 33: page* [219]]   **3–008**
See also *Melhuish v Redbridge Citizens Advice Bureau* [2005] I.R.L.R. 419,
where a voluntary worker agreed to work (without pay) for two days a week; his

expenses were to be reimbursed and he had the benefit of being allowed to take part in training courses. It was held that there was no "mutuality of obligation" (and hence no contract of employment) but at most "a limited unilateral contract" (at [18]).

3. ADEQUACY OF CONSIDERATION

Objects of trifling value

3–016   [Add to note 80: page [225]]
By virtue of s.335(1) of the Gambling Act 2005, consideration for money paid by a member of the club will be provided, on facts such as those of *Lipkin Gorman v Karpnale Ltd* [1991] 2 A.C. 548, by reason of the fact that the club's promise to the member will be legally enforceable: see below, Vol.II, paras 40–001D and 40–083 of this Supplement.

3–017   [Add to note 90: page [226]]
For the effect of the Gambling Act 2005 on the reasoning of *Lipkin Gorman v Karpnale Ltd* [1991] 2 A.C. 548, see above, para.3–016 of this Supplement.

Nominal consideration

3–019   [Add to note 94: page [228]]
See also Charities Act 1993, s.65(1)(a), requiring "full consideration in money or money's worth", a requirement not satisfied in *Bayoumi v Women's Total Abstinence Educational Union Ltd* [2003] EWCA Civ 1548; [2004] Ch. 40 at [46]–[47].

6. CONSIDERATION MUST MOVE FROM THE PROMISEE

Bar pupillage contracts

3–038   [Add to note 180: page [238]]
But an application for pupillage is not one for "membership" of chambers within the Disability Discrimination Act 1995, s.13(1)(c): *Horton v Higham* [2004] EWCA Civ 941; [2004] 3 All E.R. 863, where *Edmonds v Lawson* [2000] Q.B. 501 (discussed in Main Work para.3–038) is cited at [21].

7. Compromise and Forbearance to Sue

(b) *Invalid or Doubtful Claims*

Claims known to be invalid

[*Add to note 229: page* [244]]
Under s.335(1) of the Gambling Act 2005, contracts relating to gambling will, as a general rule, become legally enforceable: see below, Vol.II, para.40–001D. It follows that a promise not to sue a client for the amount of a lost bet will, in general, be good consideration for a promise made in return by the client. Such a case will fall within the principle stated in Main Work, para.3–047.

8. Existing Duties as Consideration

(b) *Duties Imposed by Contract with Promisor*

Cases in which there was no consideration

[*Add to note 287: page* [251]]
See also *South Caribbean Trading v Trafigura Beheer BV* [2004] EWHC 2676 (Comm); [2005] 1 Lloyd's Rep. 128 at [107], as to which see also below, paras 3–069 and 3–079 of this Supplement.

Factual benefit to the promisor

[*Add to note 305: page* [253]]
For the difficulty of reconciling *Williams v Roffey Bros & Nicholls (Contractors) Ltd* [1991] 1 Q.B. 1 with *Stilk v Myrick* (1809) 2 Camp. 317 and the cases that have followed it, see also *South Caribbean Trading v Trafigura Beheer BV* [2004] EWHC 2676 (Comm); [2005] 1 Lloyd's Rep. 128 at [107], [108]. Colman J. there accepted that the *Williams* case "appears to have introduced some amelioration" (at [107]), but said that he would not have followed the reasoning of that case if it had not been a decision of the Court of Appeal. The learned judge criticised the reasoning of the case as being "inconsistent with the . . . rule that consideration must move from the promisee" (*i.e.* the carpentry sub-contractor in that case). It is, however, respectfully submitted that the requirement that consideration must move from the promisee can be satisfied by the promisee's conferring a benefit on the promisor even though the promisee, in doing so, suffers no detriment (see Main Work, para.3–037) and that the carpentry sub-contractor had conferred such a benefit on the promisor by doing the agreed work (see *ibid.*, at n.176). Colman J.'s refusal to apply the reasoning of the *Williams* case is, however, with respect justifiable on the different ground (given by him in the *South Caribbean* case at [109]) that the promisee's "threat of non-compliance of its delivery obligation" under the original contract was in the latter case "analogous to economic duress." In the *Williams* case, there was

no such threat (see Main Work, para.3–068 after n.302) and it is clear that where the new promise is obtained by duress, it cannot be enforced by virtue of the principle enunciated in that case (see Main Work, para.3–069).

(c) *Duty imposed by Contract with a Third Party*

Performance of the duty

3–073   [*Add to note 325: page* [256]]
A "civil partnership agreement" likewise does not have contractual force: Civil Partnership Act 2004, s.73.

9. DISCHARGE AND VARIATION OF CONTRACTUAL DUTIES

Introduction

3–076   [*Add new note 344a in line 11, after "originally undertaken by A": page* [258]]
[344a] The issue discussed in *South Caribbean Trading v Trafigura Beheer BV* [2004] EWHC 2676 (Comm); [2005] 1 Lloyd's Rep. 128 at [107]–[112] appears to have been of this kind: it was whether a seller of oil had provided consideration for the buyer's promise to take delivery after the originally agreed date by promising to perform his (the seller's) duties with respect to delivery by a specified later date: see below, para.3–079 of this Supplement.

(b) *Variation*

(i) *Requirement of Consideration*

Agreements to vary contracts

3–079   [*Add new text at end of paragraph: page* [260]]
An agreement for the sale of goods can likewise be varied by mutual promises (made before the delivery date originally specified) on the part of the buyer to accept delivery and of the seller to perform his obligations with respect to delivery, on a different (later) date. This was held to be the position where a seller of fuel oil, to be produced by blending components to be provided by the buyer, had encountered "apparently insuperable"[353a] problems in completing the blending process by the originally agreed delivery date. An agreement was then made by which the seller promised to complete that process by a later date and the buyer promised to accept delivery on that date. The price remained fixed at a level which was below the market price on the date of the variation agreement but which "might exceed"[353b] the market price on the extended delivery date. It was held that the variation amounted to "a new agreement supported by mutual promises"[353c] and that "sufficient consideration [for the buyer's promise to accept delivery on the later date] moved from the promisee"[353d] (*i.e.* the seller).

[353a] *South Caribbean Trading v Trafigura Beheer BV* [2004] EWHC 2676 (Comm); [2005] 1 Lloyd's Rep. 128 at [105]. It does not appear that these difficulties were treated by the buyer as a breach of the contract.
[353b] *ibid.*
[353c] *ibid.*; for mutual promises as consideration for each other, see Main Work, para.3–008A.
[353d] *South Caribbean Trading* case, above n.353a, at [105].

(ii) *Common Law Mitigations*

Forbearance may become irrevocable

[*Add to note 369: page* [262]]   **3–083**
See also *Bottiglieri di Navagazione SpA v Cosco Quindao Ocean Shipping Co (The Bunge Saga Lima)* [2005] EWHC 244 (Comm); [2005] 2 Lloyd's Rep. 1 at [31], below para.3–097 n.438 of this Supplement.

(iii) *Equitable mitigations*

Requirement of pre-existing legal relationship

[*Add to note 378: page* [264]]   **3–088**
Evans v Amicus Healthcare Ltd has been affirmed ([2004] EWCA Civ 727; [2005] Fam. 1) on the ground that estoppel or waiver could not preclude a man from withdrawing his consent to the use of his genetic material since the right to withdraw such consent was expressly given by the Human Fertilisation and Embryology Act 1990, Sch.3 para.4(1), so that the application of waiver or estoppel "would conflict with the Parliamentary scheme" (at [37]; see also at [36] and [120]).

The promise or representation must be "clear" or "unequivocal"

[*Add to note 386, line 12: page* [266]]   **3–090**
Super Chem Products Ltd v American Life & General Insurance Co Ltd [2004] UKPC 2; [2004] 2 All E.R. 358 at [23], where the present requirement was not satisfied.

[*Add to note 387: page* [266]]
Evans v Amicus Healthcare Ltd has been affirmed [2004] EWCA Civ 727; [2005] Fam. 1: see above, para.3–088 of this Supplement.

Whether "detriment" is required

[*Add to note 22: page* [269]]   **3–094**
See also *Bottiglieri di Navigazione SpA v Cosco Quindao Ocean Shipping Co (The Bunge Saga Lima)* [2005] EWHC 244; [2005] 2 Lloyd's Rep. 1, the facts of which are stated in para.3–097 of this Supplement. Gloster J. said (at [31]) that "a failure to act by the representee may give rise to a waiver... ; it is unnecessary that the conduct of the representee should be to his detriment provided that there is some conduct which differs from that which would have occurred in the absence of the representation."

Inequitable

3–095   [*Add to note 424: page* [270]]

See also *Bottiglieri di Navigazione SpA v Cosco Quindao Ocean Shipping Co (The Bunge Saga Lima)* [2005] EWHC 244; [2005] 2 Lloyd's Rep. 1 at [31], quoted below in para.3–097 n.438 of this Supplement.

[*Add to note 428: page* [270]]

Evans v Amicus Healthcare Ltd has been affirmed [2004] EWCA Civ 727; [2005] Fam. 1: see above, para.3–088 of this Supplement.

[*Add to note 429*]

See also *South Caribbean Trading v Trafigura Beheer BV* [2004] EWHC 2676 (Comm); [2005] 1 Lloyd's Rep. 128 at [112], holding that the "estoppel" (see Main Work, para.3–103) does not prevent the promisor from going back on a promise obtained by economic duress in the form of a refusal on the promisee's part to perform the original contract.

Extinctive effect in exceptional cases

3–097   [*Add to note 438: page* [271]]

In *Bottiglieri di Navigazione SpA v Cosco Quindao Ocean Shipping Co (The Bunge Saga Lima)* [2005] EWHC 244 (Comm); [2005] 2 Lloyd's Rep. 1 a time charter contained a "cleaning clause" requiring the vessel to be clean and suitable for the charterer's cargo at the first loadport. The charterer loaded cargo there in spite of the fact that the clause had not been complied with but later claimed damages in respect of contamination caused to further cargo loaded at the second loadport by reason of the original failure to comply with the cleaning clause. The claim failed as the charterer had waived the clause. Gloster J. said at [31]:

> "Although a waiver of this kind may be retracted, no revocation can be retrospective; thus waiver may have permanent effect where it would be inequitable to permit retraction (for example because the representee can no longer resume his former position)."

Defensive nature of the doctrine

3–098   [*Add to note 455: page* [273]]

Evans v Amicus Healthcare Ltd has been affirmed ([2004] EWCA Civ 727; [2005] Fam. 1) on the ground stated in para.3–088 of this Supplement and without reference to the point discussed in para.3–098 of the Main Work.

Doctrine may deprive promisor of certain defences

3–101   [*Add to note 471a: page* [275]]

Evans v Amicus Healthcare Ltd has been affirmed ([2004] EWCA Civ 727; [2005] Fam. 1) on the ground stated in para.3–088 of this Supplement and without reference to the point discussed in para.3–101 of the Main Work.

Distinguished from estoppel by convention

[*Add to note 514: page* [281]]   **3–107**
See also *Thor Navigation Inc v Ingosstrakh Insurance* [2005] EWHC 19
(Comm); [2005] 1 Lloyd's Rep. 547 at [66], [67].

[*Add to note 515*]
See also the *Thor Navigation* case, above n.514, at [66]

"Communication" passing "across the line"

[*Add to note 518: page* [283]]   **3–109**
See also *Thor Navigation Inc v Ingosstrakh Insurance* [2005] EWHC 19
(Comm); [2005] 1 Lloyd's Rep. 547 at [66] for the requirement that "both parties
must have conducted themselves on the basis of such shared assumption."

Whether estoppel by convention creates new rights

[*Add to note 557 line 1, after "132":* [page 286]]   **3–113**
cf. *Dunford Trading A-G v OAO Atlantrybflot* [2005] EWCA Civ 24; [2005] 1
Lloyd's Rep. 289 at [39], referring to Brandon L.J.'s view in the *Amalgamated
Investment* case [1982] Q.B. 84 at [131]–[132] as the likely answer to the
argument that the estoppel was being used "as a sword rather than as a shield"
(*per* Rix L.J.).

10. PART PAYMENT OF A DEBT

(c) *Limitations in Equity*

Extinctive effects in exceptional cases

[*Add to note 658: page* [297]]   **3–132**
The statement in *Bottiglieri di Navigazione SpA v Cosco Quindao Ocean
Shipping Co (The Bunge Saga Lima)* [2005] EWHC 244 (Comm); [2005] 2
Lloyd's Rep. 1 at [31] that "no revocation can be retrospective" is made in the
context of a situation in which "it would be inequitable to permit retraction": see
the account of this case given above in para.3–097, n.438 of this Supplement.
The case was not concerned with "waiver" of an obligation to pay money.

11. PROPRIETARY ESTOPPEL

(b) *Bases of Liability*

Alternative explanation: contract

[*Add to note 709: page* [303]]   **3–141**
See also *Oxley v Hiscock* [2004] EWCA Civ 546; [2005] Fam. 211 at
[35]–[36], distinguishing between cases of proprietary estoppel and those in

which parties *before* acquiring property reach "an agreement, arrangement or understanding . . . that each is to have a beneficial share in the property."

(c) *Conditions giving rise to Liability*

Kinds of promises capable of giving rise to proprietary estoppel

3–143 [*Add to note 719–720: page* [305]]
Secretary of State for Transport v Christos [2003] EWCA Civ 1073 is reported in [2004] 1 P. & C.R. 17.

Subject-matter of the promise

3–145 [*Add to note 734: page* [307]]
In *Strover v Strover* [2005] EWHC 860 "proprietary estoppel" (at [39]) operated in relation to a life insurance policy; the case was one in which the estoppel arose, not from an "assurance" but from a "mistake" (at [42]); *cf.* Main Work para.3–138 for the distinction between the two lines of cases; our concern in this Chapter is with the "assurance" (or "encouragement") cases (*ibid.*).

Detrimental reliance

3–146 [*Add to note 737: page* [307]]
See also *H v M (Property Occupied by Wife's Parents)* [2004] EWHC 625; [2004] 2 F.L.R. 16, where a claim alleging proprietary estoppel failed for want of detrimental reliance.

12. SPECIAL CASES

Both promises defective by statute

3–167 [*Add to note 850: page* [319]]
For the repeal of s.18 of the Gaming Act 1845 by the Gambling Act 2005 ss.334(1)(c) and 356(3)(d) and Sch.17, see below Vol.II, para.40–001A.

Firm offers

3–170 [*Add to note 870: page* [321]]
For the description of an option as "an irrevocable offer that only matures into a bilateral contract upon its exercise", see *Re Gray* [2004] EWHC (Ch); [2005] 1 W.L.R. 815 at [25].

Novation of partnership debts

3–173 [*Add new text at end: page* [324]]
In *Re Burton Marsden Douglas*[892a] A practised as a solicitor and was instructed by X to act in the administration of an estate of which X was executor.

After liabilities were incurred by A to X, A went into partnership with B and C. After A had disappeared, it was held that B and C were not responsible for liabilities incurred by A before they had joined the partnership. There had been no novation of A's liabilities incurred before that time since (a) there had been no agreement to novate those liabilities; and (b) there would be no consideration for any promise by B and C to discharge those liabilities since there was no promise by X to release A.

892a [2004] EWHC 593 (Ch); [2004] 3 All E.R. 222.

Non-feasance and misfeasance

[Add new text at end: page [326]]   **3–177**
There appears to be an exception to the position stated at the end of this paragraph of the Main Work. The exception is said to arise where A's representation to B that A will take certain steps to safeguard some specific financial interest of B's amounts to an "express assumption of responsibility for a particular matter".908a A's failure to exercise due care in discharging that responsibility may then make him liable to B in tort and such liability has been said to cover "acts of omission".908b

908a *Lennon v Metropolitan Police Commissioner* [2004] EWCA Civ 130; [2004] 1 W.L.R. 2594 at [34].
908b *ibid.*, at [20]. *Quaere*, however, whether the wrongful conduct in *Lennon's* case did not amount to misfeasance in the sense in which that expression is used in para.3–177 of the Main Work (*i.e.*, "failure to achieve a *promised result*").

CHAPTER 4

FORM

2. CONTRACTS FOR THE SALE OR OTHER DISPOSITION OF AN INTEREST IN LAND

(b) *The New Law: Contracts made on or after September 27, 1989*

(i) *Contracts within Section 2 of the Law of Property (Miscellaneous Provisions) Act 1989*

Variations

4–056   [*Add new note 262a at end of paragraph: page* [354]]
262a *cf. HL Estates Ltd v Parker-Lake Homes Ltd* [2003] EWHD 604 (Ch).

[*Add new paragraph: page* [354]]
Boundary agreements between neighbours

4–056A   In *Joyce v Rigolli*262b the Court of Appeal considered whether a boundary agreement between neighbouring landowners constituted "a contract for the sale

[30]

or other disposition of an interest in land" within the meaning of s.2 of the Law of Property (Miscellaneous Provisions) Act 1989. In this respect, the court adopted the distinction drawn by Megarry J. in *Neilson v Poole*,[262c] in the context of the requirement of registration of such an agreement as an "estate contract" within s.10(1) of the Land Charges Act 1925, between agreements which constitute an exchange of land and those by which the parties merely intend to "demarcate" an unclear boundary referred to in title documents, "a contract merely to demarcate and confirm [not being] a contract to convey".[262d] According to the Court of Appeal, for a contract to be one "for" selling or disposing of land within the meaning of s.2 of the 1989 Act, "it must have been part of the parties' purposes, or the purposes to be attributed to them, in entering into such a contract that the contract should achieve a sale or other disposition of land. The fact that the effect of their contract is that land or an interest in land is actually conveyed, when that effect was neither foreseen nor intended nor was it something which ought to have been foreseen or intended, is not the acid test."[262e] However, on the facts before them it had been found that while the agreement to establish the boundary did not purport to be a contract to convey any land, one of its parties consciously thought that he was giving up a small amount of land.[262f] Nevertheless, the Court of Appeal held s.2 inapplicable: the important public policy in upholding informal boundary agreements which are "act[s] of peace, quieting strife and averting litigation"[262g] led the court to hold that Parliament could not have intended s.2 to apply to transfers of land pursuant to demarcating boundary agreements simply because a trivial transfer or transfers of land were consciously involved, and it should be presumed, until the contrary is shown, that any transfer of land effected by such an agreement is trivial for this purpose.[262h]

[262b] [2004] EWCA Civ 79; [2004] All E.R. (D) 203 (Feb).
[262c] (1969) 20 P. & C.R. 909.
[262d] *ibid.*, at [918]–[920].
[262e] [2004] EWCA Civ 79 at [31] *per* Arden L.J.
[262f] *ibid.*, at [30], [32].
[262g] *Nielson v Poole* (1969) 20 P. & C.R. 909, 919 *per* Megarry J.
[262h] [2004] EWCA Civ 79 at [32]–[34]. cf. *ibid.*, at [45] Sir Martin Nourse referring to "the de minimis principle".

Conditions in planning agreements

[*Page* [356]]   **4–060**
Criticism by *Emmet and Farrand on Title* (19th ed.) para.2–047 of the decision in *Jelson Ltd v Derby City Council*, which required the signature of the housing association, on the basis that s.2 of the 1989 Act requires only the signature of the contracting parties was said to seem valid by Waller L.J. in *Nweze v Nwoko* [2004] EWCA Civ 379; [2004] 2 P. & C.R. D1, *The Times,* May 6, 2004.

Compromises

[*Add to text at end of paragraph*: page [358]]   **4–063**
Similarly, in *Nweze v Nwoko*[295a] the Court of Appeal held that a compromise agreement between two parties to an executed contract of sale of land under which, *inter alia,* the buyer agreed to sell the property with vacant possession at

the best price available on the open market (so as to be in a position to pay the price of the earlier purchase to the sellers) was not a contract *for* the sale or other disposition of an interest in land within the meaning of s.2 of the Law of Property (Miscellaneous Provisions) Act 1989. In doing so, Waller L.J. relied on the Law Commission's Report, *Formalities for Contracts for Sale, etc. of Land*,[295b] which "is clearly concerned with contracts or dispositions under which land or an interest in land is actually sold or disposed of".[295c] While the compromise agreement required the buyer to sell the property (to a third party), it did not itself effect a sale of the property.[295d]

[295a] [2004] EWCA Civ 379; [2004] 2 P. & C.R. 33.
[295b] (1987) No. 164.
[295c] [2004] EWCA Civ 379 at [25].
[295d] *ibid.*, at [31].

[Add new paragraph 4–063A: page [358]]

4–063A　**Partnerships.** In *Kilcarne Holdings Ltd v Targetfollow (Birmingham) Ltd*[295a] it was held that an overall bargain for the creation of a joint venture involving the development of premises which consisted of a number of individual contracts could include contracts falling within and attracting the formal requirements of s.2 of the Law of Property (Miscellaneous Provisions) Act 1989 and that this remained the case even though the contract was expressed as a partnership. In so holding, the court rejected the argument based on nineteenth century authority[295b] that an oral partnership agreement can be validly made but that if the partnership assets include land, then the land is held on a constructive trust for the partnership[295c]: unlike the Statute of Frauds, the 1989 Act created a "substantive rule of law which prohibits the making of an oral contract for the sale or disposition of an interest in land" even if "it is wrapped up in an alleged partnership".[295d]

[295a] [2004] EWHC 2547 at [193]–[195], [200]–[204]
[295b] *Forster v Hale* (1800) 5 Ves. Jr. 308; *Dale v Hamilton* (1846) 5 Hare 369.
[295c] [2004] EWHC 2547 at [200]–[204].
[295d] *ibid.*, at [203], *per* Lewison J.

Composite agreements

4–064　*[Add new text at end of note 303: page* [359]]
See also the criticisms of the approach of Scott L.J. in *Tootal Clothing Ltd v Guinea Properties Ltd* (1992) 64 P. & C.R. 3513 in *Kilcarne Holdings Ltd v Targetfollow (Birmingham) Ltd* [2004] EWHC 2547 at [197]–[198].

(ii) *Formal Requirements*

Signature

4–069　*[Add at the beginning of note 320: page* [361]]
RG Kensington Management Co v Hutchinson [2002] EWHC 1180; [2003] 2 P. & C.R. 13 (signature by each party to the contract, not each party to the prospective conveyance or transfer).

[*Add new text at end of paragraph: page* [362]]

However, it has been held that a party can sign a document by writing only his initials, provided that it is clear that he intended to authenticate the full terms of the document.[325a]

[325a] *Newell v Tarrant* [2004] EWHC 772 at [47].

4–070

[*Add new text at end of paragraph: page* [362]]

Similarly, while a manuscript initialling of a document may constitute its "signature", the mere initialling of corrections at the margins of a document does not constitute its signing for the purposes of s.2 of the 1989 Act, as it does not evidence assent to the whole document.[328a]

[328a] *Newell v Tarrant* [2004] EWHC 772 at [48].

(iii) *The Effect of Failure to Comply with the Formal Requirements*

Constructive trust

[*Add new text at the end of the paragraph: page* [364]]   **4–073**

A further illustration of the way in which a constructive trust may avoid the formal requirements imposed by s.2 of the 1989 Act may be found in the application of the so-called *Pallant v Morgan* equity.[350a] Where A and B agree that A will acquire some specific property for the joint benefit of A and B, and B, in reliance on A's agreement, refrains from attempting to acquire the property, then equity will not permit A, when he acquires the property, to keep it for his own benefit, to the exclusion of B. It has been said that because this equity is in the nature of a constructive trust, it is unaffected by s.2(1) the 1989 Act.[350b]

[350a] *Pallant v Morgan* [1953] Ch. 43; *Banner Homes Group plc v Luff Developments Ltd* [2000] Ch. 372.
[350b] *Kilcarne Holdings Ltd v Targetfollow (Birmingham) Ltd* [2004] EWHC 2547 at [219] (where it was held inapplicable on the facts).

MISTAKE

2. COMMON MISTAKE

(c) *Mistake at Common Law*

(ii) *Situations in which contract may be void for Common Mistake*

Section 6 cases

5–034 [*Note 121: page* [388]]
Update reference to Atiyah, *Sale of Goods* to (11th ed., 2005), pp.106–107.

Mistakes as to law

5–042 [*Note 163, page* [393]]
The decision of Morland J. in *Brennan v Bolt Burdon* (which in the Main Work is stated incorrectly: Morland J. held that the compromise agreement was invalidated by the mistake of law) was reversed on appeal, [2004] EWCA Civ 1017; [2005] Q.B. 303. The Court of Appeal accepted that a mistake of law may render

a contract void; the principle underlying the decision in *Kleinwort Benson Ltd v Glasgow City Council (No. 2)* [1999] 1 A.C. 153 is not confined to restitution (at [12] and [26]). However, there is not a mistake of law if the relevant law was merely in doubt. The majority held that in this case the law was merely in doubt; the parties could have discovered that the relevant decision was under appeal.

In addition, when combined with the "declaratory theory of law" espoused in the *Kleinwort* case that when a decision is overturned the previous view of the law was mistaken, the mistake of law rule would threaten the finality of compromise agreements. In the view of Maurice Kay L.J. and Bodey J., a compromise agreement is one under which each party should be treated as accepting the risk that their view of the law might subsequently turn out to be mistaken (at [31] and [39]; *cf.* Main Work, para.5–015). Bodey J. would imply a term to that effect (at [42]). If the parties want to be able to withdraw from the compromise agreement should their view of the law turn out to have been mistaken, they should provide for that expressly (at [22] and [42]).

Sedley L.J. agreed that the appeal should be allowed: "a shift in the law cannot be allowed to undo a compromise of litigation entered into in the knowledge of both of how the law now stood and of the fact—for it is always a fact—that it might not remain so" (at [64]), though he preferred not to base this on an implied term but on the factual matrix of the agreement.

The court left open the question whether a mistake of law could ever invalidate a compromise agreement if, as a matter of construction, the compromise applies (*cf. Bank of Credit and Commerce International SA (In Liquidation) v Ali (No.1)* [2001] UKHL 8; [2002] 1 A.C. 251, in which the House of Lords held that a general release was not effective to release a claim for "stigma" damages that neither party could have known about: see Main Work para.5–012.) To exempt compromises altogether from the mistake of law rule might not be inconsistent with the *Kleinwort* case, as Lord Goff (at p.382G) and Lord Hope (at p.412F–G) had suggested that in a restitution case there might be a defence of "settlement of an honest claim" (at [14], [23] and [30]).

Maurice Kay L.J. doubted if a mistake of law would ever render performance impossible (at [22]). Sedley L.J. considered that in mistake of law cases the test of impossibility was too narrow; he would apply a test of whether the mistake destroyed the subject matter (at [60]).

In *S v S* [2003] Fam 1 it was held that a mistake of law was not a sufficient ground to set aside a consent order made in ancillary relief proceedings, though there was no such mistake on the facts. One ground for the decision, that the *Kleinwort* principle was confined to restitution cases, was rejected in *Brennan v Bolt Burdon* but Maurice Kay L.J. (at [12]) expressed sympathy with the other ground, that public policy favouring an end to litigation must prevail. On consent orders see Main Work, para.5–048, n.200.

(d) *No separate rule in equity*

No separate doctrine of common mistake in equity

The Court of Appeal in Singapore has hinted that it might not follow *The Great Peace*. See *Chwee Kin Keong v Digilandmall.com Pte Ltd* [2005] SGCA

5–043

2; [2005] 1 S.L.R. 502, at [66]–[73]. The case was one of unilateral mistake (see below, para.5–064). It is noted by Yeo in (2005) 121 L.Q.R. 393.

(e) *Summary of Common Mistake*

Other common mistakes

5–052   In *EIC Services Ltd v Phipps* [2004] EWCA Civ 1069; [2005] 1 W.L.R. 1377 the doctrine of common mistake in contract was applied by analogy to an issue of bonus shares. The issue had proceeded on the false assumption that all the relevant shares were fully paid up and would have the right to participate.

3. MISTAKES IN "COMMUNICATION"

(c) *Unilateral Mistake as to Terms*

(i) *When mistake will affect contract*

Mistakes which ought to have been apparent

5–064   In *Chwee Kin Keong v Digilandmall.com Pte Ltd* [2005] SGCA 2; [2005] 1 S.L.R. 502 the Singapore Court of Appeal held that the common law doctrine of mistake applies only when the non-mistaken party had actual knowledge of the other's mistake (at [53]). It appears that this would include cases of " 'Nelsonian knowledge', namely, wilful blindness or shutting one's eyes to the obvious" (*ibid.* at [42]). The court considered that there is also an equitable jurisdiction to set aside a contract for unilateral mistake in cases in which there is "sharp practice" or "unconscionable conduct" (at [76]–[77]). However, it indicated that it would not follow the view of the Canadian court in *Can-Dive Services v Pacific Coast Energy Corp* (2000) 74 B.C.L.R. (3d) 30 that constructive knowledge alone would suffice to "invoke equity's conscience" (at [78]–[80]). The practical difference between what the Court of Appeal envisaged would suffice and actual knowledge is not clear, but perhaps it would include the type of conduct described by Stuart-Smith L.J. in *Commission for New Towns v Cooper* [1995] Ch. 259, 280, quoted below, para.5–100. The *Chwee Kin Keong* case is noted by Yeo in (2005) 121 L.Q.R. 393.

(ii) *Mistaken Identity*

5–078—
5–082A   *Shogun Finance Ltd v Hudson* is now reported at [2004] 1 A.C. 919.

5. RECTIFICATION OF WRITTEN AGREEMENTS

Unilateral mistake

In *Hurst Stores & Interiors Ltd v ML Property Europe Ltd* [2004] EWCA 490;   **5–100**
[2004] Building L.R. 249 at [19], the Court of Appeal applied the dicta of Stuart-
Smith L.J. in *Commission for New Towns v Cooper* [1995] Ch. 259, 280:

> " . . . were it necessary to do so in this case, I would hold that where A intends B to
> be mistaken as to the construction of the agreement, so conducts himself that he
> diverts B's attention from discovering the mistake by making false and misleading
> statements, and B in fact makes the very mistake that A intends, then notwithstanding
> that A does not actually know, but merely suspects, that B is mistaken, and it cannot
> be shown that the mistake was induced by any misrepresentation, rectification may
> be granted. A's conduct is unconscionable and he cannot insist on performance in
> accordance to the strict letter of the contract; that is sufficient for rescission."

and of Evans L.J. (*ibid.*, at [292]) that " 'knowledge' in this context includes
'shut-eye' knowledge."

The nature of the knowledge that A must be shown to have of B's mistake if
rectification is to be granted was discussed in detail by the Court of Appeal in
George Wimpey UK Ltd v VI Construction Ltd [2005] EWCA Civ 77; [2005]
B.L.R. 135. It must be (i) actual knowledge; (ii) wilfully shutting one's eyes to
the obvious; or (iii) wilfully and recklessly failing to make such inquiries as an
honest and reasonable man would make. See the analysis of the various forms of
knowledge made by Peter Gibson J. in *Baden v Société Générale pour Favoriser
le Développement du Commerce et de l'Industrie en France SA (Note)* [1993] 1
W.L.R. 509 and cited by Millett J. in *Agip (Africa) Ltd v Jackson* [1990] Ch. 265,
293. Millett J. said that the true distinction is between honesty and dishonesty. In
cases within (i)–(iii) A would not be acting honestly. The implication is that the
same would not be true if A had merely (again using the categories of Peter
Gibson J.) (iv) knowledge of circumstances which would indicate the facts to an
honest and reasonable man or (v) knowledge of circumstances which would put
an honest and reasonable man on inquiry, though it might depend on the
comparative competence and resources of the parties (see the judgment of Sedley
L.J., [2005] EWCA Civ 77, at [65]). The type of conduct described by Stuart-
Smith L.J. in *Commission for New Towns v Cooper* [1995] Ch. 259, 280 (above)
would clearly not be honest.

MISREPRESENTATION

1. IN GENERAL

Preliminary

6–001 The Unfair Commercial Practices Directive (2005/29/EC of May 11, 2005, OJ L 149/22), which must be implemented by December 12, 2007, requires Member States to prohibit, and to provide "adequate and effective" means to combat unfair commercial practices. These are defined so as to include misleading actions (Art.6) and misleading omissions (Art.7). However it seems that unfair commercial practices within the meaning of the Directive will not give rise to civil remedies for individual consumers, as the Directive is "without prejudice to contract law and, in particular, to the rules of validity, formation or effect of a contract" (Art.3(1)). A useful summary of the Directive and its likely impact will be found in Twigg-Flesner (2005) 121 L.Q.R. 386.

2. WHAT CONSTITUTES EFFECTIVE MISREPRESENTATION

(a) *False Statement of Fact*

Statements of law

6–011 [*Note 45a, page* [435]]
See this Supplement, para.5–042, above.

Representation ceases to be true

[*Note 77: page* [439]]   **6–017**
Formerly Financial Services and Markets Act 2000, s.86 extended the provision on supplementary listing particulars (s.81) to a prospectus required by the listing rules. The issue of supplementary prospectuses is now governed by s.87G, inserted by the Prospectus Regulations 2005 (SI 2005/1443), reg.2(1), Sch.1 para.6(1), (2)). This applies to both listed and unlisted securities; the Public Offer of Securities Regulations 1995 have been revoked. See further below, para. 6–027.

(b) *Statement By or Known to Other Party*

The representor

[*Add to note 88, page* [440]]   **6–020**
An agent may have authority to make representations in relation to a particular transaction even though he has no authority to conclude the transaction: *First Energy v HIB* [1993] 2 Lloyd's Rep. 194, 204; *MCI Worldcom International Inc v Primus Telecommunications plc* [2004] EWCA Civ 957; [2004] 2 All E.R. (Comm.) 833 at [25]. For examples see Main Work, Vol. II, para.31–015.

(c) *Other Requirements*

The representee or person intended to act on the representation

[*Note 119: page* [444]]   **6–027**
The Public Offer of Securities Regulations 1995 have been revoked and replaced by new provisions inserted into the Financial Services and Markets Act 2000 by the Prospectus Regulations 2005 (SI 2005/1443). The effect of the Regulations is that unlisted securities are now within the definition of "transferable securities" in new s.102A, and the rules of the amended Pt VI of the Act apply to both listed and unlisted securities: see s.73A(4) (rules relating to transferable securities are known as the "prospectus rules") and ss.84–87R.

No requirement of materiality

In *MCI Worldcom International Inc v Primus Telecommunications plc* [2004] **6–036**
EWCA Civ 957; [2004] All E.R. (Comm.) 833 Mance L.J., delivering the judgment of the court, said that this paragraph appears "to put the position too cautiously". As he saw the position, "whether there is a representation and what its nature is must be judged objectively according to the impact that whatever is said may be expected to have on a reasonable representee in the position and with the known characteristics of the actual representee . . . The position in the case of a fraudulent misrepresentation may of course be different" (at [30]).

[*Note 166: page* [450]]
The decision of the House of Lords in *Standard Chartered Bank v Pakistan National Shipping Corp (No.2)* is now reported at [2003] 1 A.C. 959.

3. DAMAGES FOR MISREPRESENTATION

Preliminary

6–041   [*Amend note 182, line 3: page* [452]]
The reference to Lord Tenterden's Act should be to "Statute of Frauds Amendment Act 1828."

(a) *Fraudulent Misrepresentation*

Contributory negligence

6–063   [*Note 257: page* [462]]
Standard Chartered Bank v Pakistan National Shipping Corp (No.2) is now reported at [2003] 1 A.C. 959.

(b) *Negligent Misrepresentation*

Misrepresentation Act, s.2(1)

6–067   An action under s.2(1) is not an action for negligence within the meaning of the Limitation Act 1980, s.14A, since it is not necessary for the claimant to aver any negligent act or omission: *Laws v Society of Lloyd's* [2003] EWCA Civ 1887; *The Times*, January 23, 2004, at [91]. Whether it is an action in tort within s.2 of that Act was left open (see at [92]).

6–089   [*Note 362: page* [475]]
The Public Offer of Securities Regulations 1995 have been revoked: see above, para.6–027. The Financial Services and Markets Act 2000 s.86(1), which extended the provisions on listing particulars to a prospectus required by the listing rules, has been replaced by a new s.90(11), inserted by the Prospectus Regulations 2005 (SI 2005/1443), reg.2(1), Sch.1, para.5). This extends s.90 to prospectuses. A new s.90(12) provides that a person is not to be subject to civil liability solely on the basis of a summary in a prospectus unless the summary is misleading, inaccurate or inconsistent when read with the rest of the prospectus; and, for this purpose, a summary includes any translation of it.

(c) *Innocent Misrepresentation*

Exercise of court's discretion

6–099   The court may also exercise its discretion where to permit rescission would expose the misrepresentor to a large liability, even if that might in practice not be enforceable, whereas to maintain it would result in little additional loss to the misrepresentee. In *UCB Corporate Services Ltd v Thomason* [2005] EWCA Civ 225; [2005] All E.R. (D) 88 (Mar) the respondents were liable for large sums under two guarantees. As the result of misrepresentation, the appellants entered an agreement to waive their rights under the guarantees in exchange for payment of a much smaller sum. The trial judge refused to permit rescission and the Court of Appeal affirmed the decision. The judge was entitled to conclude that, had the misrepresentations not been made, the appellants would have recovered little or no more (at [37] and [52]), whereas if rescission were permitted the respondents would have faced "massive liability" (Brooke L.J. at [50]). "Loss" in s.2(2) includes financial loss and "what may loosely be described as detriment" (Latham L.J. at [37]). The damages that might be awarded to the appellants under s.2(2) were not the full sums due under the guarantees but only compensation for any loss of the chance to recover more than the appellants gave up when they entered the waiver agreement (at [38] and [51]).

6. Contracts *Uberrimae Fidei*

Companies

The Public Offer of Securities Regulations 1995 have been revoked and **6–149** replaced by new provisions inserted into the Financial Services and Markets Act 2000 by the Prospectus Regulations 2005 (SI 2005/1443): see above, paras 6–027 and 6–089.

CHAPTER 7

DURESS AND UNDUE INFLUENCE

The Unfair Commercial Practices Directive (2005/29/EC of May 11, 2005, OJ L 149/22), which must be implemented by December 12, 2007, requires Member States to prohibit, and to provide "adequate and effective" means to combat unfair commercial practices. These are defined so as to include "aggressive commercial practices" (Art.8) and "harassment, coercion and undue influence" (Art.9). However it seems that unfair commercial practices within the meaning of the Directive will not give rise to civil remedies for individual consumers, as the Directive is "without prejudice to contract law and, in particular, to the rules of validity, formation or effect of a contract" (Art.3(1)). A useful summary of the Directive and its likely impact will be found in Twigg-Flesner (2005) 121 L.Q.R. 386.

1. DURESS

(f) *Legitimacy of the Demand*

Threat to institute civil proceedings

An example of a threat to take legal proceedings which in the circumstances **7–041**
amounted to improper pressure, and thus actual undue influence, is *Drew v
Daniel* [2005] EWCA Civ 506; [2005] All E.R. (D) 84 (May).

2. UNDUE INFLUENCE

(a) *Introduction*

Unconscionable conduct

[*Add to note 215: page* [536]] **7–049**
See also *Pesticcio v Huet* [2004] EWCA Civ 372; [2004] All E.R. (D) 36
(Apr), also a case of a gift.

(b) *"Actual" Undue Influence*

Express influence

[*Add to note 243: page* [540]] **7–053**
An example of actual undue influence that seems to have amounted to illegit-
imate pressure is *Drew v Daniel* [2005] EWCA Civ 506; [2005] All E.R. (D) 84
(May). Ward L.J. pointed out that whether a vulnerable person has been exploited
is not relevant only in cases of presumed undue influence. In all cases of undue
influence, "the critical question is whether or not the influence has invaded the
free volition of the donor to accept or reject the persuasion or withstand the
influence" (at [36]).

(c) *Presumed Undue Influence*

(i) *Relationships giving rise to presumption of influence*

Guardian and ward

[*Correct note 315: page* [546]] **7–064**
Kempson v Ashbee (1874) L.R. 10 Ch. App. 15

(iii) *A Transaction not explicable by Ordinary Motives*

Transaction not explicable by ordinary motives

7–073   [*Note 361: page* [552]]
Mortgage Agency Services Number Two Ltd v Chater is now reported at
[2004] 1 P. & C.R. 4.

(f) *Undue Influence by Third Party*

Transaction not on its face to the advantage of the surety

7–099   [*Note 456: page* [562]]
Mortgage Agency Services Number Two Ltd v Chater is now reported at
[2004] 1 P. & C.R. 4.

[*Add new paragraph, page* [565]]

7–106A   **Replacement mortgages.** Where a mortgage granted by a wife to a bank was
voidable against the bank because the bank had constructive notice of undue
influence by the husband, a replacement mortgage may also be voidable against
the bank even if when the replacement was given there was no undue influence,
at least where the replacement mortgage is taken as a condition of discharging the
original mortgage.[473a] It does not matter that the new agreement is a fresh
contract rather than a variation of the old one, provided that the replacement
mortgage is between the same parties.[473b] However, it seems that the replacement
mortgage must be inseparable from the original mortgage, in the sense that the
replacement mortgage was granted before the grantor became aware that she had
a right to avoid the original one and in order to discharge it.[473c]

[473a] *Yorkshire Bank plc v Tinsley* [2004] EWCA Civ 816; [2004] 1 W.L.R. 2380 at [19].
[473b] *ibid.*, at [19]–[20].
[473c] *ibid.*, at [24], [32] and [39].

Jointly-owned homes

7–108   [*Note 478: page* [566]]
First National Bank plc v Achampong is now reported at [2004] 1 F.C.R.
18.

Part Three

CAPACITY OF PARTIES

PERSONAL INCAPACITY

4. MENTALLY DISORDERED PERSONS

The Mental Capacity Act 2005 ("the 2005 Act") has given effect to the recommendations of the Law Commission's Report No.231, *Mental Incapacity* (1995) and will have important effects on the making of contracts and deeds and the disposition of property by incapable adults (and incapable minors whom the court considers are likely still to lack capacity to make decisions in respect of the matter in question on attaining 18): 2005 Act, ss.2(5) and 18(3). It will replace the provisions governing mental patients found in Pt 7 of the Mental Health Act 1983 (and discussed at para.8–077 of the Main Work). While the Act was given Royal Assent in April 2005, its provisions are expected to be brought into force only in April 2007. Until the relevant provisions are brought into force, the law governing the making of contracts and deeds by mentally disordered persons will remain as stated in the Main Work. This Supplement will therefore note only the four most significant aspects of the Act for the making of contracts by incapable adults.

First, the 2005 Act provides that "a person lacks capacity in relation to a matter if at the material time he is unable to make a decision for himself in relation to the matter because of an impairment of, or a disturbance in the functioning of, the mind or brain": s.2(1). The Act then explains various considerations which are and are not to be taken into account for this purpose: s.2(2)–(4) and s.3. In relation to contracts, the 2005 Act removes the reference to mental incapacity in the Sale of Goods Act 1979, s.3(2), and instead provides that a person who lacks capacity to contract for the supply of goods or services must pay a reasonable price for necessary goods or services supplied to him, defining "necessary" as "suitable to a person's condition in life and to his actual requirements at the time when the goods or services are supplied": 2005 Act, s.7. This provision reflects the existing terms of the 1979 Act and clarifies the common law position as regards liability for necessary services.

Secondly, the 2005 Act makes provision for a new separate Court of Protection, with wide powers in relation to those lacking mental capacity: 2005 Act, ss.15–19, Pt 2. The new court will have a power to make declarations as to a person's capacity in relation to specified decisions or matters and on the lawfulness of any act done or to be done in relation to such a person: *ibid.*, s.15. It may itself make decisions on behalf of a person lacking capacity in relation to a matter either concerning that person's personal welfare or his property and affairs (*ibid.*, s.16(1) and 16(2)(a), 17 and 18) or appoint another person (a "deputy") to make decisions on that person's behalf in relation to such a matter: *ibid.*, s.16(2)(b). In coming to its decisions, the court must follow new statutory principles and give effect to the best interests of the person affected by the lack of capacity: *ibid.*, ss.1, 4 & 16(3).

Thirdly, the Act makes general provision to empower and to protect from liability (except for negligence) persons who "act in connection with the care or treatment of another person", which it terms "deputies": 2005 Act, ss.5–6, 19–20. As has been noted, such a deputy is to be treated as the agent of the incapable person (s.19(6)) and may be authorised to act in relation to many (but not all) of the property and affairs over which the court itself has power: *ibid.*, ss.16(2)(b), 18. Such a deputy must also follow the new statutory principles and give effect to the best interests of the person affected by the lack of capacity: *ibid.*, s.20(6).

Fourthly, the 2005 Act makes new provision for "lasting powers of attorney" which will replace the "enduring powers of attorney" provided for by the Enduring Powers of Attorney Act 1985: 2005 Act, ss.9–14.

CHAPTER 9

CORPORATIONS AND UNINCORPORATED ASSOCIATIONS

1. CORPORATIONS

(c) *Attribution of acts to a company*

[Add to note 21: page [617]]   **9–006**
Bank of India v Morris [2005] EWCA Civ 693; *The Times*, July 19, 2005.

Personal liability: estoppel

[Add to note 32: page [618]]   **9–008**
   Fiorentino Comm Guiseppe SRL v Farnesi [2005] EWHC 160 (Ch); [2005] 2
All E.R. 737.

Deeds

[Add to note 42: page [619]]   **9–010**
   The Regulatory Reform (Execution of Deeds and Documents) Order 2005 (SI
2005/1906): see above, Supplement to paras 1–077—1–082.

(d) *Registered Companies*

(i) *Contracts between Companies and Third Parties*

[Add new paragraph 9–030A: page [631]]

9–030A   An agent only has authority to act for the benefit of his principal unless the parties otherwise agree.[146a] The same rule applies to directors. As was stated by Lord Nicholls in *Criterion Properties Plc v Stratford UK Properties Ltd*[146b]:

> "If a company (A) enters into an agreement with B under which B acquires benefits from A, A's ability to recover these benefits from B depends essentially on whether the agreement is binding on A. If the directors of A were acting for an improper purpose when they entered into the agreement, A's ability to have the agreement set aside depends upon the application of familiar principles of agency and company law. If, applying these principles, the agreement is found to be valid and is therefore not set aside, questions of 'knowing receipt' by B do not arise. So far as B is concerned there can be no question of A's assets having been misapplied. B acquired the assets from A, the legal and beneficial owner of the assets, under a valid agreement made between him and A. If, however, the agreement is set aside, B will be accountable for any benefits he may have received from A under the agreement. A will have a proprietary claim, if B still has the assets. Additionally, and irrespective of whether B still has the assets in question, A will have the personal claim against B for unjust enrichment, subject always to the defence of change of position. B's personal accountability will not be dependent upon proof of fault or 'unconscionable' conduct on his part. B's accountability, in this regard, will be 'strict'."[146c]

[146a] *Bowstead and Reynolds on Agency* (17th ed.), art.23 cited with approval in *Hopkins v T L Dallas Group Ltd* [2004] EWHC 1379 (Ch); [2005] 1 B.C.L.C. 543.
[146b] [2004] UKHL 28; [2004] 1 W.L.R. 1846.
[146c] [2004] UKHL 28 at [4].

Ultra vires **and director's authority**

9–031   *[Replace last sentence of paragraph: page* [632]]

In *EIC Services Ltd v Phipps*[153] the Court of Appeal held that in the case of a bonus issue of shares, which is an internal corporate arrangement with no alteration in the assets of liabilities of the company, a shareholder could not be held as dealing with the company within the terms of s.35A.

[153] [2004] EWCA Civ 1069; [2005] 1 All E.R. 325.

CHAPTER 10

THE CROWN, PUBLIC AUTHORITIES AND THE EUROPEAN COMMUNITY

[Note 1: page [663]]
Update reference to Wade and Forsyth, *Administrative Law* to (9th ed., 2004), Chaps 20 and 21.

1. THE CROWN: STATUS AND SPECIAL RULES

Contracts between Crown and subject

[Note 1: page [663]]   **10–001**
Update reference to Wade and Forsyth, *Administrative Law* to (9th ed., 2004), Chs 20 and 21.

Update reference to Hogg, *Liability of the Crown* (1989) to Hogg and Monahan, *Liability of the Crown* (2000).

Crown Proceedings Act

[Add to note 9: page [664]]   **10–002**
s.39(1) and Sch.2, Crown Proceedings Act 1947 were repealed by Statute Law Revision Act 1950 s.1; but the 1950 Act did not reinstate those provisions repealed by s.39(1) and Sch.2 (see the proviso to Statute Law Revision Act 1950, s.1).

Fettering of discretion by contract

10–006   [*Note 35: page* [667]]
Delete reference to paras 10–007 *et seq.* and substitute para.10–017

Exercise of discretionary power in relation to a valid contract

10–008   [*Note 41: page* [667]]
Delete reference to para.10–001 and substitute para.10–011.

Crown contracting through agents

10–009   [*Add to end of note 43: page* [668]]
Marubeni Hong Kong and South China Ltd v Government of Mongolia [2004]
EWHC 472 (Comm); [2004] 2 Lloyd's Rep. 198.

2. THE *ULTRA VIRES* RULE

Statutory Modification of *ultra vires* rule

10–015
10–015A   [*Add new paragraph 10–015A: page* [671]]
    Impact of human rights on *ultra vires*. Where a public body makes an ultra vires agreement conferring a right to property, the intended recipient of that property right may have a remedy for breach of his human rights.[70a] According to European human rights jurisprudence, an ultra vires transaction purporting to confer a property right gives rise to a legitimate expectation of receiving that right; the legitimate expectation is, in itself, a possession for the purposes of Art.1, Protocol 1.[70b] The right expected to be conferred may be an interest in property,[70c] or it may relate to a component of the property, such as the existence of planning permission,[70d] or the absence of any public navigation right over a stretch of river.[70e] What is recognised as a legitimate expectation for these purposes is not dependent on domestic law definitions or classifications.[70f] Any interference with the right must be for a legitimate aim[70g] and proportionate.[70h] The mere fact that the public authority is reverting to its statutory mandate does not automatically satisfy the tests of justification and proportionality; some form of compensation may be required.[70i] The remedy for infringement of the right to property cannot require the defendant to confer the property interest which the claimant expected.[70j] If it takes the form of compensation, the European Court of Human Rights has held that the sum awarded should reflect the proportion of the initial consideration paid that can be attributed to the ultra vires element of the transaction.[70k] Such an award has been said to be based on unjust enrichment[70l]; as such, it transcends the usual requirement that restitution is only available for a total failure of consideration.[70m]

    [70a] Art.1 of Protocol No.1, European Convention for the Protection of Human Rights and Fundamental Freedoms. *Stretch v United Kingdom* (2004) 38 E.H.R.R. 12; (2003) 5 E.H.R.L.R. 554.

[70b] *Pine Valley Developments Ltd v Ireland* (1991) 14 E.H.R.R. 319. *cf. Al Fayed v Advocate General for Scotland* [2004] S.T.C. 1703 at [120], where it was conceded that a forward taxation agreement, under which the taxpayer paid a set sum per year, instead of being subject to assessment on actual transactions, created an expectation that engaged Art.1. It is difficult to reconcile this concession with the requirement that there should be the expectation of a property right.

[70c] *Stretch v United Kingdom* (2004) 38 E.H.R.R. 12; (2003) 5 E.H.R.L.R. 554.

[70d] *Pine Valley Developments Ltd v Ireland* (1991) 14 E.H.R.R. 319.

[70e] *Rowland v Environment Agency* [2003] EWCA Civ 1885; [2004] 2 Lloyd's Rep. 55.

[70f] *Beyeler v Italy* (2001) 33 E.H.R.R. 1224 at [100]. *cf. Al Fayed v Advocate General for Scotland* [2004] S.T.C. 1703 at [120], where counsel for the defender reserved the right to argue "if the case went further" that an expectation under an ultra vires agreement was a nullity and could not, therefore, give rise to a legitimate expectation. An appeal to the House of Lords was lodged on January 31, 2005.

[70g] *e.g. Al Fayed v Advocate General for Scotland* [2004] S.T.C. 1703; *Eden* [2005] B.T.R. 21 (forward taxation agreement repudiated in order to apply the taxation system equally to all taxpayers). *Pine Valley Developments Ltd v Ireland* (1991) 14 E.H.R.R. 319 (annulment of outline planning permission in order to protect the environment). Quaere, whether the aim of ceasing to act outside statutory powers should not automatically be regarded as a legitimate aim.

[70h] *e.g. Rowland v Environment Agency* [2003] EWCA Civ 1885; [2004] 2 Lloyd's Rep. 55 (reinstatement of public navigation right carried out so as to cause minimal interference to riparian owner).

[70i] *Stretch v United Kingdom* (2004) 38 E.H.R.R. 12; *cf. Pine Valley Developments Ltd v Ireland* (1991) 14 E.H.R.R. 319 (inherently risky nature of property development justified awarding no compensation where claimant deprived of planning permission).

[70j] *Rowland v Environment Agency* [2002] EWHC 2785; [2003] 1 Lloyd's Rep 427 at [80] (Lightman J.); expressly approved by the Court of Appeal, [2003] EWCA Civ 1885; [2004] 2 Lloyd's Rep. 55 at [85] (Peter Gibson L.J.) and [140] (Mance L.J.).

[70k] *Stretch v United Kingdom* (2004) 38 E.H.R.R. 12 at [47]–[50].

[70l] *Rowland v Environment Agency* [2003] EWCA Civ 1885; [2004] 2 Lloyd's Rep. 55 at [88].

[70m] See Main Work, para.29–054.

4. ESTOPPEL AND LEGITIMATE EXPECTATIONS

Estoppel and legitimate expectations

[Add to text after "contrary to statute", 7 lines from end: page [672]]   **10–017**
That there would be a substantive change is confirmed by a subsequent case, applying *Reprotech*, where it was observed that finding a legitimate expectation was "a task that is very different from an attempt to decide whether or not there is an estoppel in private law".[80a]

[80a] *R (on the application of Wandsworth LBC) v Secretary of State for Transport, Local Government and the Regions* [2003] EWHC 622 (Admin); [2004] 1 P. & C.R. 32 at [22].

[Note 80: page [672]]
Update references to *Wade and Forsyth* to (9th ed., 2004), pp.372–376, 500–505.

[Add to text at end of paragraph]
Where an authority is exercising the kind of public function that prevents it from being bound by an estoppel, it is also precluded from asserting an estoppel against an applicant.[81a]

^{81a} *Stancliffe Stone Co Ltd v Peak District National Park Authority* [2004] EWHC 1475 (QB); [2004] All E.R. (D) 232 at [35].

10–017   *[Page [672]]*

This paragraph must now be treated with caution in the light of recent cases applying the decision in *Regina (Reprotech (Pebsham) Ltd) v East Sussex County Council* [2002] UKHL 8; [2003] 1 W.L.R. 348. Since there can be no contract for planning permission (*Bielecki v Suffolk Coastal County Council* [2004] EWHC 342 (QB)), Lord Hoffmann's analysis can only be applicable to contracts where the factual matrix is analogous to a planning determination. Several important features of the planning context have been emphasised: planning determinations concern the general public interest (*South Bucks District Council v Flanagan* [2002] 1 W.L.R. 2601 at [16]); they bind the general public; and they involve participation by other planning authorities, the Secretary of State and the general public itself. (*R. (on the application of Wandsworth LBC) v Secretary of State for Transport Local Government and the Regions* [2003] EWHC 622 (Admin); [2004] 1 P. & C.R. 32 at [10]–[13]; *Stancliffe Stone Co Ltd v Peak District National Park Authority* [2004] EWHC 1475 (QB); [2005] Env.L.R. 4 at [32].) Some of these features were present in *Yarmouth (Isle of Wight) Harbour Commissioners v Harold Hayles (Yarmouth Isle of Wight) Ltd* [2004] EWHC 3375 (Ch), [2004] All E.R. (D) 66 (Dec), where it was held that an estoppel could not be relied upon against a statutory harbour authority in respect of its decision not to renew mooring licences. But many contracts made by public authorities are unlikely to share these features, and there seems to be no good reason to deny an estoppel where such features are absent. That there is still a role for estoppel in government contracts is confirmed by *Marubeni Hong Kong and South China Ltd v Government of Mongolia* [2004] EWHC 472 (Comm); [2004] 2 Lloyd's Rep. 198, which concerned a commercial guarantee issued by the Mongolian Minister of Finance. There counsel for the defendant cited *Reprotech* in support of a submission that the Minister's authority to issue the guarantee could not be determined using estoppel, but had to be analysed in terms of public law concepts (at [97]–[102]). Cresswell J. rejected the submission, and proceeded to apply the orthodox principles of ostensible authority, which, as he acknowledged (at [124]), is a species of estoppel. His analysis was not challenged on appeal: *Marubeni Hong Kong and South China Ltd v The Mongolian Government* [2005] EWCA Civ 395 at [6].

7. PUBLIC PROCUREMENT

Implied contract governing public tendering

10–025   *[Page [675]]*

This paragraph must now be read in the light of the Privy Council's decision in *Pratt Contractors Ltd v Transit New Zealand* [2003] UKPC 83; [2004] B.L.R. 143 (see Arrowsmith, (2004) 13 P.P.L.R. NA125), where (at [2]) it was conceded "in the light of modern authority" that submitting a tender in response to a request for tenders created a preliminary contract, which obliged the procuring authority to act fairly and in good faith in the selection process. This implied duty required any evaluation of the tenders to express honestly the views of the selectors. It also precluded selectors from taking steps to avoid receiving relevant information which they strongly suspected would show their opinion to be mistaken. However, there was no obligation on the procuring authority to eliminate any appearance of bias from the process, nor to avoid acting in other ways that, in different contexts, would be grounds for judicial review (at [47]). Whether the same analysis will be adopted by English courts will depend on their willingness to follow the Commonwealth authorities establishing the implied duty; they may be reluctant to go as far one Australian decision, which saw the implied duty relating to tenders as part of a more general implied obligation of good faith (at [45]: "a somewhat controversial question").

[*Note 113: page* [675]]
Fairclough Building Ltd v Port Talbot BC is reported at (1991) 62 B.L.R. 82.

EC procurement law

[*Note 116: page* [676]]   **10–026**
Arrowsmith, *The Law of Public and Utilities Procurement* is now in a second edition (2005).

[*Delete note 119: page* [676] *and substitute*]
Directive 2004/18 on the co-ordination of procedures for the award of public works contracts, public supply contracts and public service contracts [2004] OJ L 134/114, supplemented by Directive 2004/17 co-ordinating the procurement procedures of entities operating in the water, energy, transport and postal services sectors [2004] OJ L 134/1. The previous Directives have been repealed (Directive 2004/18, art.82). Both Directives must be implemented by January 31, 2006. The major change in the new legislation is the introduction of a procedure for competitive dialogue: Arrowsmith (2004) 41 C.M.L.Rev. 1277.

[*Add to last line of note 120, after* "2001/2418) *and*": *page* [676]]
Public Contracts (Works, Services and Supply) and Utilities Contracts (Amendment) Regulations 2003

[*Add to text at end of paragraph: page* [677]]
These detailed express obligations concerning transparency of process may also give rise to a general implied obligation not to act in bad faith.[120a]

[120a] *Luck t/a Luck Arboricultural & Horticultural v London Borough of Tower Hamlets* [2003] EWCA Civ 52; [2003] 2 C.M.L.R. 12 at [59]–[60].

POLITICAL IMMUNITY AND INCAPACITY

1. FOREIGN STATES, SOVEREIGNS, AMBASSADORS AND INTERNATIONAL ORGANISATIONS

Sovereign immunity and human rights

11–003   [*Add to note 11: page* [688]]
Jones v Ministry of the Interior of the Kingdom of Saudi Arabia [2004] EWCA Civ 1394; [2005] 2 W.L.R. 808.

[*Add at end of note 12: page* [688]]
Voyiakis (2003) 52 I.C.L.Q. 297; Lloyd Jones (2003) 52 I.C.L.Q. 463; *Yang* (2003) 74 B.Y.I.L. 333; *Garnett* [2005] 54 I.C.L.Q. 705. See also *Jones v Ministry of the Interior of the Kingdom of Saudi Arabia* [2004] EWCA Civ 1394; [2005] 2 W.L.R. 808.

State Immunity Act 1978

11–004   [*Add to note 13: page* [688]]
See also United Nations Convention on Jurisdictional Immunities of States and Their Property (December 2004, not yet in force).

[*Add to note 16: page* [689]]
Military Affairs Office of the Embassy of the State of Kuwait v Caramba-Coker (E.A.T./1054/02/RN, April 10, 2003).

[*Add to note 17: page* [689]]
Aziz v Republic of Yemen [2005] EWCA Civ 754; *The Times,* June 22, 2005.

[Add to note 18: page [689]]
Jones v Ministry of the Interior of the Kingdom of Saudi Arabia [2004] EWCA Civ 1394; [2005] 2 W.L.R. 808.

[Add in penultimate line of note 25: page [690]]   **11–005**
Al-Kadhimi v Government of Saudi Arabia [2003] EWCA Civ 1689; *Aziz v Republic of Yemen* [2005] EWCA Civ 754; *The Times,* June 22, 2005; Garnett (2005) 54 I.C.L.Q. 705.

[Add to note 26: page [690]]
cf. Military Affairs Office of the Embassy of the State of Kuwait v Caramba-Coker (E.A.T./1054/02/RN, April 10, 2003).

[Add at end of note 34: page [690]]
See *Svenska Petroleum Exploration A.B. v Government of the Republic of Lithuania* [2005] EWHC 9 (Comm); [2005] 1 Lloyd's Rep. 515.

[Add at end of note 35: page [691]]   **11–006**
Norsk Hydro ASA v State Property Fund of Ukraine [2002] EWHC 2120 (Comm).

Acts of sovereign states

[Add at end of note 44: page [691]]   **11–007**
R. (on the Application of Abassi) v Secretary of State for Foreign and Commonwealth Affairs [2002] EWCA Civ 1598; [2003] U.K.H.R.R. 76; *Jones v Ministry of the Interior of the Kingdom of Saudi Arabia* [2004] EWCA Civ 1394; [2005] 2 W.L.R. 808.

[Add at end of note 45: page [691]]
Briggs (2002) 6 Sing. J. Int. & Comp. L. 953; Carruthers and Crawford (2003) 52 I.C.L.Q. 761. See also *Jones v Ministry of the Interior of the Kingdom of Saudi Arabia* [2004] EWCA Civ 1394; [2005] 2 W.L.R. 808.

[Add to note 46: page [692]]
See also *Jones v Ministry of the Interior of the Kingdom of Saudi Arabia* [2004] EWCA Civ 1394; [2005] 2 W.L.R. 808.

Period of immunity

[Add in penultimate line of note 65: page [694]]   **11–014**
Jimenez v Inland Revenue Commissioners [2004] S.T.C. 371.

International organisations

[Note 85: page [695]]   **11–018**
International Organisations Act 1968 is further amended by International Organisations Act 2005.

Other persons entitled to immunity

11–019   [*First line of note 103: page* [697]]

Although immunity is conferred on the Commonwealth Secretariat, that immunity does not extend to the Commonwealth Secretariat Arbitration Tribunal, decisions of which may be reviewed under the Arbitration Act 1996: *Mohsin v Commonwealth Secretariat* [2002] EWHC 377 (Comm). The Commonwealth Secretariat Act 1966 is amended by International Organisations Act 2005, ss.1–3.

Submission to jurisdiction

11–021   [*Add to note 119: page* [698]]

Aziz v Republic of Yemen [2005] EWCA Civ 745; *The Times,* June 22, 2005.

[*Add to note 125: page* [699]]

See *Mitchell v Ibrahim Al-Dali* [2005] EWCA Civ 720 (undertaking by foreign state not to appeal a costs order made against it does not imply waiver of immunity should enforcement of the costs order be sought).

2. ALIEN ENEMIES

[*Note 137: page* [700]]

In *Ahmed Amin v Brown* [2005] EWHC 1670 (Ch); *The Times,* August 24, 2005, it was held that the procedural incapacity of an alien enemy only came into existence if a technical state of war existed as between the United Kingdom and the relevant country and that there was no warrant for extending the disability to modern armed conflict which did not involve war in this sense. Accordingly, an Iraqi citizen resident in Iraq was entitled to proceed in the English court as claimant since the court was satisfied, on the basis of Ministerial statements, that Her Majesty's government position was that there is not, and has not been, a state of war between the United Kingdom and Iraq.

Who is an alien enemy

11–024   [*Add to note 139: page* [700]]

Ahmed Amin v Brown, above.

Alien enemy as claimant

11–028   [*Add to notes 161 and 162: page* [702]]

Ahmed Amin v Brown, above.

Part Four

THE TERMS OF THE CONTRACT

CHAPTER 12

EXPRESS TERMS

2. CLASSIFICATION OF TERMS

(a) *Conditions*

Promissory and contingent conditions

[*Add at end of note 104: page* [719]]   **12–027**
   cf. Haugland Tankers AS v RMK Marine Gemi Yapim Sanayii ve Dentz Tasimaciligi Isletmesi AS [2005] EWHC 321 (Comm); [2005] 1 Lloyd's Rep. 573 (payment of commitment fee condition precedent to exercise of option).

(c) *Intermediate Terms*

Classification of time stipulations

12–037   This paragraph was approved by Langley J. in *Haugland Tankers AS v RMK Marine Gemi Yapim Sanayii ve Dentz Tasimiciligi Isletmesi AS*, above, at [31].

Effect of failure to perform on time

12–038   [*Add to note 182: page* [727]]
Contrast Stannard (2004) 120 L.Q.R. 137, 155.

3. CONSTRUCTION OF TERMS

(a) *General Rules of Construction*

Law and fact

12–046   [*Add to note 208: page* [731]]
Sun Life Assurance Co of Canada v Lincoln National Life Insurance Co [2004] EWCA Civ 1660; [2005] 1 Lloyd's Rep. 606 at [15].

(b) *Ordinary Meaning to be Adopted*

Meaning of words

12–050   [*Add to note 221; page* [732]]
Static Control Components (Europe) Ltd v Egan [2004] EWCA Civ 392; [2004] 2 Lloyd's Rep. 429 at [12]–[14]; *BP Exploration Operating Co Ltd v Kvaerner Oilfield Products Ltd* [2004] EWHC 999 (Comm); [2005] 1 Lloyd's Rep 307 at [47]–[48]; *Sirius International Insurance (Publ) v FAI General Insurance Ltd* [2004] UKHL 54; [2004] 1 W.L.R. 3251 at [19]; *Dairy Containers Ltd v Tasman Orient Line CV* [2004] UKPC 22; [2005] 1 W.L.R. 215 at [12].

[*Add to note 227; page* [733]]
Sirius International Insurance (Publ) v FAI General Insurance Ltd, above, at [19].

Adoption of the ordinary meaning of words

12–051   [*Add to note 228: page* [733]]
BP Exploration Operating Co Ltd v Kvaerner Oilfield Products Ltd [2004] EWHC 999 (Comm); [2005] 1 Lloyd's Rep. 307 at [93].

Absurdity, inconsistency, etc

[*Add to note 238: page* [734]]   **12–055**
 BP Exploration Operating Co Ltd v Kvaerner Oilfield Products Ltd [2004]
EWHC 999 (Comm); [2005] 1 Lloyd's Rep. 307 at [95]. *cf. Armitage v Staveley
Industries plc* [2004] EWHC 2320 (Comm); [2004] Pens. L.R. 385.

Mercantile contracts

[*Add to note 248: page* [736]]   **12–057**
 Sirius International Insurance (Publ) v FAI General Insurance Ltd [2004]
UKHL 54; [2004] 1 W.L.R. 3251 at [19].

(d) *Effecting the Intention of the Parties*

Modifying

The law relating to misnomer was explored by Rix L.J. in *Dumford Trading*   **12–075**
AG v OAO Atlantrybflot [2005] EWCA Civ 24; [2005] 1 Lloyd's Rep. 289,
where this paragraph was cited (at [27]); but see below, para.12–124.

[*Add to note 305: page* [743]]
 Contrast *Internaut Shipping GmbH v Fercometal SARL* [2003] EWCA Civ
812; [2003] 2 Lloyd's Rep. 430 (mistake beyond misnomer).

Clauses incorporated by reference

[*Add at end of paragraph: page* [745]]   **12–079**
 A term in a proposal for insurance which conflicts with a term of the policy
will be overriden by the term of the policy.[327a]

[327a] *Thor Navigation Inc v Ingosstrakh Insurance* [2005] EWHC 19; [2005] 1 Lloyd's Rep. 547
(applying *Izzard v Universal Insurance* [1937] A.C. 773, 780).

Grammatical errors

[*Add at end of note 330: page* [745]]   **12–080**
 See also *BP Exploration Operating Co Ltd v Kvaerner Oilfield Products Ltd*
[2004] EWHC 999 (Comm); [2005] 1 Lloyd's Rep. 307 at [95]. *cf. Armitage v
Staveley Industries plc* [2004] EWHC 2320 (Comm); [2004] Pens. L.R. 385.

4. ADMISSIBILITY OF EXTRINSIC EVIDENCE

(c) *Evidence as to the True Nature of the Agreement*

Evidence of Agency

[*Add to note 488: page* [762]]   **12–114**
 See also *Internaut Shipping v Fercometal SARL* [2003] EWCA Civ 812;
[2003] 2 Lloyd's Rep. 430 (evidence of no agency).

(d) *Evidence to Interpret or Explain the Written Agreement*

Evidence of surrounding circumstances

12–118   [*Add to end of note 503: page* [765]]
Static Control Components (Europe) Ltd v Egan [2004] EWCA 392; [2004] 2
Lloyd's Rep. 429; *UCB Corporate Services Ltd v Thomason* [2004] 2 All E.R.
(Comm.) 774; *Sirius International Insurance (Publ) v FAI General Insurance Ltd*
[2004] UKHL 54; [2004] 1 W.L.R. 3251 at [20].

12–119   [*Add in line 7, after reference to Aqua Design & Play International Ltd v Kier
Regional Ltd in note 507: page* [765]]
P&S Platt Ltd v Crouch [2003] EWCA Civ 1110; [2004] 1 P. & C.R. 18.

Identity of parties

12–122   [*Add to note 528: page* [767]]
But contrast *Shogun Finance Ltd v Hudson* [2003] UKHL 62; [2004] 1 A.C.
919 at [49]; *Dumford Trading AG v OAO Atlantrybflot* [2005] EWCA Civ 24;
[2005] 1 Lloyd's Rep. 289 at [32]; see below, para.12–124.

Subject-matter

12–123   [*Add to note 530: page* [767]]
cf. Compagnie Noga d'Importation et d'Exportation SA v Abacha (No. 4)
[2003] EWCA Civ 1100; [2003] 2 All E.R. (Comm.) 915 (where no intention to
conclude binding contract).

Equivocations

12–124   [*Add at end of paragraph: page* [768]]
However, in *Dumford Trading AG v OAO Atlantrybflot*,[537a] Rix L.J. explored
the law relating to misnomer and suggested that where there are two possible
entities intrinsic evidence would not be admissible to identify the entity referred
to, but if there is only one possible entity then it would be possible to use
extrinsic evidence to identify a misdescribed party.

[537a] [2005] EWCA Civ 24; [2005] 1 Lloyd's Rep. 289 at [32].

Subsequent acts

12–126   [*Add at end of note 547: page* [769]]
Carmichael v National Power plc [1999] 1 W.L.R. 2042, 2051.

CHAPTER 13

IMPLIED TERMS

Intention of parties

[*Add to note 5: page* [774]]   **13–004**
cf. Kramer [2004] C.L.J. 384.

Efficacy to contract

[*Add to note 10: page* [775]]   **13–005**
CEL Group Ltd v Nedlloyd Lines UK Ltd [2003] EWCA Civ 1716; [2004] 1
Lloyd's Rep. 381 at [20]–[21].

[*Add at end of paragraph: page* [775]]   **13–006**
into a contract which provided that one party should not offer design services
to any third person without the consent of the other that the consent would not
unreasonably be withheld.[21a]

[21a] *Societa Explosivi Industriale SpA v Ordnance Technologies (VIC) Ltd* [2004] EWHC 48
(Comm); [2004] 1 All E.R. (Comm.) 619.

Where term not implied

[*Add to note 36: page* [777]]   **13–009**
Holding and Management (Solitaire) Ltd v Ideal Homes Northwest Ltd [2004]
EWHC 2408; (2004) 96 Const.L.R. 114.

[*Add to note 39: page* [778]]
But in *Crossley v Faithful & Gould Holdings Ltd* [2004] EWCA Civ 293;
[2004] I.R.L.R. 377, Morritt V.C. expressed the view that, in the case of a
contract of employment, it was better to focus on questions of reasonableness,
fairness and the balance of competing policy considerations rather than on the
elusive concept of "necessity".

[*Add to note 40*]
Armitage v Staveley Industries plc [2004] EWHC 2320; [2004] Pens. L.R.
385.

[*Add to note 42*]

Hadley Design Associates Ltd v Westminster City Council [2003] EWHC 1617; [2004] T.C.L.R. 1.

13–010   [*Page* [778]]

In *Interleasing (UK) Ltd v Morris* [2002] EWHC 1086 (Ch), where a contract made provision for obtaining counsel's opinion, no term was implied that the opinion would only be valid if given on the basis of true facts or proper instructions. In *Crossley v Faithful & Gould Holdings Ltd* [2004] EWCA Civ 293; [2004] I.R.L.R. 377, no term was implied into a contract of employment that an employer ought to take reasonable care of an employee's economic well-being by advising him of the financial consequences under an insurance scheme of his early retirement. In *Ultraframe (UK) Ltd v Tailored Roofing Systems Ltd* [2004] EWCA Civ 585; [2004] 2 All E.R. (Comm.) 692, no term was implied into an exclusive purchasing agreement that the seller would not act in a way that was prejudicial to the buyer by selling directly to customers.

[*Add to note 48*]

But see the doubts expressed in *Crossley v Faithful & Gould Holdings Ltd*, above.

Co-operation

13–011   [*Add to note 66: page* [780]]

Goodway v Zurich Insurance Co [2004] EWHC 137; (2004) 96 Const.L.R. 49.

Prevention of performance

13–012   [*Add after reference to Martin-Smith v Williams in note 69: page* [780]]

CEL Group Ltd v Nedlloyd Lines UK Ltd [2003] EWCA Civ 1716; [2004] 1 Lloyd's Rep. 381 at [11], [22] and [23].

Trading Stamps

13–030   The Trading Stamps Act 1964 has been repealed by the Regulatory Reform (Trading Stamps) Order 2005 (SI 2005/871).

Package travel etc

13–034   For the relationship between the Regulations and the (Athens) International Convention on the Carriage of Passengers and their Luggage by Sea (see paras. 14–117 and 36–063, below), see *Lee v Airtours Holidays Ltd* [2004] 1 Lloyd's Rep. 683.

[*Add to note 162: page* [790]]

Chapman [2004] I.T.L.J. (3) 129.

EXEMPTION CLAUSES

2. RULES OF CONSTRUCTION

General principles

[*Add to note 19: page* [793]]   **14–005**
   Dairy Containers Ltd v Tasman Orient Line CV [2004] UKPC 22; [2005] 1 W.L.R. 215 at [12].

Inconsistency with main purpose of contract

[*Add to note 37: page* [795]]   **14–007**
   See *Mitsubishi Corp v Eastwind Transport Ltd* [2004] EWHC 2924 (Comm); [2005] 1 Lloyd's Rep. 383 at [29].

[*Add to note 44: page* [796]]
   Mitsubishi Corp v Eastwind Transport Ltd, above.

Construction contra proferentem

[*Add to note 58: page* [797]]   **14–009**
   Homburg Houtimport BV v Agrosin Private Ltd [2004] 1 A.C. 715, 779; *Dairy Containers Ltd v Tasman Orient Line CV* [2004] UKPC 22; [2005] 1 W.L.R. 215 at [12].

Liability for negligence

14–010 *[Add to note 61: page [798]]*
Frans Maas (UK) Ltd v Samsung Electronics (UK) Ltd [2004] EWHC 1502 (Comm); [2004] 2 Lloyd's Rep. 251 at [131]–[139].

Words wide enough to cover negligence

14–011 *[Add to note 80: page [800]]*
Frans Maas (UK) Ltd v Samsung Electronics (UK) Ltd, above, at [139]–[152]

Deliberate breaches

14–016 *[Add to note 110: page [803]]*
Frans Maas (UK) Ltd v Samsung Electronics (UK) Ltd [2004] EWHC 1502 (Comm); [2004] 2 Lloyd's Rep. 251 at [139]–[152]

Burden of proof

14–018 *[Add at end of note 125: page [805]]*
followed in *Euro Cellular (Distribution) plc v Danzas Ltd* [2003] EWHC 3161 (Comm); [2004] 1 Lloyd's Rep. 521.

14–019 *[Add at end of note 127: page [805]]*
Euro Cellular (Distribution) plc v Danzas Ltd, above.

4. APPLICATION OF RULES OF CONSTRUCTION TO PARTICULAR CONTRACTS

Misdelivery by carrier

14–033 *[Add at end of note 198: page [814]]*
East West Corporation v DKBS 1912 [2003] EWCA Civ 83; [2003] Q.B. 1509 at [65]–[68].

5. EXEMPTION CLAUSES AND THIRD PARTIES

Bailment

14–054 *[Add to note 274: page [824]]*
East West Corporation v DKBS 1912 [2003] EWCA Civ 83; [2003] Q.B. 1509 at [25]–[27].

[Add to note 279: page [825]]
East West Corporation v DKBS 1912, above, at [30], [69].

6. Statutory Control of Exemption Clauses

(a) *Unfair Contract Terms Act 1977*

Dealing as consumer

[Add to note 343: page [832]]   **14–066**
The *R&B* case was followed in *Feldaroll Foundry plc v Hermes Leasing (London) Ltd* [2004] EWCA Civ 747; see para.43–106, below.

Liability arising in contract

[Add to note 365: page [834]]   **14–072**
Hadley Design Associates Ltd v Westminster City Council [2003] EWHC 1617; [2004] T.C.L.R. 1.

[Add to note 377: page [835]]   **14–074**
Contrast *Hadley Design Associates Ltd v Westminster City Council*, above (one month's termination clause in architects' contract not unreasonable).

Guidelines

[Add to note 425: page [840]]   **14–085**
Frans Maas (UK) Ltd v Samsung Electronics (UK) Ltd [2004] EWHC 1502 (Comm); [2004] 2 Lloyd's Rep. 251 at [159].

[Add to note 426]
Frans Maas (UK) Ltd v Samsung Electronics (UK) Ltd, above, at [159].

[Add to note 427]
Frans Maas (UK) Ltd v Samsung Electronics (UK) Ltd, above, at [159].

Limits on amount

[Add in note 432 after Pegler Ltd v Wang: page [841]]   **14–087**
Frans Maas (UK) Ltd v Samsung Electronics (UK) Ltd [2004] EWHC 1502 (Comm); [2004] 2 Lloyd's Rep. 251 at [159].

Reasonableness under Unfair Contract Terms Act 1977

In *Frans Maas (UK) Ltd v Samsung Electronics (UK) Ltd* [2004] EWHC 1502   **14–096**
(Comm); [2004] 2 Lloyd's Rep. 251, a clause in the BIFA (freight forwarders) contract limiting the damages recoverable in respect of the loss by theft of mobile telephones from the bailee's warehouse was upheld as reasonable.

[Add to note 482: page [847]]   **14–099**
Frans Maas (UK) Ltd v Samsung Electronics (UK) Ltd, above, at [158].

(c) *Other Statutes*

Carriage by sea

14–117   In *Jindal Iron and Steel Co Ltd v Islamic Solidarity Shipping Co Jordan Inc* [2004] UKHL 49; [2005] 1 W.L.R. 1363, a term in a charterparty transferring responsibility for loading, stowage and discharge of cargo from the owner to the cargo owner was held to be valid notwithstanding art, III, r.2, of the Hague-Visby rules.

Consumer protection

14–125   [*Add to note 542: page* [855]]
Final proposals have now been made by the two Law Commissions in a joint report (Law Com. No. 292, Scot Law Com. No. 199) published in February 2005.

[*Add to note 548: page* [855]]
See *Wilson v Robertsons (London) Ltd* [2005] EWHC 1425 (Ch); *The Times*, July 28, 2005.

14–127   The Trading Stamps Act 1964 has been repealed by the Regulatory Reform (Trading Stamps) Order 2005 (SI 2005/871).

14–129   [*Add to note 554: page* [856]]
Amended by SI 2005/689. See also the Financial Services (Distant Marketing) Regulations 2004 (SI 2004/2095).

[*Add to note 555*]
Amended by SI 2003/2579.

Enterprise Act 2002

14–131   [*Add to note 571: page* [857]]
See SI 2003/1374, SI 2004/2095.

[*Add to note 575*]
SI 2003/1375, SI 2004/935; SI 2005/917. For "supercomplaints" to the OFT, see s.11 and SI 2003/1368, SI 2004/1517.

8. Force Majeure Clauses

Force majeure clauses

14–137   [*Add to note 602: page* [860]]
See Allen (2003) 147 S.J. 1416–1417.

[Add at the end of note 608: page [861]]   **14–138**

The words "beyond our control" will be construed to apply to the specific as well as to the non-specific events: *Frontier International Shipping Corp v Swissmarine Corporation Inc* [2004] EWHC 8 (Comm); [2005] 1 Lloyd's Rep. 390 at [27]–[28].

"Prevented" clauses

[Add to end of note 627: page [864]]   **14–141**

Contrast *Mamidoil-Jetoil Greek Petroleum Co SA v Okta Crude Oil Refinery AD* [2003] 1 Lloyd's Rep. 1 (Comm Ct.); [2003] EWCA Civ 1031; [2003] 2 Lloyd's Rep. 635.

CHAPTER 15

UNFAIR TERMS IN CONSUMER CONTRACTS

2. THE UNFAIR TERMS IN CONSUMER CONTRACTS REGULATIONS 1999

[Add new paragraph 15–010A: page [879]]

15–010A   **Proposals for reform.** The Law Commissions have published a joint report on proposed reforms to the legislation on unfair terms in contracts.[46a] The proposals include the creation of a unified regime for the control of unfair terms in consumer contracts, putting together the controls at present found in the Unfair Contract Terms Act 1977 and the Unfair Terms in Consumer Contracts Regulations 1999; preserving the protection given by the Unfair Contract Terms Act 1977 in business contracts; and extending existing protection against unfair contract terms for consumers to small businesses.

[46a] Law Commission, Scottish Law Commission, *Unfair Terms in Contracts,* Law Com. No.292, Scot Law Com. No.199 (2005).

(a) *The Contracts Governed by the Regulations*

Contracts for the sale, etc. of an interest in land

15–014—   *[Pages [880]–[882]]*
15–017   Paragraphs 15–014—15–017 need to be read in the light of the decision of the Court of Appeal in *London Borough of Newham v Khatun* [2004] EWCA Civ 55;

[2005] Q.B. 37. In that case, the question arose whether the 1993 Directive (and therefore the 1999 Regulations) applies to the terms on which accommodation is let by a local authority pursuant to its duty under the homeless persons legislation contained in Pt VII of the Housing Act 1996. Having looked at the *travaux préparatoires* of the Directive, the Court of Appeal noted the differences of terminology used by some of its different language versions to describe its subject matter (*e.g.* "seller of goods" and *"vendeur des biens"*, as identified in para.15–014 of the Main Text) and considered that these "effectively demolish" the textual argument that the English version's reference to "seller of goods" point to the exclusion of contracts relating to land: [2004] EWCA Civ 55, at [78]–[83]. The Court of Appeal therefore held that the 1999 Regulations apply equally to contracts relating to land. Moreover, a few weeks after this decision, the European Court of Justice in *Freiburger Kommunalbauten GMbH Bauge-sellschaft & Co KG v Hofstetter* Case C-237/02 [2004] 2 C.M.L.R. 13 was apparently content to assume that a contract for the purchase of a building to be constructed falls within the ambit of the 1993 Directive, although the issue of the application of the 1993 Directive to contracts relating to land was not before the court.

"Sellers or suppliers"

[Add to text after note 82: page [884]]

15–021

In *London Borough of Newham v Khatun*[82a] the Court of Appeal held that the provision of accommodation by a local authority under a contract of tenancy, pursuant to its duty under the homeless persons legislation contained in Pt VII of the Housing Act 1996, falls within the scope of the 1993 Directive, as this activity comes within the words "trade, business or profession" under art.2(c) of the Directive, despite the statutory context of this provision.

[82a] [2004] EWCA Civ 55; [2005] Q.B. 37.

(b) *Contract Terms Governed by the Regulations*

[Add new paragraph 15–032A: page [892]]

Standard terms put forward by the consumer. In *Bryen & Langley Ltd v Boston* the question arose as to how the 1999 Regulations would apply to standard terms put forward by a consumer (or rather by his professional advisers) and incorporated into a consumer contract, on the facts, the standard terms stemming from one of the JCT standard building contracts.[150a] The High Court considered that in these circumstances any term contained in the standard contract would usually not fail the test of fairness found in reg.5 of the 1999 Regulations as it would not cause a significant imbalance in the rights and obligations of the parties to the detriment of the consumer *contrary to the requirement of good faith*.[150b] However, it was also seen as "at least arguable that where the 'consumer' has been able to influence the substance of the relevant term because he chose to use the standard form of contract in which it is contained, the term does not fall to be regarded as not having been individually

15–032A

negotiated."[150c] However, with respect, it is submitted that the provisions of the1999 Regulations and the 1993 Directive governing the exclusion of individually negotiated terms from the ambit of their controls do not bear out this argument, particularly bearing in mind that these exclusions should be interpreted strictly following the general approach of the European Court of Justice to exceptions[150d]: for while a consumer who proposes a set of standard terms may sometimes be thought to have "been able to influence the substance of the term" (by amending or deleting the standard terms which he himself proposes), this may not always be the case. Moreover, the exclusion found in reg.5(1) of the 1999 Regulations is for contract terms which have been the object of "individual negotiation", whereas a term in a set of standard terms proposed by the consumer remains standard (and often unknown to or not understood by the consumer and possibly even his professional advisers) and cannot easily be said to be "*individually* negotiated".[150e] For this reason, it is submitted that the better approach is to take into account the fact that a consumer has proposed the terms of a contract as a matter of the test of fairness and the requirement of good faith.[150f]

[150a] [2004] EWHC 2450 (TCC); 98 Con L.R. 82.

[150b] *ibid.*, at [43], below, Supplement to para.15–060

[150c] *ibid.*, *per* Judge Richard Seymour Q.C.

[150d] 1993 Directive, art.3(1) and (2); 1999 Regulations, reg.5(1)–(4). On the strict interpretation of exceptions see, *e.g.* Case C-203/99, *Veedfald v Århus Amtskommune,* para.15 in the context of Directive 84/374/EEC concerning liability for defective products, Art.7.

[150e] *cf.* the condition for the application of the controls found in the Unfair Contract Terms Act 1977, s.3(1) that the term be on the written standard terms of the business relying on a particular term ("the *other's* written standard terms of business"): see Main Work, para.14–073.

[150f] Below, Supplement to para.15–060.

[*Add new paragraphs after paragraph 15–036*: page [895]]

15–036A   **The relevance of construction of the contract.** In *Bairstow Eves London Central Ltd v Darlingtons,*[165a] the House of Lords' approach to reg.6(2) of the 1999 Regulations in the *First National Bank plc* case[165b] was applied to clauses setting the contract price in an estate agency contract. There a vendor of a flat (the "consumer") had entered a contract with an estate agent by which the latter undertook the sole agency to sell the flat on their behalf. Under its standard terms, the "standard commission" payable to the estate agent was set at 3 per cent of the sale price of the property, but "early payment" attracted a "discount rate" of 1.5 per cent of the sale price, early payment being defined as payment of the full sum payable within 10 working days of completion of the sale. It was further expressly specified that if such a full sum was not paid within this time, the "standard commission" would become payable together with interest at 3 per cent above base rate. After completing a sale, the vendor's solicitors did not pay the agent the *full* sum of the "discount rate" within the 10 day period (falling short by a mere £387) even though they were in funds to do so, and so the estate agent claimed the "standard rate" plus interest. It was then claimed that the terms of the contract setting the 3 per cent commission rate were unfair within the meaning of the 1999 Regulations, but to this the estate agents countered that these terms fell within the exclusion from the requirement of fairness contained in reg.6(2) of terms which relate to the "adequacy of the price or remuneration, as against the goods or services supplied in exchange."

[165a] [2004] EWHC 263; [2004] 2 E.G.L.R. 25.

[165b] *Director General of Fair Trading v First National Bank plc* [2001] UKHL 52; [2002] 1 A.C. 481.

Having looked at the treatment of this provision by the House of Lords in the **15–036B** *First National Bank plc* case as described in para.15–036 of the Main Text, Gross J. held that the applicability of reg.6(2) turned on an issue of construction of the contract, *viz* whether the agreement provided for a 3 per cent commission rate (or price) with the vendors having an option (but no obligation) to pay 1.5 per cent (in which case reg.6(2) *would* apply) or an obligation to pay a price of 1.5 per cent, with a "default" provision exercisable at the estate agents' option to insist on payment of 3 per cent (in which case reg.6(2) *would not* apply).[165c] In his view, the prevailing market, the pre-contractual negotiations between the parties, and their expectation that the 1.5 per cent commission would be paid within 10 days all indicated that *both* the parties to the contract contemplated an agreed operative price of 1.5 per cent with a default provision of 3 per cent.[165d] This view of the parties' intention was not precluded by the language used by the agreement as set in its contractual matrix, even though "at first blush" the reference to the higher price as the "standard commission rate" and the lower as the "early payment discounted rate" suggested the opposite conclusion[165e]: the idea that there was merely an option in the consumer (not an obligation) to pay the lower rate was "simply fanciful."[165f] As a result, reg.6(2) did not exclude this "default provision" from the requirement of fairness. Given that the view of the judge below that the clauses in question were unfair had not been appealed, the estate agent's claim to the higher commission rate failed.

[165c] [2004] EWHC 263 at [26].
[165d] *ibid.*, at [27].
[165e] *ibid.*, at [29].
[165f] *ibid.*, at [30].

(c) *The Requirement of Fairness*

(i) *The Test of Unfairness*

[*Add new paragraph after paragraph 15–047*: page [903]]

The relative roles of the European Court of Justice and national courts. In **15–048A** *Freiburger Kommunalbauten GmbH Baugesellschaft & Co KG v Hofstetter*[207a] the European Court of Justice was asked by a national court to decide whether a clause in a particular consumer contract before it was unfair within the meaning of the 1993 Directive. This the European Court refused to do, noting that "in referring to concepts of good faith and significant imbalance between the rights and obligations of the parties, Article 3 of the [1993] Directive merely defines in a general way the factors that render unfair a contractual term that has not been individually negotiated."[207b] Given the range of factors which the Directive requires to be taken into account in assessing the fairness of a contract term, "the consequences of the term under the law applicable to the contract must also be taken into account. This requires that consideration be given to the national law."[207c] So, while the European Court "may interpret general criteria used by the Community legislation in order to define the concept of unfair terms, . . . it should not rule on the application of these general criteria to a particular term, which must be considered in the light of the particular circumstances of the case in question."[207d] As a result, it is generally for a national court to decide whether a contract term satisfies the requirements for it to be regarded as unfair within the meaning of art.3(1) of the 1993 Directive.[207e]

[207a] Case C-237/02 of April 1, 2004 [2004] 2 C.M.L.R. 13.

[207b] *ibid.*, at paras 19–21.

[207c] *ibid.*, at para.21. For an example of this, see *Director General of Fair Trading plc v First National Bank plc* [2001] UKHL 52; [2002] 1 A.C. 481, discussed Main Text, para.15–061.

[207d] Case C-237/02 at para.22, "distinguishing" (at para.23) its earlier decision in *Océano Grupo Editorial SA v Murciano Quintero*, Joined Cases C-240/98 to C-244/98 of June 27, 2000 [2000] E.C.R. 1–4941, Main Text para.15–063, where it had held an internal territorial jurisdiction clause unfair on the basis that such a clause satisfied all the criteria necessary for it to be judged unfair for the purposes of the 1993 Directive without consideration of all the circumstances in which the contract was concluded or the advantages and disadvantages which the term would have under the applicable national law.

[207e] Case C-237/02, para.25.

"The nature of the goods or services"

15–054   [*Add new text at end of paragraph: page* [906]]
Furthermore, in *Bryen & Langley Ltd v Boston*[225a] it was considered material to the issue of fairness of a term that the transaction was not of a "normal 'consumer' type, like buying a television set", but, for the individual or individuals concerned, a major project such as the costly construction of a building which would be undertaken only with the benefit of appropriate professional advice.

[225a] [2004] EWHC 2450 (TCC) at [45]; 98 Con L.R. 82.

Other factors in the assessment of good faith or fairness

15–060   [*Add new text at end of paragraph: page* [910]]
It has also been said that where a professionally advised consumer has put forward a standard set of terms which are then incorporated into the contract, then "it is difficult to envisage circumstances" in which it could be said that the business was acting "contrary to the requirement of good faith" by agreeing to them.[247a] The argument would be that even if a particular contract term caused a "significant imbalance in the parties' rights and obligations under the contract, to the detriment of the consumer" as envisaged by reg.5(1) of the 1999 Regulations, it would not be contrary to good faith and so the contract term not unfair within the meaning of the Regulations. Such a view can be supported by the significance of good faith in the Regulations, as this requires an "overall evaluation of the different interests involved", and by reg.6's requirement that the assessment of unfair terms should take into account "all the circumstances attending the conclusion of the contract".[247c] On the other hand, where a business agrees to a set of terms proposed by a consumer which the business knows to be

very prejudicial to the consumer's interests and also that the consumer is ignorant of this effect (especially where the consumer is not professionally advised), then it is submitted that the mere fact that the terms were proposed by the consumer should not be allowed to determine the issue of the fairness of the terms.

247a *Bryen & Langley Ltd v Boston* [2004] EWHC 2450 (TCC) [43]; 98 Con L.R. 82.
247b 1999 Directive, recital 16, quoted in Main Work, para.15–046.
247c Main Work, para.15–055.

(ii) *The "Indicative List" of terms*

Arbitration and adjudication clauses

[*Note 289: page* [917]]   **15–072**
  Picardi v Cuniberti [2002] EWHC 2923 is reported at (2003) 19 Const. L.J. 350; *Bryen & Langley Ltd v Boston* [2004] EWHC 2450 (TCC); 98 Con L.R. 82.

[*Add to text at end of paragraph: page* [917]]
  On the other hand, in *Westminster Building Co Ltd v Beckingham*[291a] a private individual (the "consumer") who had commissioned a firm of builders to renovate his property under a contract falling outside the Housing Grants, Regeneration and Construction Act 1996 was held bound by an adjudication clause which it contained since this clause was not unfair in the circumstances: its terms were couched in plain and intelligible language and had been decided upon by the consumer's professional agents, chartered surveyors, who could have given him competent and objective advice as to its existence and effect.

291a [2004] EWHC 138 (TCC) esp. at [31]. See similarly *Lovell Projects Ltd v Legg* (TCC) [2003] B.L.R. 452.

Penalty clauses

[*Add new text at end of paragraph: page* [919]]   **15–076**
  So, for example, it has been held that a clause which requires a consumer to pay interest at 8 per cent over the Bank of England current base rate on sums due to the business under the contract 30 days after the issue of an account is unfair within the meaning of the 1999 Regulations, even though it constituted a genuine pre-estimate of damage likely to be suffered by the claimant in the event of non-payment and therefore not a penalty clause at common law,[301a] this decision on the unfairness of the term resting principally on the grounds that the term was unusual and not balanced by a similar term governing unpaid monies such as damages which may fall due *to* the consumer.[301b]

301a *Munkenbeck & Marshall v Harold* [2005] EWHC 356 (TCC); [2005] All E.R. (D) 227.
301b *ibid.*, [12] & [15]

Other potentially unfair terms

[*Add new text at end of paragraph: page* [925]]   **15–086**
  It has also been held that a contract term which provides that the consumer must indemnify the business in respect of its legal or other costs in any action or

proceedings and pay it a reasonable sum in respect of time spent in connection with such an action or proceedings was unfair within the meaning of the 1999 Regulations, even though the court saw the force of the argument that such a term could protect the business against unfair treatment of the business by the customer who could use the business's unrecoverable costs to negotiate a discount on the unpaid contract price: the term remained unbalanced by any similar provision for the benefit of the consumer.[338a]

[338a] *Munkenbeck & Marshall v Harold* [2005] EWHC 356 (TCC) at [12]–[15]; [2005] All E.R. (D) 227.

(d) *The requirement of Plain and Intelligible Language*

(ii) *The Effects of Failure to Comply with the Requirement of Plain and Intelligible Language*

Other possible effects

15–092   [*Note 353: page* [928]].
The argument in this note that a failure of a written contract to conform to the requirement of plainness and intelligibility can in itself attract the preventative measures foreseen by Art.7 of the 1993 Directive appears to run contrary to the approach of the European Court of Justice in Case C-70/03, *Commission v Spain* of September 9, 2004, on the effect of Art.5(2) of the Directive, as the court there held that the reason why the rule of interpretation *contra proferentem* of ambiguous terms should not apply in proceedings under Art.7 was to be found in the need to enhance the effectiveness of preventive proceedings against *unfair* terms (*ibid.*, at paras 16 and 17) as otherwise a potentially unfair term could be rescued by interpretation. This reasoning appears to assume, therefore, that proceedings under Art.7 can not be founded *merely* on a failure of term to be plain and intelligible. On the other hand, the European Court in this case did not consider the impact of the Consumer Injunctions Directive (Dir. 98/27/EC of the European Parliament and of the Council of May 19, 1998, on injunctions for the protection of consumers' interests), a list which required the introduction of injunctions aimed at the protection of the collective interests of consumers where there is "any act contrary" to the directives listed in its annex, which includes the 1993 Directive in toto: Dir. 98/27/EC, Art.1(2); Annex, No.9. This suggests that the measures provided in English law for the implementation of the Consumer Injunctions Directive (which are explained at para.15–099 of the Main Text) could be used for a mere failure of plainness or intelligibility of a term of a consumer contract, on the basis that this would appear to be an "act contrary" to Art.5(1) of the 1993 Directive.

(e) *Choice of Law Clauses*

Choice of law clauses ineffective

15–093   [*Add new text at end of paragraph: page* [929]]
In Case C-70/03, *Commission v Spain* of September 9, 2004 the European Court of Justice noted that Art.6(2) of the Unfair Terms in Consumer Contracts

Directive 1993 (implemented in English law by reg.9 of the 1999 Regulations) "merely states that the contract is to have a close connection with the territory of the Member States" in order to attract the application of the 1993 Directive's provisions.[356a] This "deliberately vague" "general expression seeks to make it possible to take account of various ties depending on the circumstances of the case" and so while the legislature of a Member State may properly seek to give it concrete effect by the use of presumptions, it cannot circumscribe it by "a combination of predetermined criteria for ties such as the cumulative conditions as to residence and conclusion of the contract referred to in Article 5 of the Rome Convention".[356b]

[356a] Case C-70/03, para.32.
[356b] ibid., paras 32, 33.

Part Five

ILLEGALITY AND PUBLIC POLICY

CHAPTER 16

ILLEGALITY AND PUBLIC POLICY

2. The Position at Common Law

(a) Generally

Public policy

[*Add to note 12: page* [939]]
Kellar v Williams [2004] UKPC 30.

16–004

How illegality may affect a contract.

[*Add to text at end of paragraph: page* [942]]
The Law Commission has stated that "Generally, it seems that the commission of a legal wrong, or acting otherwise contrary to public policy, in the course of performing a contract does not, at common law, affect enforcement".[35a] Illegality will only preclude the enforcement of the contract where it has been "entered into with the purpose of doing [an] . . . unlawful or immoral act or the contract itself (as opposed to the mode of . . . performance) is prohibited by law."[35b]

16–007

[35a] *Illegal Transactions: The Effect Of Illegality On Contracts And Trusts* (LC CP No. 154, para.2.29) cited with approval in *Colen v Cebrian (U.K.) Ltd.* [2003] EWCA Civ 1676 at [44].
[35b] *Coral Leisure Group Ltd v Barnett* [1981] I.C.R. 503, 509.

(b) *Objects which are Illegal by Common Law or Statute*

Fraud

[*Add to the text at end of the paragraph: page* [949]]
However, where the contract in question is remote from the illegality, the court will enforce the contract.[92a]

16–017

[92a] *21st Century Logistic Solutions Ltd v Madysen Ltd* [2004] EWHC 231 (QB); [2004] 2 Lloyd's Rep. 92. (In this case a company that intended to evade the payment of VAT could nevertheless enforce a contract for the supply of goods, the avoidance of VAT not being an integral part of the contract.)

(c) *Objects Injurious to good Government*

(ii) *Foreign Affairs*

Performance contrary to public policy in place for performance

[*Add to note 138: page* [953]]
Tekron Resources Ltd v Guinea Investment Co Ltd [2004] 2 Lloyd's Rep. 26

16–028

Illegality under foreign applicable law to contract

[*Add to note 149: page* [954]]
See also *Mahonia Ltd v J.P. Morgan Chase Bank* [2003] 2 Lloyd's Rep. 911; *Mahonia Ltd v West LB AG* [2004] EWHC 1938 (Comm); *JSC Zestafoni G*

16–031

Nikoladze Ferroalloy Plant v Ronly Holdings Ltd [2004] EWHC 245 (Comm); [2004] 2 Lloyd's Rep. 335.

(d) *Objects Injurious to the Proper Working of Justice*

(iv) *Maintenance and Champerty*

Public policy today respecting maintenance and champerty

16–049   [*Add at end of paragraph; page* [964]]
In *Kellar v Williams*[237a] Lord Carswell stated *obiter* that the "content of public policy can change over the years, and it may now be time to reconsider the accepted [common law] prohibition [on conditional fees] in the light of modern practising conditions"[237b]

[237a] [2004] UKPC 30.
[237b] *ibid.*, at [21].

Effect of maintenance

16–053   [*Add to note 267: page* [966]]
The court could make an order under s.51 against a shareholder of a company as a shareholder who, unlike directors, was under no duty as regards the conduct of litigation on behalf of a company and thus the principle of limited liability would not be undermined by such an order: see *CIBC Mellon Trust Co v Stolzenberg* [2005] EWCA Civ 628; *The Times*, June 8, 2005.

Non-champertous agreements between solicitor and client

16–056   [*Add to note 293: page* [968]]
For techniques available to the court to regulate costs in an action involving a conditional fee agreement: see *King v Telegraph Group Ltd* [2004] EWCA Civ 613; [2005] 1 W.L.R. 2282.

[*Replace note 295: page* [968]]
[295] *ibid.*, s.58(3). Various statutory instruments have been made with respect to conditional fee orders: see *Sharratt v London Central Bus Co Ltd* [2003] EWCA Civ 718; [2003] 4 All E.R. 590 where the law is fully analysed.

Agreements savouring of champerty: assignment of the right to litigate

16–057   [*Add to note 307: page* [969]]
24 Seven Utility Services Ltd v Rosekey Ltd [2003] EWHC 3415 (QB); [2004] All E.R. (D) 288 (Feb).

(f) Contracts in Restraint of Trade

(i) Scope of the Doctrine

Criteria for application of doctrine

[*Add at end of paragraph: page* [984]]   **16–083**
However, the absence of reciprocal obligation may be a factor in determining
whether a restraint is reasonable.[447a]

[447a] *Societa Explosivi Industriali SpA v Ordnance Technologies (U.K.) Ltd* [2004] EWHC 48 (Ch);
[2004] 1 All E.R. (Comm.) 619.

Legitimate interests of the parties

[*Add to note 481: page* [988]]   **16–092**
Countryside Assured Financial Services Ltd v Deanne Smart [2004] EWHC
1214.

(ii) Employer and Employee

Employee's activities after determination of employment

[*Add to text after note 539: page* [995]]   **16–103**
Post termination restraints if reasonable are enforceable.[539a]

[539a] *Leeds Rugby Ltd v Harris* [2005] EWHC 1591 (QB); [2005] All E.R. (D) 286 (Jul.).

[*Add to text at end of paragraph: page* [997]]   **16–104**
The court will not imply a term in order to save a covenant restraining an
employee's post-employment conduct.[557a] Nor will the court re-write a covenant
in restraint of trade where the contract provides that the covenant, if unenforceable, should be rewritten with such minimum amendment as renders it enforceable.[557b] A provision that the restraint should apply "for as long as permitted by
law" was too uncertain to have effect.[557c]

[557a] *Townends Group Ltd v Cobb* [2004] All E.R. (D) 421 (Nov.)
[557b] *Townends Group Ltd v Cobb* [2004] All E.R. (D) 421 (Nov.)
[557c] *Days Medical Aids Ltd v Pihsiang Machinery Manufacturing Co Ltd* [2004] EWHC 44
(Comm); [2004] All E.R. (Comm.) 95.

Competition

[*Add to note 560: page* [997]]   **16–105**
Axiom Business Computers Ltd v Jeannie Frederick (November 20, 2003,
Court of Session).

Trade secrets and connection with customers

[*Add to note 574: page* [999]]   **16–107**
Brake Bros Ltd v Ungless [2004] EWHC 2799 (QB); [2004] All E.R. (D) 586
(Jul).

[*Add to note 577: page* [999]]
Fibrenetix Storage Ltd v Davis [2004] EWHC 1359 (QB) (protection of pricing policies).

Restraints during currency of employment

16–114   [*Add to note 645: page* [1005]]
TFS Derivatives Ltd v Morgan [2004] EWHC (QB) 3181; [2005] I.R.L.R. 246.

(iv) *Partners*

Analogous Agreements

16–119   [*Add to text at end of paragraph: page* [1010]]
In *Buchanan v Alba Diagnostics Ltd*[680a] Lord Hoffmann upheld as valid a perpetual restraint in the assignment of a patent entitling the assignee to the rights of any improvement in the patent. He considered that it was in the public interest for inventors to be able to borrow money on the security of future rights,[680b] and a clear implication of his reasoning is that the agreement was treated as being analogous to the sale of the goodwill of a business.

[680a] [2004] UKHL 5; 2004 S.C.(H.L.) 9.
[680b] *ibid.*, at [29].

(v) *Supply and Acquisition of Goods: Restraints in Vertical Agreements*

Application of doctrine

16–120   [*Add to note 681 at end: page* [1010]]
The court held in *Days Medical Aids Ltd v Pihsiang Machinery Co Ltd* [2004] EWHC 44 (Comm) that an agreement not invalidated by Art.81 of the EU Treaty could not be subject to the common law restraint of trade doctrine.

3. CONTRACTS UNENFORCEABLE BY STATUTE

(a) *General principles*

Aids to statutory interpretation

16–146   [*Add to note 773, page* [1023]]
See also *Estate of Anandh v Barnet Primary Health Care Trust* [2004] EWCA Civ 5; [2004] All E.R. (D) 242 (Jan.).

Statute: one party only affected

[*Add to note 798: page* [1026]]   **16–153**
   Crehan v Inntrepreneur Pub Company CPC [2004] EWCA Civ 637; [2004]
E.C.C. 28, the claimant, as a matter of Community Law, could claim damages
from his co-contractor with respect to an agreement which breached Art.81 of the
EU Treaty. The claimant in *Crehan* was not significantly responsible for any
distortion of competition.

4. ENFORCEMENT OF COLLATERAL AND PROPRIETARY RIGHTS

(a) *The Maxim Ex Turpi Causa Non Oritur Actio and Related Rules*

Tainting

[*Delete note 825 and replace: page* [1030]]   **16–161**
825 *Vakante v Addey & Stanhope School* [2004] EWCA Civ 1065; [2004] 4 All E.R. 1056 where
the Court of Appeal (Civil Division) upheld the decision of the Employment Appeal Tribunal that
illegality precluded the claimant from pursuing his racial discrimination claim. See also *Wheeler v
Quality Deep Ltd* [2004] EWCA Civ 1085 where the lack of English and limited knowledge of tax
and national insurance provisions were considered relevant in determining the extent to which the
employee participated in an illegality.

[*Add to note 826: page* [1030]]
   Hunt v Power Resources Ltd [2005] All E.R. (D) 23 (Apr.).

(c) *Recovery of Money Paid or Property Transferred under Illegal Contracts*

Transfer of property under illegal transactions

[*Add to note 901: page* [1039]]   **16–172**
   The court will not enforce a claim by a person claiming funds held by a person
in the position of trustee (in this case a solicitor) where the claimant has to rely
on his fraud: see *Halley v Law Society* [2003] EWCA Civ 97.

Determination of limited interests created by illegal transactions

[*Note 904: page* [1040]]   **16–173**
   Update the reference to *Treitel* to (11th ed., 2003), p.496.

[*Note 914: page* [1041]   **16–174**
   Update reference to *Treitel* to (11th ed., 2003), p.496.

[*Note 916: page* [1041]]
   Update reference to *Treitel, op. cit.*, at p.496.

16–175   *[Add at end of paragraph: page* [1042]]

Although collateral rights, as in *Tinsley v Milligan*[919a], may arise out of an illegal contract, a collateral right normally involves a proprietary right and does not include a right of action on the contract itself.[919b]

[919a] *ibid.*

[919b] *Mahonia Ltd v J P Morgan Chase Bank* [2003] 2 Lloyd's Rep. 911, at [27]. See also *Mahonia Ltd v West LB AG* [2004] EWHC 1938 (Comm).

Oppression and fraud

16–180   *[Note 942: page* [1045]]

Update reference to *Treitel* to (11th ed., 2003), pp.492–493.

Mistake

16–181   *[Note 943: page* [1045]]

Update reference to *Treitel, op. cit.,* at p.493.

6. PLEADING AND PRACTICE

Pleading of illegality

16–199   *[Add at end of note 1029: page* [1055]]

Bim Kemi AB v Blackburn Chemicals Ltd [2004] EWHC 166 (Comm); [2004] EWCA Civ 1490 (court could take notice that agreement was illegal under Art.81 of the EU Treaty); *Western Power Investments Ltd v Teeside Power Ltd* (February 18, 2005) (unreported).

Part Six

JOINT OBLIGATIONS, THIRD PARTIES AND ASSIGNMENT

[N.B. THERE ARE NO AMENDMENTS TO CHAPTER 17]

CHAPTER 18

THIRD PARTIES

1. INTRODUCTION

Preliminary

[Add to note 1: page [1073]]
Furmston, *Third Party Rights* (2005).

18–001

Present structure of the subject

[Add to note 7: page [1073]]
For the nature of the right of enforcement created by the Contracts (Rights of Third Parties) Act 1999 as an exception to the common law doctrine of privity of contract, see also *Ramco (UK) Ltd v International Insurance Co of Hanover* [2004] EWCA Civ 675; [2004] 2 All E.R. (Comm.) 866 at [32].

18–002

2. The Common Law Doctrine

(a) *Parties to the Agreement*

Collateral contracts

18–005
[Add to note 24: page [1076]]
Morin v Bonhams & Brooks Ltd has been affirmed on the ground that the governing law was that of Monaco: [2003] EWCA Civ 1802; [2004] 1 All E.R. (Comm.) 880.

[Add to text at end of paragraph: page [1077]]
Similarly, in *Brook Street Bureau v Dacas*[31a] an employment agency entered into contracts with workers whom it supplied to a local authority. It was held that there was not only an express contract between the workers and the agency, but also an implied contract between the workers and the authority.

[31a] [2004] EWCA Civ 217; [2004] I.C.R 1437.

Agency

18–012
[Add to note 60: page [1080]]
Vitesse Yacht Charterers SL v Spiers (The Deverne II) [2003] EWHC 2426 (Admlty); [2004] 1 Lloyd's Rep. 179 (contract to charter yacht for holiday to be taken by two persons together made by one of them on behalf of both).

[Add to note 61: page [1080]]
cf. Richards v Hughes [2004] EWCA Civ 266; [2004] P.N.L.R. 35 (arguable that accountant advising parent about the setting up of a trust fund for the education of children owed a contractual duty, not only to the parent, but also to the children).

3. Scope

(a) *Liability in Negligence to Third Parties*

Duty of care may be owed to third party

18–022
[Add to note 117, line 6: page [1087]]
Niru Battery Manufacturing Co v Milestone Trading Ltd [2003] EWCA Civ 1446 is now reported in [2004] 1 Lloyd's Rep. 344.

Requirement of "proximity"

18–032
[Add to note 161: page [1093]]
See also *Architype Projects Ltd v Dewhurst MacFarlane & Partners* [2003] EWHC 3341; [2004] P.N.L.R. 38 (subcontractor not liable in tort to building owner).

Defects in the very thing supplied insufficient

[*Add to note 166: page* [1094]] **18–033**
See also *Holding Management (Solitaire) Ltd v Ideal Homes Northwest Ltd* [2004] EWHC 2408; 96 Con. L.R. 114 (T&CC)

Damages in "disappointed beneficiary" cases

[*Add to note 201: page* [1099]] **18–037**
But a claim by a person in a position analogous to that of a disappointed beneficiary may be available where the consequences of the adviser's negligence do not become apparent for many years after the transaction in question: *Richards v Hughes* [2004] EWCA Civ 266; [2004] P.N.L.R. 35.

Analogous situations

[*Add to note 209: page* [1100]] **18–038**
For a further possible extension of the principle of the "disappointed beneficiary" cases, see *Richards v Hughes* [2004] EWCA Civ 266; [2004] P.N.L.R. 35 (accountant advising client about the setting up of a trust fund to pay for the education of client's children).

4. Contracts For The Benefit Of Third Parties

(a) *Effects of a Contract for the Benefit of a Third Party*

(i) *Promisee's Remedies*

Damages in respect of promisee's loss

[*Add new text at end of paragraph: page* [1107]] **18–046**
The question whether the loss had been suffered by the promisee or by a third party was discussed in *De Jongh Weill v Mean Fiddler Holdings*.[239b] The claimant in that case had been engaged as a financial consultant by the defendant company; he was to be remunerated partly by a specified fee, but the main element of his remuneration was that "in addition warrants to purchase shares in the [defendant company] will be granted to a company representing my family interests."[239c] The antecedent negotiations made it clear that the grant of those warrants was to be the claimant's (own) principal remuneration[239d] and that "it was *he* who was to benefit in reality and the idea of a nominated company was just the way that *he* was to be paid."[239e] Judge Bruce Coles Q.C., after referring to paras 18–042—18–047 above,[239f] held that the loss resulting from the defendant's failure to issue the warrants had been suffered by the claimant himself and that damages in respect of it were therefore recoverable by him under the principle stated in para.18–046.

[239b] [2005] All E.R. (D) 331 (Jul).
[239c] *ibid.*, at [2], [25].

[239d] *ibid.*, at [30].
[239e] *ibid.*
[239f] *ibid.*, at [26].

Damages in respect of third party's loss: general rule

18–047   [*Add to note 242: page* [1107]]
    See also *Ramco (UK) Ltd v International Insurance Co of Hanover* [2004] EWCA Civ 675; [2004] 2 All E.R. (Comm.) 866 at [32] where the actual decision (that an insurance policy issued to a bailee of goods did not cover loss suffered by the bailor in circumstances in which the bailee was not liable to the bailor in respect of that loss) turned on the wording of the policy.

Damages in respect of third party's loss: exceptions in general

18–050   [*Add to note 269: page* [1109]]
    In *Rolls Royce Power Engineering plc v Ricardo Consulting Engineers Ltd* [2003] EWHC 2871 (T.C.C.); [2004] 2 All E.R. (Comm.) 129 it was held that a contracting party could not recover damages in respect of a third party's loss as trustee for the third party where the other contracting party at the time of the contract did not know or have reason to know that the former party was contracting as trustee.

    [*Add to note 272, line 10, after reference to* [1977] C.L.J. 24: *page* [1110]]
    In the *Rolls Royce Power* case, above, n.269, it was held that the "rule in *Dunlop v Lambert*" ((1839) 2 Cl. & F. 626, 627) applied only if at the time of the contract it was "in the actual contemplation of the parties that an identified third party or a third party who was a member of an identified class might suffer damage in the event of a breach of the contract" (at [124]).

Scope of the "broader ground"

18–059   [*Add to note 324: page* [1116]]
    In *Rolls Royce Power Engineering plc v Ricardo Consulting Engineers Ltd* [2003] EWHC 2871 (TCC); [2004] 2 All E.R. (Comm.) 129, Judge Seymour Q.C. said (at [128]) that the "broader ground" for the decision in the *Linden Gardens* case ([1994] 1 A.C. 85) was not easy to apply "where the alleged damage is damage to, or failure to repair, property and there is no suggestion of consequential loss."

(b) *Exceptions to the Doctrine*

(ii) *Contracts (Rights of Third Parties) Act 1999*

Term conferring benefit on third party

18–087   [*Add new note 471b in line 18 at "property owned by C.": page* [1133]]
    [471b] A similar problem arose, apparently under Brazilian law, in *Petromec Inc v Petroleo Brasileiro SA Petrobas* [2004] EWHC 1180 (Comm); [2005] 1 Lloyd's Rep. 219. A, a sub-bareboat charterer of an oil production platform, took out a policy of insurance with B, relating to the platform. It was

held that no claim could be brought on the policy in his own right by C, a subcontractor engaged to do upgrading work on the platform, as A had not purported to insure for the benefit of C. In a case governed by English law, similar reasoning could be applied, on such facts, to a claim brought by C under s.1(1)(b) of the Contracts (Rights of Third Parties) Act 1999.

[*Add new text at end of paragraph: page* [1134]]
    The operation of ss.1(1)(b) and 1(2) is illustrated by *The Laemthong Glory (No.2)*[473b] where goods had been carried on a voyage chartered ship and difficulties had arisen with regard to their delivery at the end of the transit as the bill of lading had not reached the prospective receiver by the time of the arrival of the ship at the contractual destination. The shipowners delivered the goods to the receiver against letters of indemnity one of which was addressed by the receiver to the charterer and so amounted to a contract between these parties. It contained a promise by the receiver to indemnify "you [*i.e.*, the charterer], your servants or agents" in respect of liability which might be incurred by reason of delivery of the goods at the receiver's request without production of the bill of lading. The Court of Appeal held that this promise on its true construction purported to confer a benefit on the shipowner within s.1(1)(b) of the 1999 Act since the shipowner had acted as one of the charter's "agents" in delivering the goods to the receiver and that the receiver had failed to discharge the burden imposed on him by s.1(2) of proving that letter of indemnity was not intended by the parties to it (*i.e.*, the receiver and the charterer) to be enforceable by the shipowner. The receiver's promise in that letter was accordingly enforceable by the shipowner against the receiver under the 1999 Act.

[473b] *Laemthong International Lines Co Ltd v Artis (The Laemthong Glory) (No.2)* [2005] EWCA Civ 519; [2005] 1 Lloyd's Rep. 632.

(iii) *Other Statutory Exceptions*

Insurance by persons with limited interests

[*Add to note 608: page* [1152]]   **18–120**
    For the possibility of displacing the principle of *Waters v Monarch Insurance Co* (1856) 5 E. & B. 870 by the terms of the policy, see *Ramco (UK) Ltd v International Insurance Co of Hanover* [2004] EWCA Civ 675; [2004] 2 All E.R. (Comm.) 866 at [32].

Third parties' rights against insurers

[*Note 615, line 14: page* [1153]]   **18–123**
    In *Centre Reinsurance International Co v Curzon International Ltd* [2004] EWHC 200 (Ch); [2004] 2 All E.R. (Comm.) 28 it was held that a transfer of rights under the Third Parties (Rights against Insurers) Act 1930 could occur "notwithstanding that the insured's liability to the third party has yet to be established" (at [29]). The contrary view in *Nigel Upchurch Associates v Aldridge Estates Investment Co Ltd* [1993] 1 Lloyd's Rep. 533 (cited in Main Work, p.1153, n.615) was rejected. The decision in the *Centre Reinsurance* case, above, was varied, but not on the point here under discussion, on appeal [2005] EWCA Civ 115; [2005] 2 All E.R. (Comm.) 65, where the Court of Appeal also held that s.1(3) of the 1930 Act was not intended to strike down provisions in the

insurance contract itself designed to put the third party in a better position than that in which the insured would have been immediately before the statutory transfer of the insured's rights to the third party (at [83]).

5. Enforcement Against Third Parties

Scope of the rule

18–127   [*Add to note 635: page* [1156]]

For the requirements of knowledge of the contract and intention to procure its breach, see also *Unique Pub Properties Ltd v Beer Barrels & Mineral Waters Ltd* [2004] EWCA Civ 586; [2005] 1 All E.R. (Comm.) 181.

[*Add to note 636*]

For the requirement of "wrongfulness", see also *OBG Ltd v Allan* [2005] EWCA Civ 106; [2005] 2 All E.R. 602.

Lack of causal connection

18–134   [*Add to note 667: page* [1160]]

The mortgagee of a ship is not obliged to defer the exercise of his power of sale under the mortgage even though such exercise interferes with contracts made by the mortgagor for the carriage of goods in the ship with the shippers of those goods: *Den Norske Bank ASA v Acemex Management Co* [2003] EWCA Civ 1559; [2004] All E.R. (Comm.) 904, at [22].

CHAPTER 19

ASSIGNMENT

1. ASSIGNMENT

(b) *Equitable Assignments*

Formalities for equitable assignments

[*Add to note 98; page* [1173]]   **19–025**

In *Coulter v Chief of Dorset Police* [2003] EWHC 3391 (Ch); [2004] 1 W.L.R. 1425 it was held that the benefit of a judgment (for costs) had been assigned in equity by a retiring chief constable to his successor. Patten J., after referring to the need for there to be "a sufficient expression of an intention to assign" for an equitable assignment, said (at [16]): "What, in my judgment, acts as the trigger, if trigger is needed, is the manifest event of the resignation or retirement of the existing office holder, and the assumption of office by his successor. That is, as I see it, a sufficient outward manifestation of an intention that the successor office holder should obtain the benefits held on trust by a predecessor, for there to be an equitable assignment of the benefit of the judgment."

(c) *Principles Applicable to Statutory and Equitable Assignments*

(i) *What Rights are Assignable*

Rights declared by contract to be incapable of assignment

19–043   [*Add to note 159; page* [1182]]
Thomas, "Contractual Prohibitions on the Assignment of Copyright" (2004) 120 L.Q.R. 222

19–045   [*Add to note 168: page* [1183]]
For criticism of this decision, making the argument that one cannot have a trust of, or charge over, unassignable rights, see Turner, "Charges of Unassignable Rights" (2004) 20 J.C.L. 97.

[N.B. THERE ARE NO AMENDMENTS TO CHAPTER 20]

Part Seven

PERFORMANCE AND DISCHARGE

CHAPTER 21

PERFORMANCE

1. IN GENERAL

Promises in the alternative

[Add to note 22: page [1235]]   **21–006**
Mora Shipping Inc v Axa Corporate Solutions Assurance SA [2005] EWHC
315 (Comm); [2005] All E.R. (D) 251 (Mar) at [18].

2. TIME OF PERFORMANCE

Time made expressly or implicitly "of the essence"

[Add to note 82: page [1241]]   **21–013**
*Re Simoco Digital UK Ltd: Thunderbird Industries LLC v Simoco Digital UK
Ltd* [2004] EWHC 209 (Ch); [2004] 1 B.C.L.C. 541 at [14]; *Haugland Tankers
AS v RMK Marine Gemi Yapim Sanayii ve Deniz Taşimaciliì İşletmesi AS* [2005]
EWHC 321 (Comm); [2005] 1 Lloyd's Rep. 573; *Peregrine Systems Ltd v Steria
Ltd* [2005] EWCA Civ 239; [2005] All E.R. (D) 215 (Mar) at [15].

[Add to end of note 83: page [1241]]
Tennara Ltd v Majorarch Ltd [2003] EWHC 2601 (Ch) (on the facts it was
held that time was not expressly or impliedly of the essence). Where time is not
of the essence and there has been unreasonable delay in performance, a court

may be able to infer that the delay nevertheless amounts to a repudiation of the contract where the consequences of the delay are sufficiently serious. When deciding whether or not the delay amounts to a repudiation of the contract, the court will have regard to all the facts and circumstances of the case: *ibid.*

Consequences of time being "of the essence"

21–015   [*Add to note 101: page* [1243]]
State Securities plc v Initial Industry Ltd [2004] All E.R. (D) 317 (Jan).

Where no precise time for performance is specified

21–020   [*Add to note 128 after reference to Jolley v Carmel Ltd: page* [1246]]
National Car Parks Ltd v Baird (Valuation Officer) [2004] EWCA Civ 967; [2005] 1 All E.R. 53 at [58].

[*Add to text at the end of the paragraph*]
When deciding whether or not performance has taken place within a reasonable time, a court is not limited to what the parties contemplated or ought to have foreseen at the time of entry into the contract but can, with the benefit of hindsight, take account of a broad range of factors, including any estimate given by the performing party of the time which it would take for it to perform, whether the party for whose benefit the relevant obligation was to be performed needed to participate in the performance, whether it was necessary for a third party to collaborate with the performing party in order to enable it to perform, and the nature of the cause or causes of any delay in performance.[130a]

[130a] *Peregrine Systems Ltd v Steria Ltd* [2005] EWCA Civ 239; [2005] All E.R. (D) 215 (Mar) at [15]; *Astea (UK) Ltd v Time Group Ltd* [2003] EWHC 725 (TCC); [2003] All E.R. (D) 212 (Apr) at [144].

3. PARTIAL PERFORMANCE OF AN ENTIRE OBLIGATION

Partial performance of entire obligations

21–030   [*In note 180, delete text after first sentence and substitute: page* [1252]]
The Court of Appeal in *Item Software (UK) Ltd v Fassihi* [2004] EWCA Civ 1244; [2004] I.R.L.R. 928 held that the effect of s.2 of the Act is that, unless the parties agree otherwise, the salary of an employee whose employment terminates part way through a pay period shall be apportioned and paid in respect of the period actually worked (with payment only becoming due and payable at the end of the relevant pay period). The decision of the Court of Appeal in *Boston Deep Sea Fishing and Ice Co Ltd v Ansell* (1888) 39 Ch. D. 339 was held not to stand in the way of this conclusion because the Act was not mentioned at any point in the case: it is therefore not an authority on the construction, scope or effect of the Apportionment Act.

4. PAYMENT

(a) *In General*

Payment

[*Add to end of note 234: page* [1257]]
    The current edition of Mann (6th ed., 2005) at paras 3.04–3.05 does, however, recognise that frustration may have a limited role to play in such cases.

21–039

(b) *Appropriation of Payments*

Creditor's right to appropriate

[*In note 344, insert after reference to Lowther v Heaver: page* [1267]]
    Potomek Construction Ltd v Zurich Securities Ltd [2003] EWHC 2827 (Ch); [2004] 1 All E.R. (Comm.) 672 at [69].

21–061

Current account: Clayton's Case

[*Add to note 363: page* [1269]]
    Commerzbank Aktiengesellschaft v IMB Morgan plc [2004] EWHC 2771 (Ch); [2005] 1 Lloyd's Rep. 298 at [42]–[48].

21–066

Appropriation as between principal and interest

[*Add to note 364: page* [1270]]
    Potomek Construction Ltd v Zurich Securities Ltd [2003] EWHC 2827 (Ch); [2004] 1 All E.R. (Comm.) 672 at [69].

21–067

(c) *Revalorisation: Gold Clauses and Index-Linking*

The nominalistic principle

[*Note 365: page* [1270]]
    Update reference to Mann *The Legal Aspect of Money* to (6th ed., 2005), Chs 9–13.

21–068

Gold clauses

[*Note 379: page* [1271]]
    Update reference to Mann *The Legal Aspect of Money* to (6th ed., 2005), paras 11.19 *et seq.*

21–070

Index-linking in domestic contracts

21–072 [*Note 396: page* [1273]]
Update reference to Mann *The Legal Aspect of Money* to (6th ed., 2005), paras
11.38–11.46.

(d) *Payment by Negotiable Instrument or Documentary Credit*

Conditional payment

21–074 [*Add to note 404 after reference to Re Charge Card Services Ltd: page* [1274]]
*Fusion Interactive Communication Solutions Ltd v Venture Investment Place-
ment Ltd* [2005] EWHC 736 (Ch); [2005] All E.R. (D) 111 (May) at [91].

CHAPTER 22

DISCHARGE BY AGREEMENT

3. ACCORD AND SATISFACTION

Ineffective accord

[Add to note 75, at end: page [1292]]   **22–021**
This is likely to be a difficult hurdle to overcome (see, for example, *Champion Investments Ltd v Ahmed* [2004] All E.R. (D) 28 (Aug)). In the rare case in which it is overcome, compromise may be vitiated by a mistake of law as well as a mistake of fact: *Brennan v Bolt Burden (a firm)* [2004] EWCA Civ 1017; [2004] 1 All E.R. (D) 551 (Jul) at [17].

4. RESCISSION

Substituted contract

[Add to note 101: page [1295]]   **22–028**
Sookraj v Samaroo [2004] UKPC 50.

5. VARIATION

Unilateral power of variation

[Add to end of note 154: page [1300]]   **22–039**
See also *Paragon Finance plc v Pender* [2005] EWCA Civ 760; [2005] All E.R. (D) 307 (Jun).

6. Waiver

[Insert new paragraph: page [1303]]

22–044A   **Contracting out of waiver.** It would appear that there is no general principle of law that parties to a contract cannot restrict the operation of the doctrine of waiver by the terms of their contract.[182a] In *State Securities plc v Initial Industry Ltd*[182b] Jonathan Gaunt Q.C., sitting as a Deputy Judge of the High Court, stated,

> "I can, however, see no reason in principle why the parties to an equipment lease . . . or other commercial contract, should not be free to stipulate that a particular act, such as payment of a rental instalment should not be taken to waive a right to terminate for an earlier breach. After all, such a provision may be very convenient and operate to the benefit of both parties. The finance company may want to encourage the lessee to correct the breach but not want him to fall behind with his payments while he does so. It may be in the interests of the lessee that the finance company should not have to take an early decision whether to terminate."[182c]

However it cannot be assumed that the courts in all cases will give effect to a term of the contract which purports to exclude or limit the operation of the doctrine of waiver; in some circumstances the term of the contract may not suffice to deny effect to a clear and unequivocal representation made by one party to the contract.[182d]

[182a] *State Securities plc v Initial Industry Ltd* [2004] All E.R. (D) 317 (Jan).
[182b] [2004] All E.R. (D) 317 (Jan).
[182c] At [57].
[182d] *I-Way Ltd v World Online Telecom Ltd* [2002] EWCA Civ 413 (Court of Appeal refused to give summary judgment in a case in which the court was asked, in effect, to enforce a term of the contract which provided that "no addition, amendment or modification of this Agreement shall be effective unless it is in writing and signed by or on behalf of both parties.")

Waiver of condition for benefit of one party

22–045   *[Add to end of note 184: page* [1304]]
Wessex Reserve Forces and Cadets Association v White [2005] EWHC 983 (QB); [2005] All E.R. (D) 310 (May).

7. Provision for Discharge in the Contract Itself

Express provision

22–047   *[Add to end of note 195: page* [1305]]
More OG Romsdal Fylkesbatar AS v The Demise Charterers of the Ship "Jotunheim" [2004] EWHC 671 (Comm); [2005] 1 Lloyd's Rep. 181.

CHAPTER 23

DISCHARGE BY FRUSTRATION

1. INTRODUCTION

Introduction

[Note 1: page [1311]]   **23–001**
Update reference to Treitel, *Frustration and Force Majeure* to (2nd. ed., 2004).

Historical development

[Note 10: page [1312]]   **23–004**
Update reference to Treitel to (2nd. ed., 2004), Chap.2.

2. THE TEST FOR FRUSTRATION

[Note 24: page [1314]]
Update reference to Treitel, *Frustration and Force Majeure* to (2nd. ed., 2004), paras 16–006—16–016.

Practical differences between the tests

23–018   [*Note 76: page* [1321]]
Update reference to Treitel, *Frustration and Force Majeure* to (2nd. ed., 2004), paras 16–013—16–016.

3. ILLUSTRATIONS OF THE DOCTRINE

(b) *Common Types of Frustrating Events*

(i) *Subsequent Legal Changes and Supervening Illegality*

Changes affecting employment

23–022   [*Note 104: page* [1324]]
Update reference to Treitel to (2nd. ed., 2004), Chap.8.

(ii) *Cancellation of an Expected Event*

The "coronation cases"

23–032   [*Note 130: page* [1327]]
Update reference to Treitel to (2nd. ed., 2004), paras 7–006—7–014.

(iii) *Delay*

Delay

23–034   [*Note 142: page* [1329]]
Update reference to Treitel to (2nd. ed., 2004), paras 5–036—5–056.

(c) *Application of the Doctrine to Common Types of Contracts*

(i) *Personal Contracts*

Death

23–036   [*Note 162: page* [1330]]
Update reference to Treitel to (2nd. ed., 2004), para.2–015.

Illness or incapacity

23–037   [*Add to Note 168: page* [1331]]
It may be that permanent incapacity alone will not suffice to frustrate a contract of employment, on the basis that the contract itself may, exceptionally, envisage the possibility that the employee will continue to be employed notwithstanding the fact that he or she is suffering a permanent incapacity: see *R (Verner)*

v Derby City Council [2003] EWHC 2708 (Admin); [2004] I.C.R. 535 at [66]. Lindsay J. concluded (at [68]) that in such a case the contract of employment continues to exist "in an entirely shadowy form in which, by reason of the employee's incapacity and retirement, the employer cannot require any performance and the employee cannot offer it."

(ii) *Charterparties*

[Note 184: page [1333]]
Update reference to Treitel to (2nd. ed., 2004), paras 5–052—5–054.

(iii) *Sale and Carriage of Goods*

Sale and carriage of goods

[Note 202: page [1336]]   23–045
Update reference to Atiyah, *The Sale of Goods* to (11th ed., 2005), pp.360–365.

(v) *Leases and Tenancies*

[Note 220: page [1339]]
Update reference to Treitel to (2nd. ed., 2004), Chap.11.

Prohibition on intended use

[Note 234: page 1340]]   23–052
Update reference to Treitel to (2nd. ed., 2004), paras 7–023—7–0024 and 11–022.

4. THE LIMITS OF FRUSTRATION

Express provision

[Note 253: page [1343]]   23–056
Update reference to Treitel to (2nd. ed., 2004), Chap.12.

[Add to the end of Note 254]
cf. *R (Verner) v Derby City Council* [2003] EWHC 2708 (Admin); [2004] I.C.R. 535 at [66].

Significance of a foreseen event

[Note 264: page [1344]]   23–057
Update reference to Treitel, *Frustration and Force Majeure* to (2nd. ed., 2004), Chap.13.

Event foreseeable but not foreseen

23–058   [*Note 273: page* [1345]]
Update reference to Treitel to (2nd. ed., 2004), para.13–012.

Self-induced frustration

23–059   [*Note 274: page* [1345]]
Update reference to Treitel to (2nd. ed., 2004), Chap.14.

Partial excuse at common law

23–066   [*Note 311: page* [1350]]
Update reference to Treitel, *Frustration and Force Majeure* to (2nd. ed., 2004), para.5–060.

5. THE LEGAL CONSEQUENCES OF FRUSTRATION

23–068   [*Note 318: page* [1351]]
Update reference to Treitel to (2nd. ed., 2004), Chap.15.

Law Reform (Frustrated Contracts) Act 1943

23–072   [*Note 329: page* [1353]]
Update reference to Treitel to (2nd. ed., 2004), paras 15–049—15–096.

Contracts excluded from the Act

23–094   [*Note 398: page* [1363]]
Update reference to Atiyah, *The Sale of Goods* to (11th ed., 2005), pp.365–368.

CHAPTER 24

DISCHARGE BY BREACH

1. IN GENERAL

Affirmation

[*Add to note 19: page* [1368]]   **24–003**
State Securities plc v Initial Industry Ltd [2004] All E.R. (D) 317 (Jan)
(acceptance of rental payment held not to have amounted to an election to
continue with the contract).

Acceptance of repudiation

[*Add to note 91: page* [1377]]   **24–013**
When deciding whether or not inconsistent actions amount to an acceptance of
a repudiation, the courts apply an objective test: *Enfield London Borough Council
v Sivanandan* [2004] EWHC 672 (QB); [2004] All E.R. (D) 73 (April) at
[38]–[39].

[*Add to note 93: page* [1377]]
Sookraj v Samaroo [2004] UKPC 50 at [17]; *South Caribbean Trading Ltd v
Trafigura Beheer BV* [2004] EWHC 2676 (Comm); [2005] 1 Lloyd's Rep. 128
at [129]–[130].

[*Add to note 95*]
In such a case the contractor may be absolved from his contractual obligation
before he communicates his acceptance: *Potter v RJ Temple* [2003] All E.R. (D)
327 (Dec.)

No reason or bad reason given

24–014   *[Add to note 100 after reference to Sheffield v Conrad: page [1378]]*
South Caribbean Trading Ltd v Trafigura Beheer BV [2004] EWHC 2676 (Comm); [2005] 1 Lloyd's Rep. 128 at [133]–[134].

Both parties in breach

24–015   *[Add to note 108: page [1379]]*
Total Spares & Supplies Ltd v Antares SRL [2004] EWHC 2626 (Ch) at [147].

3. IMPOSSIBILITY CREATED BY ONE PARTY

Anticipatory breach

24–030   *[Add to note 174 after [1957] 2 Q.B. 401, 449–450: page [1389]]*
Re Simoco Digital UK Ltd: Thunderbird Industries LLC v Simoco Digital UK Ltd [2004] EWHC 209 (Ch); [2004] 1 B.C.L.C. 541 at [22]–[23].

5. CONSEQUENCES OF DISCHARGE

Effect on contract

24–048   *[Add to note 258: page [1399]]*
Similarly, an adjudication provision in a contract will survive the discharge of the contract: *Connex South Eastern Ltd v MJ Building Services Group plc* [2004] EWHC 1518 (TCC) at [25].

Rights acquired before discharge

24–051   *[Add to note 274: page [1401]]*
Odfjfell Seachem A/S v Continental des Petroles et D'Investissements [2004] EWHC 2929 (Comm); [2005] 1 Lloyd's Rep. 275 at [35].

CHAPTER 25

OTHER MODES OF DISCHARGE

1. Merger

Estoppel by judgment

[*Note 44: page* [1409]]   **25–011**
Update reference to *Cross and Tapper on Evidence* to (10th ed., 2005), p.95.

Requirements

[*Note 55: page* [1411]]   **25–012**
Update reference to *Cross and Tapper on Evidence* to (10th ed., 2005), pp.106–108.

2. Alteration or Cancellation of a Written Instrument

Material alteration

[*Insert new note 111a after "alteration" at the beginning of line 12: page* [1417]   **25–020**
[111a] It may be necessary in certain cases to distinguish between an "alteration" to a document and an "appendage" to the contract. Thus the addition of an incorrect date after the document has been signed may amount to an "appendage" rather than an alteration: *Moussavi-Azad v Sky Properties Ltd* [2003] EWHC 2669 (QB); [2003] All E.R. (D) 38 (Dec) at [49]. This may be thought to introduce an unnecessary element of sophistry into the rule and that the better view is that such an addition is an "alteration" and the vital question then becomes whether that alteration is "material".

Immaterial alteration

[*Add to note 128: page* [1418]]   **25–023**
Moussavi-Azad v Sky Properties Ltd [2003] EWHC 2669 (QB); [2003] All E.R. (D) 38 (Dec) at [48]–[51].

Part Eight

REMEDIES FOR BREACH OF CONTRACT

CHAPTER 26

DAMAGES

1. NATURE AND KINDS OF DAMAGES

(g) *Exemplary Damages and Depriving the Defendant of his Profit*

Exemplary damages

26–019   [*Add to note 94 at end: page* [1433]]
and in *Borders (UK) Ltd v Metropolitan Police Commissioner* [2005] EWCA Civ 197 (see below, para.26–022, n.128)

The extension made by *Att-Gen v Blake*

[*Add to note 128 at end; page* [1436]]   **26–022**
In *Borders (UK) Ltd v Metropolitan Police Commissioner*, above, *Blake* was
used to justify the extension of exemplary damages to cover disgorgement of
some of the profits made by D through tortious activity.

Partial disgorgement on the *Wrotham Park* basis

[*Add to note 139 at end; page* [1437]]   **26–024**
A substantial level of damages has been awarded on the *Wrotham Park* basis:
Lane v O'Brien Homes [2004] EWHC 303 (QB). The claimant had lost "the
value of [her] bargaining position"; damages of £150,000 were awarded against
a builder whose profit was at least £280,000 (case noted by Campbell, (2004) 67
M.L.R. 817). See also *Gafford v Graham* (1999) 77 P. & C.R. 73; *Amec
Developments Ltd v Jury's Hotel Management (UK) Ltd* [2001] 1 E.G.L.R. 81

2. Causation and Contributory Negligence

The claimant's lost opportunities: hypothetical consequences

[*Add to note 208 after the Bank of Credit and Commerce case: page* [1445]]   **26–039**
Maden v Clifford Coppock & Carter (a firm) [2004] EWCA Civ 1037; [2005]
2 All E.R. 43 (80 per cent chance of obtaining a particular level of damages in
an out of court settlement).

[*Add to the text at the end of the paragraph: page* [1446]]   **26–040**
or where, but for the breach, there was a real or substantial chance that the
claimant would have continued to make profits from "repeat orders" from
customers.[215a]

[215a] *Jackson v Bank of Scotland* [2005] UKHL 3; [2005] 1 W.L.R. 377 (see below, para.
26–062A).

The contract-breaker's opportunity to minimise the cost of performance

[*Add to note 222 at end: page* [1446]]   **26–041**
The *Mihalis Angelos* case was applied in *The Golden Victory* [2005] EWHC
161 (Comm); [2005] 1 Lloyd's Rep. 443 (after repudiation by the contract-
breaker, the war clause would have entitled him to cancel before the end of the
charter period).

3. Remoteness of Damage

(a) *General rules*

Modern statement of the rule

[*Add to note 248 at end: page* [1450]]   **26–047**
On the time when the test is applied, see *Jackson v Bank of Scotland*, above,
at [35]–[36].

Actual and imputed knowledge

26–052   [*Add to note 278 after The Heron II: page* [1453]]
   Louis Dreyfus Trading Ltd v Reliance Trading Ltd [2004] EWHC 525 (Comm); [2004] 2 Lloyd's Rep. 243 (see Vol.II, para.43–442, n.1999).

Actual knowledge of special circumstances

26–054   [*Add to note 288 after the Victoria Laundry case: page* [1454]]
   See *Jackson v Bank of Scotland*, above, at [35]–[36].

   [*Add to note 289 after Wroth v Tyler: page* [1454]]
   See *Jackson v Bank of Scotland*, above, at [36].

   [*Add to the end of the text of the paragraph: page* [1454]]
   There is now authority in the House of Lords that the two rules in *Hadley v Baxendale* are not mutually exclusive.[289a]

   [289a] *Jackson v Bank of Scotland*, above, at [46]–[49].

Knowledge and assumption of risk

26–055   [*Add to the text of the paragraph after note 293: page* [1455]]
   "Where knowledge of special circumstances is relied on, the assumption is that the defendant undertook to bear any special loss which was referable to those special circumstances".[293a]

   [293a] *Jackson v Bank of Scotland*, above, at [26].

(c) *Loss of Profits*

[*Add new paragraph after paragraph 26–062: page* [1460]]

26–062A   **Loss of future business.** Subject to the rules on causation and remoteness, the contract-breaker may be liable for the claimant's loss of future profits from "repeat orders" from his previous customers which loss was caused by the particular breach of contract.[336a] When loss of future profits is not too remote, the period of time for which the loss should be assessed is until the question whether any loss has been sustained has become "too speculative to permit the making of any award".[336b]

   [336a] *Jackson v Bank of Scotland*, above (breach of obligation to maintain confidence). See above, para.26–040; and Vol.II, paras 43–430, 43–452.
   [336b] *Jackson v Bank of Scotland*, above, at [37].

(d) *Expenditure Wasted or Incurred as a Result of the Breach*

Damages assessed on a "no transaction" basis

26–070   [*Add to note 383: page* [1466]]
   (followed in *Hok Sport Ltd v Aintree Racecourse Co Ltd* [2002] EWHC 3094; [2003] Lloyd's Rep. P.N. 148).

(e) *Non-pecuniary Losses*

Mental distress and disappointment: nervous shock

[Add to note 409 after the reference to Malik's case: page [1468]]   **26–074**
In *Eastwood v Magnox Electric plc* [2004] UKHL 35; [2005] 1 A.C. 503, Lord
Nicholls said (at [11]) that if the facts of *Addis* occurred today, the claimant
would have a remedy at common law for breach of contract: see para.26–077,
below.

[Add to note 412]
On *Johnson v Unisys*, see the text added to para.26–077, below.

[Add to text after note 417: page [1469]]
Damages for breach of contract may be awarded to a mother for the mental
distress caused by the loss of the company of her child.[417a]

[417a] *Hamilton-Jones v David & Snape* (a firm) [2003] EWHC 3147 (Ch); [2004] 1 W.L.R. 924
(solicitor's failure allowed father to remove children from the UK).

[Add to note 419: page [1469]]
Barber v Somerset County Council [2004] UKHL 13; [2004] 1 W.L.R. 1089
(employee's psychiatric injury caused by work-related stress).

Loss of reputation

[Add to text at the end of the paragraph: page [1470]]   **26–077**
But this case has later been distinguished by the House of Lords, which held
that an employee may have a common law claim for financial loss where his
employer has acted unfairly towards him prior to, and independently of, his
subsequent unfair dismissal.[430a] However, it should be noted that in another case
the House of Lords held that in his unfair dismissal claim an employee cannot
recover compensation for non-economic or non-pecuniary loss, such as distress,
humiliation or loss of reputation.[430b]

[430a] *Eastwood v Magnox Electric plc* [2004] UKHL 35; [2005] 1 A.C. 503.
[430b] *Dunnachie v Kingston upon Hull City Council* [2004] UKHL 36; [2005] 1 A.C. 226 (interpreting s.123 of the Employment Rights Act 1996).

[Add to note 434: page [1471]]   **26–078**
Jackson v Bank of Scotland, above (see above, para.26–062A)

5. MITIGATION OF DAMAGE

"Reasonable steps"

[Add to note 518: page [1480]]   **26–095**
See also paras 26–095A—26–095D below.

[After paragraph 26–095, add new paragraphs: page [1481]]
Impecuniosity of the claimant. A recent tort case in the House of Lords leads   **26–095A**
to the question whether the impecuniosity of the claimant could be relevant in a

contractual claim. In *Lagden v O'Connor*[523a] the House of Lords held that it would not follow the dicta in *The Liesbosch* case[523b] to the effect that the plaintiff's impecuniosity was not relevant to the assessment of damages. *Lagden v O'Connor* was a claim in tort where the claimant's car had been damaged by the defendant's negligence. Since the claimant could not afford simply to hire a replacement car while his was being repaired (the car-hire firm would require him to make an up-front payment) he entered into a more expensive hire arrangement with an "accident hire" insurance company under which he need not pay anything in advance. The majority of their Lordships held that it was reasonably foreseeable that an impecunious claimant might reasonably incur the higher cost of credit hire because he had no other choice in obtaining a replacement car. Thus the claimant's foreseeable impecuniosity resulted in his entitlement to higher damages in tort than would have been awarded to others who could afford to pay for ordinary hire. This rule "requires the wrongdoer to bear the consequences if it was reasonably foreseeable that the injured party would have to borrow money or incur some other kind of expenditure to mitigate his damages".[523c] This language ("wrongdoer", "injured party") is not appropriate to a claim in contract where the main remoteness rule (the first rule in *Hadley v Baxendale*) is different from that in tort: the kind of loss within the reasonable contemplation of the parties at the time of making the contract.[523d] But even in contract the claimant's impecuniosity might be relevant if it prevented him from choosing a cheaper form of mitigation. The rules on mitigation and those on remoteness are entwined in some cases, where what was "within reasonable contemplation" and what was "reasonable" mitigation are treated as interchangeable concepts. In the *Monarch S.S.* case,[523e] Lord Wright said (with reference to the decision of the House of Lords in *Muhammad Issa el Sheikh Ahmad v Ali*[523f]) that "damages consequent on impecuniosity were held not too remote because . . . the loss was such as might reasonably be expected to be in the contemplation of the parties as likely to flow from breach of the obligation undertaken".[523g] This means that the claimant's impecuniosity will be relevant in contract if it falls within the defendant's reasonable contemplation (as at the time of contracting) as not unlikely to affect the claimant's ability to mitigate after a breach of the particular undertaking, *viz.*, that the claimant would be likely to incur greater than usual expense (or higher than normal interest charges) in a reasonable attempt to mitigate. This test will not be easy for the claimant to satisfy if he cannot prove that the defendant actually knew of his impecuniosity (which is the situation examined in the next paragraph.) Thus, there is no reported case holding his impecuniosity to be relevant in relation to the market price rule in the sale of goods[523h] or to the similar market price rule for breach of a contract of hire.[523i]

[523a] [2003] UKHL 64; [2004] 1 A.C. 1067.
[523b] [1933] AC 449, 460.
[523c] *per* Lord Hope, at [61].
[523d] See paras 26–045—26–051.
[523e] [1949] A.C. 196.
[523f] [1947] A.C. 427.

523g [1949] A.C. 196, 224; see para.26–056, n.295.
523h See paras 26–097, 43–415.
523i See para.26–097, n.530.

Actual knowledge of the claimant's impecuniosity. The claimant's impecuniosity will be relevant in contract if the second rule in *Hadley v Baxendale* is satisfied *viz.*, if, at the time of contracting, the contract-breaker had actual knowledge of special circumstances under which a breach was likely to cause the claimant greater or different loss from that to be normally expected under normal circumstances.[523j] The claimant's impecuniosity could be a "special circumstance" under this rule if, with his knowledge of it, the defendant could foresee that the claimant could mitigate his loss caused by the breach only by incurring greater expense than would be incurred by a financially secure person. The claimant must act "reasonably" in his mitigating actions but what is reasonable for a claimant known to be impecunious may be different from the case of a person with financial resources.[523k] One of the mitigation rules is that the claimant is entitled to damages for any loss or expense incurred by him in reasonably attempting to mitigate his loss, even where this attempt was unsuccessful or led to greater loss.[523l]

26–095B

523j See paras 26–054—26–056.
523k On the question of actual knowledge, see para.26–089, text at n.495.
523l See para.26–105.

Several cases illustrate the position.[523m] In *Wadsworth v Lydall*,[523n] on the dissolution of a farming partnership between the parties, the defendant was obliged to pay £10,000 to the plaintiff on a fixed date. The defendant knew that the plaintiff needed another farm and would be dependent on payment of that sum on that date to finance any purchase. When the defendant failed to pay, the Court of Appeal awarded the plaintiff as special damages the extra interest charges and legal costs incurred by him as a result of the breach.[523o] In *Bacon v Cooper*[523p] the rotor of the plaintiff's machine was damaged beyond repair as a result of the defendant's breach of contract. The only available replacement cost £41,500 which the plaintiff, a dealer in scrap metal, could not finance out of his own resources. It was held that the plaintiff had acted reasonably in obtaining it on hire purchase at a high rate of interest.[523q] A further authority is *Trans Trust S.P.R.L. v Danubian Trading Co Ltd*.[523r] The buyers undertook that a confirmed credit was to be opened forthwith in favour of the firm from which the sellers were obtaining the goods. The buyers knew that the sellers were not in a position themselves to open the necessary credit. The Court of Appeal held that the loss due to this impecuniosity of the sellers was not too remote because it was within the reasonable contemplation of the parties as likely to flow from the buyer's breach of contract in failing to obtain the credit.

26–095C

523m See also para.26–097 below.
523n [1981] 1 W.L.R. 598.
523o See para.26–089: the House of Lords approved the decision, *ibid.*, n.490.
523p [1982] 1 All E.R. 397; see also para.26–145)

[523q] The case was not explicitly put on the ground of the second rule in *Hadley v Baxendale* but on the reasonableness of mitigation, as was *Robbins of Putney Ltd v Meek* [1971] R.T.R. 345 (see para.26–097, below.)

[523r] [1952] 2 Q.B. 297.

26–095D   Another case appears to accept the principle but it was found on the facts that the defendants did not know of the plaintiff's special financial arrangements. In *Compania Financiera "Soleada" S.A. v Hamoor Tanker Corporation Inc.*[523s] the plaintiff's vessel was arrested in breach of contract: since it was reasonably foreseeable that the plaintiff would seek to obtain its release and for that purpose would obtain a guarantee for payment of the debt, the Court of Appeal held that the expense in doing so, if reasonable, would be recoverable either because it was within the remoteness rules, or as the expense of reasonable mitigation.[523t] But because the particular financial arrangements between the plaintiffs and their bank were not known to the defendants, the high interest charges actually incurred by the plaintiffs were held to be "wholly unreasonable" and so not recoverable.

[523s] [1981] 1 W.L.R. 274.

[523t] Although Lord Denning preferred the former, his colleagues seemed to use the two concepts interchangeably.

Sale of goods

26–097   [*Add to text at the end of the paragraph: page* [1482]]
The relevance of the claimant's impecuniosity is discussed above.[532a] The market price rule is fundamental to the sale of goods: if the seller fails to deliver, the buyer's damages are *prima facie* the difference between the contract price and the market price at the date of breach.[532b] The rule assumes that the buyer should be able to finance the purchase of substitute goods at the time of the breach, even though he may not receive the damages until much later. The rule works reasonably well if he retains the balance of the price and there has not been a substantial rise in the market price. But the buyer's lack of financial resources could prevent his purchase of a substitute if he had paid the price (or a substantial deposit) in advance, or if the rise in price has been substantial. But to date none of these factors has prevented the application of the prima facie rule.[532c] Actual knowledge of the buyer's lack of resources has been treated as relevant to the purchase of a house[532d]; and the seller's decision to re-sell quickly because he was short of liquid resources was held to be reasonable mitigation in *Robbins of Putney Ltd v Meek*.[532e]

[532a] This Supplement, paras 26–095A—26–095D above.

[532b] See Vol.II, para.43–415.

[532c] See Benjamin's *Sale of Goods* (6th ed.) §17–008. On the *prima facie* nature of the rule, see Vol.II, 43–416.

[532d] *Wroth v Tyler* [1974] Ch. 30: see this Supplement, para.26–098A below.

[532e] [1917] R.T.R. 345 (sale of goods).

[*After paragraph 26–098, add new paragraph: page* [1482]]

26–098A   **Sale of land.** In *Wroth v Tyler*[536a] the contract-breaker's knowledge of the plaintiffs' lack of resources was treated as relevant to their ability to mitigate.[536b] Both the seller and the purchasers of a house contemplated at the date of the

THOMSON
™
SWEET & MAXWELL

Thank you for purchasing **Chitty on Contracts, 2nd supplement to the 29th Edition**.

Supplements to your main work

Chitty is supplemented regularly in order to keep your main work up-to-date with ongoing developments.

In order to receive your updating supplements to **Chitty** automatically on publication *you need to register*. Supplements will be invoiced on publication. You can cancel your request at any time.

How to register

Either complete and return this FREEPOST card, or, if you have purchased your copy of **Chitty** from a bookshop or other supplier, please ask your supplier to ensure that you are registered to receive your supplements.

Yes, please send me updating supplements to **Chitty on Contracts** on publication, unless countermanded.

Name:

Organisation:

Address:

Postcode:

Telephone:

Email:

S&M account number: (if known)

Signed: Date:

LBU0975E

ORDERS

SWEET & MAXWELL

FREEPOST

PO Box 2000

ANDOVER

SP10 9AH

UNITED KINGDOM

contract that there would be a rise in house prices after the contract; the seller knew that the purchasers "had no financial resources beyond [the price] that they could have put together for the purchase of [the seller's house] . . . [The purchasers] were therefore to the [seller's] knowledge unable at the time of breach to raise a further £1500 to purchase an equivalent house forthwith, and so . . . mitigate their loss".[536c]

[536a] [1974] Ch. 30 (mentioned in para.26–096, n.527).
[536b] On the relevance of this knowledge, see this Supplement, para.26–095B, above.
[536c] [1974] Ch. 30, 57.

Recovery of sum due on performance

[*Add to note 572: page* [1487]]   **26–107**
The *White and Carter* case was further distinguished where one party's obligation to pay a definite sum was not dependent on performance by the other party of its own obligations: *Ministry of Sound (Ireland) Ltd v World On-line Ltd* [2003] EWHC 2178 (Ch); [2003] 2 All E.R. (Comm.) 823.

6. PENALTY OR LIQUIDATED DAMAGES

Statement of penalty rules

[*Add to note 599: page* [1490]]   **26–110**
The law laid down in the *Dunlop* case has not been significantly altered by the *Philips Hong Kong* case (cited in para.26–109, n.589 above): *Jeancharm Ltd v Barnet Football Club Ltd* [2003] EWCA Civ 58; [2003] 92 Con. L. R. 26.

[*Add to note 605: page* [1491]]
cf. Jeancharm Ltd v Barnet Football Club Ltd, above, n.599 (interest rate for late payment of 5 per cent per week held to be a penalty).

8. INTEREST AND RATE OF EXCHANGE

Finance charges on particular transaction contemplated

[*Add to note 788: page* [1511]]   **26–145**
On the relevance of the impecuniosity of the claimant, see paras 26–095A—26–095D, above.

CHAPTER 27

SPECIFIC PERFORMANCE AND INJUNCTION

2. THE "ADEQUACY" OF DAMAGES

Difficulty of quantifying damages

27–008   [*Add to note 32: page* [1525]]

In *Laemthong International Lines Co Ltd v Artis (The Laemthong Glory) (No.2)* [2004] EWHC 2738 (Comm); [2005] 1 Lloyd's Rep. 632 goods were delivered from a chartered ship against letters of indemnity, one of which, addressed by the receiver to the character, was held to be enforceable by the shipowner against the receiver under the Contracts (Rights of Third Parties) Act 1999: see above, para.18–087 of this Supplement. One of the terms of this letter provided that, if the ship should be arrested in consequence of the shipowner's delivering the goods without production of the bill of lading, then the receiver would provide bail or other security to secure her release. Cooke J. held that this promise was specifically enforceable as the assessment of damages for detention was "never an entirely straightforward matter" (at [47]) and as the "very purpose" of the letter of indemnity was "to prevent the detention that occurred" (at [49]; *cf.* at [51]). The decision was affirmed, but without any discussion on appeal of the issue of specific enforceability: see [2005] EWCA Civ 519; [2005] 1 Lloyd's Rep. 688 where the shipowner's claim is said at [19] to have been one for a declaration that the promisors under the letters of indemnity were obliged to take the specified steps to secure the release of the ship.

[112]

[*Add to note 36: page* [1526]]

For the difficulty of enforcing a judgment for damages as a ground for ordering specific performance, see also *Laemthong International Lines Co. Ltd v Artis (The Laemthong Glory) (No.2)* [2004] EWHC 2738 (Comm); [2005] 1 Lloyd's Rep. 632 at [47]: "the enforcement of judgments in Yemen is a matter of some difficulty"; affirmed without reference to the issue of specific enforceability [2005] EWCA Civ 519; [2005] 1 Lloyd's Rep. 688, above para.27–008, n.32 of this Supplement.

Availability of substitute

[*Add to note 45: page* [1527]]   **27–011**

See also *Pena v Dale* [2003] EWHC 1065; [2004] 2 B.C.L.C. 508 at [135] (option to purchase shares in private company specifically enforced).

Sale of goods: non-delivery

[*Add to note 52, line 6, after reference to Lingen v Simpson: page* [1528]]   **27–014**

cf. Land Rover Group Ltd v UPF (UK) Ltd [2002] EWHC 3183; [2003] B.C.L.C. 222 at [52] (mandatory injunction to enforce obligation to supply chassis to car manufacturer).

Specific enforcement of contracts not within section 52

[*Add to note 70: page* [1530]]   **27–017**

cf. Land Rover Group Ltd v UPF (UK) Ltd [2002] EWHC 3183; [2003] 2 B.C.L.C. 222, above para.27–014 of this Supplement. For the question whether the goods in that case were indeed specific (as was there agreed: see at [52]) *cf.* Main Work, para.43–031.

3. Contracts not Specifically Enforceable

Exceptions

[*Add to note 107: page* [1534]]   **27–022**

For recognition of the exceptions referred to in the Main Work, para.27–022, see also *Lauritzencool AB v Lady Navigation Inc* [2005] EWCA Civ 579; [2005] 2 All E.R. (Comm.) 183 at [10].

Other contracts involving "personal" service

[*Add to note 110: page* [1535]]   **27–023**

cf. A v Lord Grey's School [2004] EWCA Civ 382; [2004] Q.B. 1231, where *damages* were recovered by a pupil whose expulsion from a state school was found to amount to a breach of the Human Rights Act 1998, Sch.1 Pt II, Art.2 and whose requests for *reinstatement* had been denied.

[*Add to note 113*]

In *Pena v Dale* [2003] EWHC 1065; [2004] 2 B.C.L.C. 508 specific perform-ance was ordered of an agreement by which A, a shareholder in a private company, granted an option to B to acquire a minority shareholding in the company. The existence of personal animosity between A and B was no bar to such specific enforcement since B would not, by virtue of exercising the option, acquire any right to participate in the day to day management of the company: see *ibid.*, at [136].

Services not of a "personal" nature

27–024   [*Add to note 116: page* [1535]]

Lauritzencool AB v Lady Navigation Inc [2005] EWCA Civ 579; [2005] 2 All E.R. (Comm.) 183, below n.119.

[*Add to note 119*]

See also *Lauritzencool AB v Lady Navigation Inc* [2005] EWCA Civ 579; [2005] 2 All E.R. (Comm.) 183, where it was said at [9] to be "common ground . . . that *The Scaptrade* stands as authority for the proposition that specific performance will not be ordered of a time charter" though counsel reserved the right "to ask the House [of Lords] to review this proposition, should that matter go that far" (*ibid.*). For the injunctive relief granted in the *Lauritzencool* case, see below, para.27–068 of this Supplement.

4. OTHER GROUNDS FOR REFUSING SPECIFIC PERFORMANCE

Inutility

27–039   [*Add new text after note 201: page* [1544]]

Specific performance of a promise to issue share warrants has likewise been refused where "the time for the exercise of the option in any warrants which ought to have been issued" had "long since expired".[201a]

[201a] *De Jongh Weill v Mean Fiddler Holdings* [2005] All E.R. (D) 331 (Jul) at [75].

7. SPECIFIC PERFORMANCE WITH COMPENSATION

Condition against error or misdescription

27–056   [*Substitute for note 306: page* [1554]]

The Court of Appeal has held that the Unfair Terms in Consumer Contracts Regulations 1999 (SI 1999/2083), apply to contracts for the sale of an interest in land by a commercial supplier to a consumer: *London Borough of Newham v Khatun* [2004] EWCA Civ 55; [2005] Q.B. 37, see above, para.15–014.

8. INJUNCTION

Negative contracts

[Add to note 323: page [1556]]   **27–059**
For the application of the "balance of convenience" test to a mandatory injunction to enforce a position obligation (to maintain supplies of components to the supplier of motor vehicles), see *Land Rover Group Ltd v UPF (UK) Ltd* [2002] EWHC 3183; [2003] B.C.L.C. 222 at [60]. The injunction there granted was an interim injunction (at [65]), so that the "balance of convenience" test was applicable also on the principle stated in Main Work, para.27–060.

[Add to note 324: page [1557]]
cf. Mortimer v Bailey [2004] EWCA Civ 1514; [2005] 02 E.G. 102, where a mandatory injunction was granted to order the defendant to pull down an extension built in breach of a restrictive covenant. The point at issue was whether there had been undue delay in applying for this form of relief.

Injunction imposing undue pressure on employee

[Add new text at end of paragraph: page [1560]]   **27–065**
The above discussion is concerned with contracts of employment and reflects the reluctance of the courts to put undue pressure on the employee to render personal service. Where the contract is one for services which are not of a personal nature, an injunction may be available against the party who has promised to provide the services, even though the practical effect of the injunction is to "compel performance". A shipowner who has let him ship out under a time charter may, for example, be restrained by injunction from employing the ship inconsistently with the charterparty.[356a]

[356a] *Lauritzencool AB v Lady Navigation Inc* [2005] EWCA Civ 579; [2005] 2 All E.R. (Comm.) 183, below para.27–068 of this Supplement.

Implied negative promises

[Add to note 372: page [1562]]   **27–068**
In *Lauritzencool AB v Lady Navigation Inc* [2005] EWCA Civ 579; [2005] 2 All E.R. (Comm.) 183 disputes under two time charters were submitted to arbitration and interim injunctions were granted restraining the shipowners from (a) employing the vessels inconsistently with the charterparties, or (b) fixing the vessels with any third party during the period of the charterparties, pending the final award in the arbitration. The contract was not one of personal service, but "a commercial arrangement between two independent companies involving the employment of no named individuals" (at [35]). It was therefore no objection to the grant of an injunction that the "practical effect" of this form of relief would be to "compel performance" (at [19], [20]) in the sense that the "only realistic course" (at [33]) which the injunction left to the owners was to continue to perform the charterparties. A distinction was to be drawn between an injunction resulting in such practical compulsion to perform and one which was "as a matter

of law pregnant with an affirmative obligation to perform the charterparty" (at [6]) such as one "not to break the contract" or "not to take steps to prevent its performance". Such an injunction was "tantamount to" (at [6]) or "juristically indistinguishable from" an order of specific performance (at [10], quoting from *The Scaptrade* [1983] 2 A.C. 694 at 700) and was therefore not available in respect of contracts which were not specifically enforceable: see Main Work para.27–069 and this Supplement para.27–069. An injunction which did not result in such *legal* compulsion to perform the contract was available to restrain breach of a contract of the present kind even though it resulted in practical compulsion of the kind described above. Such practical compulsion was a ground for refusing injunctive relief in personal service cases of the kind described in paras 27–064 and 27–068 at n.371 above, but not where the services were not of a personal nature.

27–069   [*Add new text after note 379: page* [1563]]
Similarly, an injunction will not be granted against "taking any step preventing the performance of" a contract.[379a]

[379a] See the decision at first instance in *Lauritzencool AB v Lady Navigation Inc* [2004] EWHC 2607 (Comm); [2005] 1 All E.R. (Comm.) 77, so far as it relates to para.12(a) of the relief claimed. There was no appeal against this aspect of the case when the decision was affirmed and injunctions were granted in the more restricted form, "not pregnant with an affirmative obligation to perform", discussed in para.27–068 above: [2005] EWCA Civ 579 at [6].

Statutory provisions against refusal to contract

27–072   [*Add to note 386, line 3, after reference to SI 1996/438: page* [1564]]
For the unlawfulness of discrimination on grounds of religion or belief, and for remedies in respect of such discrimination, see Employment Equality (Religion or Belief) Regulations 2003 (SI 2003/1660). Regulation 30 falls short of providing for injunctive relief: it enables an employment tribunal to make a "recommendation" that steps should be taken to obviate or reduce the adverse effect on the complainant of the discrimination (reg.30(1)(c)); but the only effect of failure to comply with the recommendation is to increase the compensation payable to the complainant or to enable him to get compensation where no order for compensation was originally made (reg.30(3)). The position is the same in cases of unlawful discrimination on grounds of sexual orientation: see Employment Equality (Sexual Orientation) Regulations 2003 (SI 2003/1661), reg.30.

Chapter 28

LIMITATION OF ACTIONS

1. PERIODS OF LIMITATION

Specialities

[*Add to note 19: page* [1573]]   **28–003**
On s.20, see *West Bromwich Building Society v Wilkinson* [2005] UKHL 44;
[2005] 1 W.L.R. 2303.

Latent damage in actions for the tort of negligence

[*Add to note 47: page* [1575]]   **28–010**
It has also been held that the Limitation Act 1980, s.14A does not apply to a
claim for damages under s.2(1) of the Misrepresentation Act 1967 because under
s.2(1) there is no onus on the claimant to prove negligence: *Laws v The Society
of Lloyd's* [2003] EWCA Civ 1887; *The Times*, January 23, 2004, at
[78]–[93].

[*Add to note 58: page* [1576]]   **28–011**
Section 14A(10) therefore makes clear that constructive knowledge is sufficient.

Action on a judgment

28-015   [*Add to note 68: page* [1577]]
In *Ridgeway Motors (Isleworth) Ltd v ALTS Ltd* [2005] EWCA Civ 92; [2005] 2 All E.R. 304 it was held that, following *Lowsley v Forbes* [1999] 1 A.C. 329 and impliedly disapproving *Re a Debtor* [1997] Ch. 310, a winding up or bankruptcy petition by a judgement creditor was not "an action upon a judgment" within s.24(1) of the 1980 Act. "An action upon a judgment" had the special meaning of a "fresh action" brought upon a judgment in order to obtain a second judgment, which could be executed. Insolvency proceedings, whether personal or corporate, did not fall within the scope of that special meaning.

2. ACCRUAL OF THE CAUSE OF ACTION

Concurrent liability in tort

28-033   [*Add to note 142: page* [1584]]
For consideration of when a cause of action accrues against an accountant in the tort of negligence, see *Law Society v Sephton & Co* [2004] EWCA Civ 1627; [2005] 3 W.L.R. 212. For a consideration of s.14A(10), see *Gravgaard v Aldridge & Brownlee* [2004] EWCA Civ 1529; [2005] P.N.L.R. 19.

5. EXTENSION OF THE PERIOD

(b) *Fraud, Concealment or Mistake*

Concealment

28-086   [*Add to note 329: page* [1602]]
In *Williams v Fanshaw Porter & Hazelhurst* [2004] EWCA Civ 157; [2004] 2 All E.R. 616, the decision in *Cave v Robinson Jarvis & Rolf* [2002] UKHL 18; [2003] 1 A.C. 384 was considered and applied to a professional negligence claim. It was held that a trainee legal executive, employed by the defendants, had deliberately concealed a relevant fact within the meaning of s.32(1)(b) of the Limitation Act 1980.

(c) *Acknowledgement and Part Payment*

Parties to the acknowledgement or part payment

28-100   [*Add to note 391: page* [1607]]
In *UCB Corporate Services Ltd v Kohli* [2004] EWHC 1126 (Ch); [2004] 2 All E.R. (Comm.) 422 it was held that the part payments were not made by an agent of the debtor, so that the limitation period did not run afresh under s.29 and s.30(2) of the Limitation Act 1980.

Effect of acknowledgement and part payment on other persons

[*Add to note 404: page* [1609]]   **28–103**
   This sentence in the text was approved in *UCB Corporate Services Ltd v Kohli*
[2004] EWHC 1126 (Ch); [2004] 2 All E.R. (Comm.) 422, in which it was held
that part payment by a principal debtor bound the surety for the purposes of
s.31(7) of the Limitation Act 1980.

(d) Agreement of the Parties

Estoppel

[*Add to note 427; page* [1611]]   **28–109**
   Super Chem Products Ltd v American Life and General Insurance Co Ltd
[2004] UKPC 2; [2004] 2 All E.R. 358.

7. C<small>OMMENCEMENT OF</small> P<small>ROCEEDINGS</small>

Amendments to statement of case after the end of the limitation period

[*Add to note 471: page* [1615]]   **28–118**
   Laws v The Society of Lloyd's [2003] EWCA Civ 1887; *The Times,* January 23,
2004; *Furini v Bajwa* [2004] EWCA Civ 412; [2004] 1 W.L.R. 1971; *P&O
Nedlloyd BV v Arab Metals Co* [2005] EWHC 1276; [2005] All E.R. (D) 237
(Jun.) (in which it was held that a claim for a declaration of different rights than
those originally pleaded constituted a new claim under CPR Pt 17, r.4.2).

[*Add to note 474: page* [1616]]   **28–119**
   Parsons v George [2004] EWCA Civ 912; [2004] 1 W.L.R. 3264; *Morgan Est
(Scotland) Ltd v Hanson Concrete Products Ltd* [2005] EWCA Civ 134; [2005]
3 All E.R. 135.

9. L<small>IMITATION IN</small> E<small>QUITY</small>

Introductory

[*Add to note 536: page* [1621]]   **28–134**
   The point in *Re Pauling's Settlement Trusts* [1964] Ch. 303, 353, was applied
in *Re Loftus* [2005] EWHC 406 (Ch); [2005] 1 W.L.R. 1890 at [161]–[162].

[*Add to note 537*]
   In *P&O Nedlloyd BV v Arab Metals Co* [2005] EWHC 1276; [2005] All E.R.
(D) 237 (Jun.) Colman J. held that a declaration was not "equitable relief" within
s.36(1). Rather it was statutory so that normal time limits within the Limitation
Act 1980 apply.

The statute applied by analogy

28–135   *[Add to note 543: page* [1622]*]*
    In *P&O Nedlloyd BV v Arab Metals Co* [2005] EWHC 1276; [2005] All E.R. (D) 237 (Jun.) the usual contractual limitation period of six years was applied by analogy under s.36(1) to a claim for specific performance, so that it was time-barred.

Part Nine

RESTITUTION

Chapter 29

RESTITUTION

1. Introduction

(a) *Nature of Restitution*

Common law

[*Add to note 7: page* [1632]]   **29–002**

   Taylor v Motability Finance Ltd [2004] EWHC 2619 (Comm), at [23] (Cooke J.); *Mowlem plc v Stena Line Ports Ltd* [2004] EWHC 2206; *S and W Process Engineering Ltd v Cauldron Foods Ltd* [2005] EWHC 153 (TCC).

Equity

29–003   [*Add to note 15: page* [1633]]
For the history of the unjust enrichment principle in the United States see Kull [2005] O.J.L.S. 297.

(c) *The Theoretical Basis of Restitution*

The principle of unjust enrichment

29–012   [*Add to note 47: page* [1638]]
See Kull [2005] O.J.L.S. 297.

Statutory recognition

20–015   [*Add to line 11, after note 65: page* [1641]]
It has been recognised that the rationale of the Civil Liability (Contribution) Act 1978 is to ensure that a defendant is not unjustly enriched where the defendant's liability to a third party has been discharged by the claimant.[65a]

[65a] *Dubai Aluminium Co Ltd v Salaam* [2002] UKHL 48; [2003] 2 A.C. 366 at [76] (Lord Hobhouse).

The state of the unjust enrichment principle

29–016   [*Note 69: page* [1641]]
Update reference to Birks, *Unjust Enrichment* to (2nd ed., 2005).

Different causes of action within restitution

29–017   [*Add to note 79: page* [1642]]
See also *Criterion Properties Ltd v Stratford UK Properties* [2004] UKHL 28; [2004] 1 W.L.R. 1846, at [4] (Lord Nicholls).

2. UNJUST ENRICHMENT

(a) *The Content of the Unjust Enrichment Principle*

The elements of unjust enrichment

29–018   [*Note 81: page* [1642:]]
McDonald v Coys of Kensington is now reported at [2004] 1 W.L.R. 2775.

Defences and bars

29–019   [*Note 92, line 3: page* [1643]]
Portman BS v Hamlyn Taylor Neck is reported at [1998] 4 All E.R. 202.

(b) *Enrichment*

Non-monetary benefits

[Note 105: page [1644:]]
McDonald v Coys of Kensington is now reported at [2004] 1 W.L.R. 2775.

29–021

[Add to note 107: page [1645]]
See *S and W Process Engineering Ltd v Cauldron Foods Ltd* [2005] EWHC
153 (TCC), at [51]–[55].

Service resulting in incontrovertible benefit

[Notes 114 and 116: page [1645]]
McDonald v Coys of Kensington is now reported at [2004] 1 W.L.R. 2775.

29–022

[Add to end of note 116: page [1645]]
See Virgo (2004) C.L.J. 280.

(c) *At the expense of the claimant*

Rejection of "passing on" defence

[Add to note 128: page [1647]]
However, in *Marks and Spencer plc v Commissioners of Customs and Excise*
[2005] UKHL 53, at [25] Lord Walker of Westingthorpe recognised that passing
on is recognised as a possible defence to any restitutionary claim. His Lordship
cited *Roxborough v Rothmans of Pall Mall Australia Ltd, ibid.*, in support of this
conclusion, but that decision expressly rejected the passing on defence in Australia.

29–026

(e) *Mistake*

Burden of proof

[Add to note 174, after reference to Kleinwort Benson case: page [1652]]
Cobbold v Bakewell Management Ltd [2003] EWHC 2289 (Ch), at [19]
(Rimer J.).

29–034

Examples of payments under a mistake of law

[Delete last sentence: page [1657]]

29–041

Exceptions to the mistake of law bar

[Add to note 221: page [1658]]
Following the decision of the Court of Appeal in *IRC v Deutsche Morgan
Grenfell Group plc* [2005] EWCA Civ 78; [2005] S.T.C. 329 such a claim for

29–042

restitution against public authorities can only be founded on the *ultra vires* nature of the receipt and not on mistake either of law or fact. See paras. 29–083—29–086. The consequence of this is that the claimant cannot rely on the extended limitation period under s.32(1)(c) of the Limitation Act 1980 which applies to claims involving mistake and for which time does not begin to run until the mistake could reasonably have been discovered. See para.28–088.

Mistake of law: principles governing recovery

29–047   *[Add to note 249: page* [1661]]
In *Brennan v Bolt Burdon* [2004] EWCA Civ 1017; [2005] Q.B. 303 Maurice Kay L.J. stated that he was "reluctant to countenance as a mistake of law a situation in which it is generally known or ought to be known that the law in question is about to be reconsidered on appeal."

[Add new note 249a after "compromise" in line 10: page [1661]]

[249a] See *Brennan v Bolt Burdon* [2004] EWCA Civ 1017.

Changes in the law

29–048   *[Add to note 261 in line 3, after reference to Derrick v Williams: page* [1662]]
See also *Brennan v Bolt Burdon* [2004] EWCA Civ 1017; [2005] Q.B. 303 especially at [50] (Bodey J.).

(f) *Failure of Consideration*

General principles

29–054   *[Add to note 283: page* [1665]]
cf. Taylor v Motability Finance Ltd [2004] EWHC 2619 (Comm), at [25] (Cooke J.), where the judge appears to suggest that the test of whether the consideration has failed totally depends on substantial performance by the claimant, whereas the true position is that it typically depends on whether there has been performance by the other party to the contract.

Bad bargains

29–068   *[Delete paragraph and replace with the following: page* [1675]]
Bad Bargains. Where the innocent party has made a bad bargain the damages for breach may well be less than the reasonable value of the work he has done. In such circumstances the claimant would wish to obtain a restitutionary remedy rather than damages which would be affected by the contractual limit. It has been unclear whether a restitutionary remedy is available to the innocent party in such circumstances or whether any claim for reasonable remuneration will be limited to a rateable proportion of the contract price. The weight of United States authority favours the view that the *quantum meruit* should not be limited in this way,[369] the Privy Council has held that the measure of relief in a *quantum meruit*

is the actual value of the work and that the profitability of the contract is irrelevant[370] and the Law Commission has recommended that a *quantum meruit* granted to an innocent party should not be based on the contract price.[371] Until recently the matter does not appear to have been considered explicitly in England.[372] However, in *Taylor v Motability Finance Ltd*[372a] Cooke J. stated that there is no justification for the award of a restitutionary remedy which is in excess of the contractual limit since the award of such a remedy would put the claimant in a better position than he would have been in had the contract been fulfilled which would be unjust. He emphasised that, when determining the *quantum meruit*, regard should be had to the contract both as a guide to the value which the parties put on the service and to ensure justice between the parties.

[369] The most notable instance is *Boomer v Muir* 24 P. 2d 570 (1933), in which $258,000 was awarded as the value of the work done over and above the price paid although only $20,000 was still due under the contract. See also the authorities cited by Palmer, *The Law of Restitution* (1978), Vol.I, pp.389–390.

[370] *Slowey v Lodder* [1904] A.C. 442; affirming (1900) N.Z.L.R. 321; *Reynard Construction (ME) Pty Ltd v Minister of Public Works* (1992) 26 N.S.W.L.R. 234; *Newton Woodhouse v Trevor Toys Ltd*, December 20, 1991, CA; *Rover International Ltd v Cannon Film Sales Ltd (No.3)* [1989] 1 W.L.R. 912 (below, para.29–076; see also above, para.29–055) supports this approach although the contract in that case was void.

[371] Law Comm. No.121, para.2.52 on which see Birks *op. cit.* pp.262–263. See in general, Birks [1987] L.M.C.L.Q. 421.

[372] *Inchbold v Western Neilgherry Coffee, etc.* (1864) 17 C.B. (N.S.) 733 may suggest the use of the contract price as a ceiling but the judgments make no clear distinction between damages and a *quantum meruit*. See also *Burchall v Gowrie & Blockhouse Collieries* [1910] A.C. 614 (contract price used to value services). *cf. De Bernardy v Harding* (1853) 8 Ex. 822; *Prickett v Badger*, above.

[372a] [2004] EWHC 2619 (Comm) at [26].

Claim of the party in breach

[*Add to note 384: page* [1676]]   **29–070**
See also *Item Software v Fassihi* [2004] EWCA Civ 1244; [2004] I.R.L.R. 928, where the Apportionment Act 1870 was applied to enable an employee who had been dismissed to recover a proportionate part of his monthly salary for the period he had actually worked, despite his breach of the contract of employment.

Absence of consideration

[*Note 412: page* [1679]]   **29–075**
Update reference to Birks, *Unjust Enrichment* to (2nd ed., 2005).

(g) *Ultra vires Receipts by the Revenue and Public Authorities*

Ultra vires demands

[*Add to note 452: page* [1684]]   **29–083**
See further *Sempra Metals Ltd v Inland Revenue Commissioners* [2005] EWCA Civ 389.

Scope of right

29–084   [*Replace the first sentence with the following: page* [1684]]

Scope of right. The *Woolwich* principle is applicable when money has been paid to a public authority as a result of a mistake of law.[454] In *IRC v Deutsche Morgan Grenfell Group plc*[454a] the Court of Appeal recognised that claims for restitution of tax paid by mistake can only arise by reference to particular statutory provisions, where the demand for payment was lawful,[454b] or at common law by virtue of the *Woolwich* principle, where the demand was unlawful. In reaching this decision the Court of Appeal drew a distinction between public and private transactions and recognised that, for the recovery of overpaid taxes at least, restitution occurs by virtue of a specific public law regime which is distinct from the private law regime which governs the bulk of the law of unjust enrichment. The practical consequence of this decision is that the claimant cannot rely on the extended limitation period under s.32(1)(c) of the Limitation Act 1980 which applies to claims involving mistake and for which time does not begin to run until the mistake could reasonably have been discovered.[454c]

[454] [1993] A.C. 70, 177, 205.
[454a] [2005] EWCA Civ 78; [2005] S.T.C. 329. See Virgo [2005] B.T.R. 281.
[454b] See para.29–085.
[454c] See para.28–088.

Defences

29–086   [*Delete note 472: page* [1686], *and replace with*]

As amended by the Finance (No.2) Act 2005, s.3. See *Marks and Spencer plc v Commissioners of Customs and Excise* [2005] UKHL 53, where the House of Lords referred the question of the validity of the unjust enrichment defence to the European Court of Justice. For the present operation of the defence see *Baines and Ernst Ltd v Commissioners of Customs and Excise* [2004] U.K.V.A.T. V18769.

(h) *Compulsion*

Unlawful or illegitimate compulsion

29–088   [*Add new note 482a, on line 7, after 'act': page* [1687]]
See *R v Attorney-General for England and Wales* [2002] UKPC 22.

Extortion colore officii

29–094   [*Replace second and third sentences, lines 4–6: pages* [1690]-[1691], *with*]
Following the decision of the Court of Appeal in *IRC v Deutsche Morgan Grenfell Group plc*[513] such a fee is probably only recoverable under the principle laid down in *Woolwich Equitable Building Society v IRC*[514] although the point was not expressly considered.

513 [2005] EWCA Civ 78, [2005] S.T.C. 329.
514 [1993] A.C. 70; above para.29–083.

Compulsory payments to a third person

[Delete final sentence in note 539: page [1693], and replace with:]   **29–099**
See also *Niru Battery Manufacturing Co v Milestone Trading Ltd (No.2)* [2004] EWCA Civ 487; [2004] 2 All E.R. (Comm.) 289 where the "principles of recoupment" were applied, although the effect was to recognise a restitutionary claim founded on the ground of legal compulsion.

The defendant must be primarily or ultimately liable to pay the third person

[Add to the end of note 551: page [1695]]   **29–102**
See also *Niru Battery Manufacturing Co v Milestone Trading Ltd (No.2)* [2004] EWCA Civ 487; [2004] 2 All E.R. (Comm.) 289 where restitution was available even though the claimant and the defendant were not subject to a common demand.

The right to contribution

[Delete the final sentence in note 631: page [1705] and replace with:]   **29–121**
However, in *Niru Battery Manufacturing Co v Milestone Trading Ltd (No.2)* [2004] EWCA Civ 487; [2004] 2 All E.R. (Comm.) 289 the Court of Appeal suggested that, if it had been necessary to decide the point, the dicta in *Royal Brompton Hospital Trust* concerning the meaning of "damage" were *obiter* and that it was bound by the earlier decision of the Court of Appeal in *Friends' Provident Life Office v Hillier Parker May and Rowden (a firm)* [1997] Q.B. 85, which held that a claim for restitution could be treated as a claim for compensation for the purposes of the 1978 Act, so that claims for breach of contract or tort and for unjust enrichment could be treated as claims for the same damage.

(i) Necessity

Agency of necessity

[Add to note 661: page [1708]]   **29–130**
See *Guildford Borough Council v Hein* [2005] EWCA Civ 979, at [33] (Clarke L.J.), and [80] (Waller L.J.).

(j) Exploitation

Undue influence

[Add to note 698: page [1712]]   **29–137**
See *Yorkshire Bank plc v Tinsley* [2004] EWCA Civ 816; [2004] 1 W.L.R. 2380.

[Add to note 699: page [1712]]
See *National Commercial Bank (Jamaica) Ltd v Hew* [2002] UKPC 51, at [43].

3. RESTITUTION FOR WRONGS

(a) *General Principles*

Disgorgement for wrongs

29–139　　*[Add to note 702: page* [1713]]
See *Murad v Al-Saraj* [2005] EWCA Civ 1235, at [108] (Jonathan Parker L.J.).

(b) *Tort*

Which torts may give rise to a restitutionary claim

29–142　　*[Add to note 732: page* [1715]]
In *Severn Trent Water Ltd v Barnes* [2004] EWCA Civ 570 damages for trespass to land were awarded to compensate the claimant for the loss of opportunity to bargain with the defendant for the price of interfering with the claimant's land rather than to deprive the defendant of any gain made by committing the tort.

The nature of the benefit

29–144　　*[Add to note 751, line 6 after reference to Wrotham Park Estate case: page* [1717]]
Severn Trent Water Ltd v Barnes [2004] EWCA Civ 570.

(c) *Breach of Contract*

Restitution for breach of contract

29–151　　*[Add to note 796, at end: page* [1721]]
Amec Developments v Jury's Hotel Management [2001] E.G.L.R. 81. See also *O'Brien Homes Ltd v Lane* [2004] EWHC 303 (QB) where damages for breach of a collateral contract not to build more than three houses were assessed by reference to what the defendant would have been prepared to pay the claimant to be released from the contractual obligation.

(d) *Equitable Wrongdoing*

Types of equitable wrongdoing

29–155　　*[Add to note 809: page* [1723]]
Crown Dilmun, Dilmun Investments Ltd v Nicholas Sutton, Fulham River [2004] EWHC 52 (Ch); *Re Quarter Master UK Ltd* (Paul Morgan Q.C.) (July 15, 2004); *Murad v Al-Saraj* [2005] EWCA Civ 1235.

[*Add to text at end of the paragraph: page* [1723]]
A fiduciary who has profited from his breach of duty will be liable to account for all the profits made, even if they would have been made had the defendant not breached his fiduciary duty.[810a]

[810a] *Murad v Al-Saraj* [2005] EWCA Civ 1235.

Receipt of a bribe, secret profit or commission

[*Text to note 817: page* [1724]]
In *Daraydan Holdings Ltd v Solland* [2004] EWHC 622 (Ch); [2005] Ch. 119 Lawrence Collins J. recognised that a defendant who had received a secret commission from the claimants in breach of fiduciary duty held that commission on constructive trust for the claimants, following the decision of the Privy Council in *Attorney General for Hong Kong v Reid* [1994] 1 A.C. 324.

29–156

Equitable allowance

[*Add to note 822: page* [1735]]
Murad v Al-Saraj [2005] EWCA Civ 1235.

29–157

[*Add to note 823: page* [1725]]
The award of an equitable allowance was declined in *Re Quarter Master UK Ltd* (July 15, 2004) on the ground that directors should not profit from their breach of fiduciary duty and that the directors concerned had not demonstrated special skills or taken unusual risks.

4. Proprietary Restitutionary Claims

(a) *Establishing proprietary rights*

Constructive trusts

[*Add to note 837, in line 10, after reference to Att.-Gen. (HK) v Reid: page* [1726]]
: approved in *Daraydan Holdings Ltd v Solland International Ltd* [2004] EWHC 622 (Ch) (Lawrence Collins J.).

29–160

[*Add to note 837, line 16, after 107: page* [1726]
Oxley v Hiscock [2004] EWCA Civ 546; [2005] Fam. 211.

[*Add to note 838, line 4, after 'void)': page* [1726]]
; *Commerzbank AG v IMB Morgan plc* [2004] EWHC 2771 (Ch); [2005] 1 Lloyd's Rep. 298 at [36] (Lawrence Collins J.); *Sinclair Investment Holdings SA v Versailles Trade Finance Ltd* [2005] EWCA Civ 722.

[*Add to note 843: page* [1727]]
Cobbold v Bakewell Management Ltd [2003] EWHC 2289 (Ch), at [17] (Rimer J.).

(b) *Following and Tracing*

Following and Tracing

29–162   [*Note 853: page* [1728]]
Shalson v Russo is reported at [2005] Ch. 281.

Withdrawals from a mixed fund in a bank account

29–167   [*Add to note 891: page* [1731]]
Commerzbank AG v IMB Morgan plc [2004] EWHC 2771 (Ch); [2005] 1
Lloyd's Rep. 298, at [50] (Lawrence Collins J.).

[*Add to note 894*]
Campden Hill Ltd v Chakrani [2005] EWHC 911 (Ch).

(c) *Proprietary Restitutionary Claims*

Subrogation

29–173   [*Add to note 919: page* [1734]]
Cheltenham and Gloucester plc v Appleyard [2004] EWCA Civ 291.

[*Add to note 920, after reference to Eagle Star Insurance v Karasiewicz*]
Filby v Mortgage Express (No.2) Ltd [2004] EWCA Civ 759 (where, although
the claim was characterised as grounded on unjust enrichment, the court treated
it as a claim founded on the vindication of property rights).

[*Add to note 919*]
See also *Niru Battery Manufacturing Co v Milestone Trading Ltd (No.2)*
[2004] EWCA Civ 487; [2004] 2 All E.R. (Comm.) 289, where the remedy of
subrogation was ordered to prevent the defendant's unjust enrichment arising
from the discharge of a liability owed by the defendant. It is unclear, however,
why this remedy was sought or obtained since the claimant had a direct restitutionary claim to recover the value of the benefit obtained by the defendant and
did not need to step into the shoes of any other party to bring such a claim.

[*In note 925, replace reference to Niru Battery Manufacturing Co v Milestone
Trading Ltd (No.2): page* [1735] *with*]
[2004] EWCA Civ 487; [2004] 2 All E.R. (Comm.) 289.

[*Add to note 927*]
See also *Cheltenham and Gloucester plc v Appleyard* [2004] EWCA Civ 291,
at [32] (Neuberger L.J.).

[*Add to the end of note 930*]
See also *Filby v Mortgage Express (No.2)* [2004] EWCA Civ 759, where a
mortgage was a nullity by virtue of a forged signature; and *Cheltenham and
Gloucester plc v Appleyard* [2004] EWCA Civ 291, where a mortgage had not
been registered.

[Add to the end of note 932]
Compare *Cheltenham and Gloucester plc v Appleyard* [2004] EWCA Civ 291, where the claimant's mortgage had not been registered as required by statute but it was subrogated to another mortgage because, *inter alia*, the claimant had not obtained the legal charge for which it had bargained but only an equitable charge and the failure to register was not the result of the claimant's negligence.

[Add to note 935, after reference to Banque Financière de la Cité case: page [1736]]
Cheltenham and Gloucester plc v Appleyard [2004] EWCA Civ 291, at [36] (Neuberger L.J.).

[Add to the text at the end of the paragraph]
Principles relating to the award of the equitable remedy of subrogation were usefully summarised by the Court of Appeal in *Cheltenham and Gloucester plc v Appleyard*.[936a] These include that a lender cannot claim subrogation if he obtains all of the security for which he bargained[936b] or where the lender bargained on the basis that no security would be received.[936c]

[936a] [2004] EWCA Civ 291, at [32]–[44] (Neuberger L.J.).
[936b] *Capital Finance Co Ltd v Stokes* [1969] 1 Ch. 261.
[936c] *Paul v Speirway Ltd (in liquidation)* [1976] 1 W.L.R. 220.

Personal restitutionary remedies

[Add to note 937, at the end: page [1736]]

29–174

The House of Lords concluded that the case was not concerned with the question of unconscionability but whether directors had authority to sign an agreement: [2004] UKHL 28; [2004] 1 W.L.R. 1846. On the interpretation of the test of unconscionability see also *Crown Dilmun, Dilmun Investments Ltd v Nicholas Sutton, Fulham River* [2004] EWHC 52 (Ch), at [200] (Peter Smith J.).

5. Defences

(b) *Change of Position*

Change of position as a separate defence

[Add to note 972: page [1740]]

29–179

Barros Mattos Jnr v McDaniels Ltd [2004] EWHC 1188 (Ch); [2005] 1 W.L.R. 247, at [16] (Laddie J.).

[Add to the text after note 973 in line 4]
In *Commerzbank AG v Gareth Price-Jones*[973a] Mummery L.J. recognised that "the decided cases steer a cautious course, aiming to avoid the dangers of a diffuse discretion and the restrictions of rigid rules." Munby J. stated that the defence was "intended to be a broadly stated concept of practical justice" and that "technicality and black letter law are to be avoided."[973b]

973a [2003] EWCA Civ 1663; [2004] 1 P. & C.R. D. 15, at [32].
973b *ibid.*, at [48]

Illustrations of change of position

29–180   [*Add to note 984: page* [1741]]
The Court of Appeal expressly recognised that an anticipatory change of position is a good defence in *Commerzbank AG v Gareth Price-Jones* [2003] EWCA Civ 1663; [2004] 1 P. & C.R. D. 15, at [38] (Mummery L.J.) and [64] (Munby J.).

Link between receipt and specific expenditure unnecessary

29–181   [*Add to end of paragraph: page* [1742]]
In *Commerzbank AG v Gareth Price-Jones*992a the Court of Appeal recognised that a non-pecuniary change of position may be sufficient to establish the defence, although, on the facts of the case, the defendant's change of position in staying in his job rather than seeking more lucrative employment elsewhere was not sufficient for it to be inequitable to require him to make restitution since there was no relevant connection between the anticipated receipt of money and the decision to stay in his job and that decision did not have a significant, precise or substantial impact on the defendant.

992a [2003] EWCA Civ 1663; [2004] 1 P. & C.R. D. 15, at [39], [40], [43] (Mummery L.J.) and [59] (Munby J.).

Bad faith

29–183   [*Notes 1002 and 1002a: page* [1743]]
McDonald v Coys of Kensington is now reported at [2004] 1 W.L.R. 2775.

[*Add to note 1002a: page* [1743]]
See also *Commerzbank AG v Gareth Price-Jones* [2003] EWCA Civ 1663; [2004] 1 P & C.R. D. 15, para.[53] where Munby J. stated that this was an exercise in judicial evaluation rather than judicial discretion. Cp. Birks (2004) 120 LQR 373, Burrows (2004) C.L.J. 276.

[*Add to text at end of paragraph*]
The defence is not available where a defendant's change of position is tainted since it involves the commission of an illegal act, other than where the illegality can be characterised as *de minimis*.1004a

1004a *Barros Mattos Jnr v McDaniels Ltd* [2004] EWHC 1188 (Ch); [2004] 3 All E.R. 299.

Relative fault

29–184   [*Add to text at end of paragraph: page* [1744]]
However, in *Commerzbank AG v Gareth Price-Jones*1011a Munby J., whilst acknowledging that relative fault was irrelevant, was clearly influenced by the fact that the defendant changed his position as a result of his own negligent mistake, which was not shared or induced by the claimant, in reaching his

conclusion that it was not equitable to allow the defendant to rely on the defence.

1011a [2003] EWCA Civ 1663; [2004] 1 P & C.R. D. 15. See also *Niru Battery Manufacturing Co v Milestone Trading Ltd (No.2)* [2004] EWCA Civ 487, at [33] (Clarke L.J.).

(c) *Settlement of an Honest Claim*

Payer has doubts but nevertheless pays

[*Add to note 1020: page* [1746]]   **29–187**
    Cobbold v Bakewell Management Ltd [2003] EWHC 2289 (Ch) at [19] (Rimer J.); *Brennan v Bolt Burdon* [2004] EWCA Civ 1017.

Compromise

[*Add to text at end of paragraph: page* [1747]]   **29–189**
    A compromise may be invalidated by a mistake, but not where the compromise was agreed on the basis of an erroneous assumption about the law.1030a

1030a *Brennan v Bolt Burdon* [2004] EWCA Civ 1017; [2005] Q.B. 303.

Part Ten

CONFLICT OF LAWS

CHAPTER 30

CONFLICT OF LAWS

1. PRELIMINARY CONSIDERATIONS

Sources of the law

30–002   [*Add to note 3: page* [1758]]

For an extensive discussion of all aspects of the conflict of laws relating to sale of goods, apart from consumer sales, see Fawcett, Harris and Bridge, *International Sale of Goods in the Conflict of Laws* (2005).

[*Add in line 2 of note 4: page* [1758]]
King v Brandywine Reinsurance Co [2005] EWCA Civ 235; [2005] 1 Lloyd's Rep. 655; *Zebrarise Ltd v De Nieffe* [2005] 1 Lloyd's Rep. 154.

2. COMMON LAW: THE DOCTRINE OF THE PROPER LAW OF A CONTRACT

Incorporation by reference

30–008   [*Add at end of note 38: page* [1763]]
Shamil Bank of Bahrain v Beximco Pharmaceuticals Ltd [2004] EWCA Civ 19; [2004] 1 W.L.R. 1784 (a case on the Rome Convention).

Relevant factors

[*Add at end of note 46: page* [1764]]   **30–010**
King v Brandywine Reinsurance Co [2005] EWCA Civ 235; [2005] 1 Lloyd's
Rep. 655.

[*Add to note 52: page* [1765]]
cf. *King v Brandywine Reinsurance Co,* above.

[*Add at end of note 60: page* [1765]]
Zebrarise Ltd v De Nieffe [2005] 1 Lloyd's Rep. 154.

3. THE ROME CONVENTION

(a) *In General*

[*Add to note 94: page* [1769]]
Meeusen, Pertegas and Straetmans (eds.), *Enforcement of International Con-
tracts in the European Union* (2004), Fawcett, Harris and Bridge, *International
Sale of Goods in the Conflict of Laws* (2005), Ch.13.

History and purpose

[*Text at notes 100 and 101: page* [1769]]   **30–016**
Belgium finally ratified the Brussels Protocol on May 5, 2004. The Protocol
entered into force on August 1, 2004, internationally, and is brought into force in
UK law by SI 2004/3448 as from March 1, 2005.

Revision of the Rome Convention

[*Add to note 108: page* [1770]]   **30–018**
Meeusen, Pertegas and Straetmans (eds.), *Enforcement of International Contracts in the European Union* (2004).

[*Add at beginning of note 113: page* [1771]]
See the Opinion of the European Economic and Social Committee on the
Green Paper at [2004] OJ C108/1.

[*Note 114: page* [1771]]
On the proposed "Rome II", see House of Lords, European Union Committee,
The Rome II Regulation: Report with Evidence, HL Paper 66 (2004). See also
European Parliament legislative resolution on the proposal for a regulation of the
European Parliament and of the Council on the law applicable to non-contractual
obligations ("Rome II") (P6_TA-PROV (2005)0284, July 6, 2005).

Interpretation: European Court of Justice

30–019   [*Text at notes 117 and 118: page* [1771]]
As a result of Belgian ratification of the Protocols on May 5, 2004, the Protocols entered into force on August 1, 2004. For implementation in UK law with effect from March 1, 2005, see SI 2004/3448.

Uniformity of interpretation and application

30–020   [*Add to note 131: page* [1773]]
European Bank of Reconstruction & Development v Tekoglu [2004] EWHC 846 (Comm); *Apple Corps Ltd v Apple Computer Inc* [2004] EWHC 768 (Ch); [2004] I.L.Pr. 597; *Base Metal Trading Ltd v Shamurin* [2004] EWCA Civ 1316; [2005] 1 W.L.R. 1157; *Opthalmic Innovations International (United Kingdom) Ltd v Opthalmic Innovations International Inc* [2004] EWHC 2948 (Ch); [2005] I.L.Pr. 10; *Atlantic Telecom GmbH, Noter,* 2004 S.L.T. 1031.

Incorporation by reference

30–029   [*Add at beginning of note 154: page* [1776]]
Shamil Bank of Bahrain v Beximco Pharmaceuticals Ltd [2004] EWCA Civ 19; [2004] 1 W.L.R. 1784.

[*Note 154: page* [1776]]
The principle of incorporation by reference only applies where the parties have sufficiently indicated the provisions of a foreign law or international convention which are apt to be incorporated as terms of the contract. A broad reference to principles of Sharia law is insufficient to incorporate such principles: *Shamil Bank of Bahrain v Beximco Pharmaceuticals Ltd,* above.

(b) *Exclusions*

Introduction

30–030   [*Add at end of note 157: page* [1777]]
Fawcett, Harris and Bridge, *International Sale of Goods in the Conflict of Laws* (2005), Ch.18.

Meaning of "contractual obligations"

30–031   [*Add in first line of note 158: page* [1777]]
Base Metal Trading Ltd v Shamurin [2004] EWCA Civ 1316; [2005] 1 W.L.R. 1157. See also *Atlantic Telecom GmbH, Noter,* 2004 S.L.T. 1031.

[*Add at end of note 159: page* [1777]]
Pertegas in Meeusen, Pertegas and Straetmans (eds.) *Enforcement of International Contracts in the European Union* (2004), pp.175–190; Briggs [2003] L.M.C.L.Q. 12.

[*Add at end of note 160: page* [1778]]
As to unilateral contracts, see Maher, 2002 Jur. Rev. 317.

Concurrent liability

[*Add in first line of note 163: page* [1778]]   **30–032**
Base Metal Trading Ltd v Shamurin [2004] EWCA Civ 1316; [2005] 1 W.L.R.
1157. See also *Booth v Phillips* [2004] EWHC 1437 (Comm); [2004] 1 W.L.R.
3292.

[*Add in line 2 of note 163: page* [1778]]
Fawcett, Harris and Bridge, *International Sale of Goods in the Conflict of
Laws* (2005), Ch.20.

Restitution

[*Add to note 165: page* [1778]]
cf. Fawcett, Harris and Bridge, *International Sale of Goods in the Conflict of
Laws,* Ch.19.

[*Add at end of note 170: page* [1779]]   **30–033**
cf. Caterpillar Financial Services Corporation v SNC Passion [2004] EWHC
569 (Comm); [2004] 2 Lloyd's Rep. 99, at [16].

Wills, succession, etc.

[*Add to note 175: page* [1779]]   **30–036**
Bogdan in Meeusen, Pertegas and Straetmans (eds.), *The Enforcement of
International Contracts in the European Union* (2004), pp.211–223.

[*Add to note 177: page* [1779]]
Waldwiese Stiftung v Lewis [2004] EWHC 2589 (Ch).

Bills of exchange, cheques and promissory notes

[*Add to note 185: page* [1780]]   **30–037**
See *Zebrarise Ltd v De Nieffe* [2005] 1 Lloyd's Rep. 154.

Arbitration agreements and agreements on the choice of court

[*Add to note 190; page* [1780]]   **30–039**
Morse in Meeusen, Pertegas and Straetmans (eds.), *The Enforcement of International Contracts in the European Union* (2004), pp.191–209.

Questions governed by the law of companies, etc.

[*Add to note 202: page* [1781]]   **30–040**
Benedetelli in Meeusen, Pertegas and Straetmans (eds.), *The Enforcement of
International Contracts in the European Union* (2004), pp.225–254.

[*Add to note 205: page* [1782]]
Base Metal Trading Ltd v Shamurin [2004] EWCA Civ 1316; [2005] 1 W.L.R. 1157; *Atlantic Telecom GmbH, Noter,* 2004 S.L.T. 1031.

Insurance

30–044   [*Note 224: page* [1784]]
Update reference to *Dicey & Morris* to *Dicey & Morris op. cit. Fourth Supplement to the 13th ed.* (2004), r.184, pp.398–411.

[*Add to note 226: page* [1784]]
For amendments to UK legislation consequent on Directive 2002/83/ EC of the European Parliament and of the Council of November 5, 2002, see SI 2004/3379.

[*Note 228: page* [1784]]
Update reference to *Dicey & Morris* to *Dicey & Morris op. cit. Fourth Supplement to the 13th ed.* (2004), r.185, pp.412–426, r.186, pp.427–435.

Identification of *situs*

30–045   [*Note 232: page* [1785]]
Update reference to *Dicey & Morris* to *Dicey & Morris op. cit. Fourth Supplement to the 13th ed.* (2004), pp.403–405.

(c) *Choice of Law by the Parties*

Choice must be of law of a country

30–047   [*Add to note 236: page* [1786]]
Shamil Bank of Bahrain v Beximco Pharmaceuticals Ltd [2004] EWCA Civ 19; [2004] 1 W.L.R. 1784.

[*Add to note 237: page* [1786]]
Shamil Bank of Bahrain v Beximco Pharmaceuticals Ltd, above (choice of principles of Sharia law not a choice of the law of a country).

Law neither pleaded nor proved

30–048   [*Add to note 245: page* [1786]]
cf. Shaker v Al-Bedrawi [2002] EWCA Civ 1452; [2003] Ch. 350.

Meaning of a "choice" of law: express

30–049   [*Add to note 249: page* [1786]]
The parties may make an express oral agreement as to the applicable law: *Oakley v Ultra Vehicle Design Ltd* [2005] EWHC 872 (Ch).

"Implied choice"

[Add to note 253: page [1787]]   **30–050**
Travelers Casualty & Surety Co of Europe v Sun Life Insurance Co of Canada (UK) Ltd [2004] EWHC 1704 (Comm); [2004] I.L.Pr. 50.

[Add in line 5 of note 256: page [1787]]
Evialis S.A. v S.I.A.T. [2003] EWHC 863 (Comm); [2003] 2 Lloyd's Rep. 377; *Tonicstar Ltd v American Home Insurance Co* [2004] EWHC 1234 (Comm); [2005] Lloyd's Rep. I.R. 32; *Munchener Ruckversicherungs Gesellschaft v Commonwealth Insurance Co* [2004] EWHC 914 (Comm); [2004] C.L.C. 665; *Tryg Baltica International (UK) Ltd v Boston Compania De Seguros SA* [2004] EWHC 1186 (Comm); [2005] Lloyd's Rep. I.R. 40.

[Add in line 7 of note 260: page [1788]]
European Bank of Reconstruction & Development v Tekoglu [2004] EWHC 846 (Comm).

[Add at end of note 262: page [1788]]
See also Morse in Meeusen, Pertegas and Straetmans (eds.), *The Enforcement of International Contracts in the European Union* (2004), pp.191, 204–206.

"Implied" choice or "no" choice

[Add in line 2 of note 274: page [1790]]   **30–053**
Tryg Baltica International (UK) Ltd v Boston Compania De Seguros SA [2004] EWHC 1186 (Comm); [2005] Lloyd's Rep. I.R. 40.

Partial choice of law

[Add in line 7 of note 283: page [1790]]   **30–054**
Travelers Casualty & Surety Co v Sun Life Assurance Co of Canada (UK) Ltd [2004] EWHC 1704 (Comm); [2005] I.L.Pr. 50.

Mandatory rules

[Add to note 307: page [1793]]   **30–059**
For a case where the application of Art.3(3) of the Rome Convention was considered but rejected, see *Caterpillar Financial Services Corporation v SNC Passion* [2004] EWHC 569 (Comm); [2004] 2 Lloyd's Rep. 99.

When is a rule mandatory?

[Note 322: page [1796]]   **30–063**
Directive 2002/65/EC of the European Parliament and of the Council of September 23, 2002 concerning the distance marketing of consumer financial services is implemented in the UK in Financial Services (Distance Marketing) Regulations 2004 (SI 2004/2095). The anti-avoidance provision is contained in reg.16(3). Consumer Protection (Distance Selling) Regulations 2000 (SI 2000/2334), are amended by SI 2005/689.

Public policy

30–067   [*Add to note 340: page* [1798]]
See also *Re COLT Telecom Group plc* [2002] EWHC 2815 (Ch); [2003] B.P.I.R. 324; *Tekron Resources Ltd v Guinea Investment Co Ltd* [2003] EWHC 2577 (Comm); [2004] 2 Lloyd's Rep. 26.

"Community public policy"

30–068   [*Add to note 341: page* [1798]]
Peruzzetto in Meeusen, Pertegas and Straetmans (eds.), *The Enforcement of International Contracts in the European Union* (2004), pp.343–361; Meidanis (2005) 30 E.L.Rev. 95.

(d) *Applicable Law in the Absence of Choice by the Parties*

[*Add in line 4 of note 346: page* [1799]]
Hill (2004) 53 I.C.L.Q. 325; Atrill (2004) 53 I.C.L.Q. 549.

General principle

30–069   [*Add in last line of note 351: page* [1799]]
Travelers Casualty & Surety Co of Europe Ltd v Sun Life Assurance Co of Canada (UK) Ltd [2004] EWHC 1704 (Comm).

Characteristic performance

30–072   [*Add to note 358: page* [1801]]
Hill (2004) 53 I.C.L.Q. 325; Atrill (2004) 53 I.C.L.Q. 549.

Performance for which payment due "characteristic"

30–073   [*Add to note 364: page* [1801]]
See Maher, 2002 Jur. Rev. 317.

[*Add to note 365: page* [1801]]
See *Waldweise Stiftung v Lewis* [2004] EWHC 2589 (Ch) (gift); *Opthalmic Innovations International (United Kingdom) Ltd v Opthalmic Innovations International Inc* [2004] EWHC 2948 (Ch); [2005] I.L.Pr. 10 (indemnification agreement).

Characteristic performance not determinable

30–074   [*Add to note 367: page* [1802]]
Apple Corps Ltd v Apple Computer Inc [2004] EWHC 768 (Ch); [2004] I.L.Pr. 597 (characteristic performance of an agreement between two companies regulating the use of their respective trade marks cannot be determined).

Specific applications

[Add to note 380: page [1803]] 30–075
Tonicstar Ltd v American Home Assurance Co [2004] EWHC 1234 (Comm).

[Add in line 5 of note 386: page [1803]]
PT Pan Indonesia Bank Ltd Tbk v Marconi Communications International Ltd [2005] EWCA Civ 235; *The Times,* May 18, 2005.

[Add in first line of note 387: page [1803]]
PT Pan Indonesia Bank Ltd Tbk v Marconi Communications International Ltd, above.

[Add to note 389: page [1804]]
Atlantic Telecom GmbH, Noter, 2004 S.L.T. 1031.

[Add in text at end of paragraph: page [1804]]
In a contract of gift, the characteristic performance is that of the donor[398a]; in a contract to provide an indemnity, the characteristic performance is that of the party who is to provide the indemnity.[398b]

[398a] *Waldwiese Stiftung v Lewis* [2004] EWHC 2589 (Ch).
[398b] *Opthalmic Innovations International (United Kingdom) Ltd v Opthalmic Innovations International Inc* [2004] EWHC 2948 (Ch); [2005] I.L.Pr. 10.

Habitual residence

[Add in line 2 of note 403: page [1805]] 30–077
Mark v Mark [2005] UKHL 42; [2005] 3 W.L.R. 111.

[Add in line 4 of note 404: page [1805]]
Mark v Mark, above.

[Add in first line of note 406: page [1806]]
Mark v Mark, above.

Immovables

[Add in line 4 of note 417: page [1807]] 30–080
Case C-518/99 *Gaillard v Chekili* [2001] E.C.R. I-2771.

Characteristic performance cannot be determined

[Add to notes 436 and 437: page [1810]] 30–087
Apple Corps Ltd v Apple Computer Inc [2004] EWHC 768 (Ch); [2004] I.L.Pr. 597.

Rebutting the presumptions

30–088 [*Add to note 438: page* [1810]]
Hill (2004) 53 I.C.L.Q. 325; Atrill (2004) 53 I.C.L.Q. 549.

[*Add in line 4 of note 447: page* [1811]]
Waldwiese Stiftung v Lewis [2004] EWHC 2589 (Ch); *Opthalmic Innovations International (United Kingdom) Ltd v Opthalmic Innovations International Inc* [2004] EWHC 2948 (Ch); [2005] I.L.Pr. 10.

[*Add to note 456: page* [1812]
cf. PT Pan Indonesia Bank Ltd Tbk v Marconi Communications International Ltd [2005] EWCA Civ 422; *The Times,* May 18, 2005 (letter of credit issued by Indonesian bank which became insolvent, confirmed by another Indonesian bank with no place of business in England, the credit to be advised through an English bank which did not confirm credit, documents to be presented in England and payment to be made there, led to conclusion that although presumptively the contract between the beneficiary and the confirming bank was governed by Indonesian law, pursuant to Art.4(2) of the Rome Convention, the above connections with England justified disregarding the presumption, pursuant to Art.4(5). There appear to be no circumstances justifying displacement of the presumption in relation to the contract between the issuing bank and the confirming bank: *ibid.* at [67]).

[*Add to note 459: page* [1812]]
See also *PT Pan Indonesia Bank Ltd Tbk v Marconi Communications International Ltd,* above.

(e) *Certain Consumer Contracts and Individual Employment Contracts*

"Certain consumer contracts"

30–090 [*Add in line 5 of note 462: page* [1812]]
Basedow in Meeusen, Pertegas and Straetmans (eds.), *The Enforcement of International Contracts in the European Union* (2004), pp.269–288; Straetmans *ibid.* pp.295–322.

[*Add in line 6 of note 465: page* [1813]]
Case C-27/02 *Engler v Janus Versand GmbH* [2005] I.L.Pr. 83; Case C-464/01 *Gruber v Bay Wa AG* [2005] I.L.Pr. 144.

Article 5(2): first condition: advertising

30–094 [*Add to note 495: page* [1817]]
cf. King v Lewis [2004] EWCA Civ 1329; [2005] I.L.Pr. 185.

Mandatory rules

[*Add to note 508: page* [1819]]
cf. *Office of Fair Trading v Lloyds TSB Bank plc* [2004] EWHC 2600 (Comm);
[2005] 1 All E.R. 843.

30–099

EC consumer protection legislation

[*Add to note 512: page* [1820]]
Directive of the European Parliament and of the Council of September 23,
2002, concerning the distance marketing of consumer financial services is implemented in the UK by Financial Services (Distance Marketing) Regulations 2004
(SI 2004/2095). The anti-avoidance provision is contained in reg.16(3).

30–100

[*Add to note 514: page* [1820]]
In Case C-70/03 *Commission of the European Communities v Kingdom of
Spain* the European Court found that Spain had not properly transposed the anti-
avoidance provision in the Directive into national law.

[*Add to note 515: page* [1820]]
SI 2000/2334 is amended by SI 2005/689.

Individual employment contracts

[*Add in line 4 of note 526: page* [1822]]
Polak in Meeusen, Pertegas and Straetmans (eds.), *The Enforcement of International Contracts in the European Union* (2004), pp.323–342.

30–105

"Employment": autonomous meaning

[*Note 538: page* [1823]]
Base Metal Trading Ltd v Shamurin [2003] EWHC 2419 (Comm) is now
reported at [2004] 1 All E.R. (Comm.) 159, rvsd. in part, but not on this point,
[2004] EWCA Civ 1316; [2005] 1 W.L.R. 1157.

30–107

Choice of law by the parties and mandatory rules

[*Note 541: page* [1824]]
See previous entry.

30–109

[*Note 548: page* [1825]]
Serco Ltd v Lawson is now reported at [2004] I.C.R. 204. See on this case,
which is the subject of an appeal to the House of Lords, *Crofts v Cathay Pacific
Airways Ltd* [2005] EWCA Civ 599; *The Times,* May 31, 2005; *Botham v
Ministry of Defence* (UKEAT/0503/04/DM), November 12, 2004; *Shekar v
Satyam Computer Services Ltd* [2005] I.C.R. 737 (EAT).

[*Note 549: page* [1825]]
Race Relations Act 1976 is amended by Race Relations Act 1976 (Amendment) Regulations 2003 (SI 2003/1626), reg.11, inserting a new s.8(1A) into the

principal Act. Disability Discrimination Act 1995 is amended by Disability Discrimination Act 1995 (Amendment) Regulations 2003 (SI 2003/1673), inserting a new s.68(1) and (2)–(4A) into the 1995 Act which is further amended by Disability Discrimination Act 2005.

[*Add in line 4 of note 549: page* [1825]]
Employment Equality (Religion or Belief) Regulations 2003 (SI 2003/1660, as amended by SI 2004/437 and SI 2004/2520), reg.9; Employment Equality (Sexual Orientation) Regulations 2003 (SI 2003/1661, as amended by SI 2004/2519), reg.9. For consideration of the territorial reach of the Race Relations Act 1976, which may well apply to the other legislation cited in this note, see *Saggar v Ministry of Defence* [2005] EWCA Civ 413; [2005] I.C.R. 1073.

Applicable law in absence of choice

30–112 [*Add at beginning of note 559: page* [1826]]
See *Booth v Phillips* [2004] EWHC 1437 (Comm); [2004] 1 W.L.R. 3292.

[*Add to note 560: page* [1826]]
Booth v Phillips, above.

30–113 [*Add to note 561: page* [1827]]
cf. Booth v Phillips, above.

[*Note 563: page* [1827]]
Base Metal Trading Ltd v Shamurin [2003] EWHC 2419 (Comm) is now reported at [2004] 1 All E.R. (Comm.) 159, rvsd. in part, but not on this point, [2004] EWCA Civ 1316; [2005] 1 W.L.R. 1157.

Contract and tort

30–114 [*Note 564: page* [1827]]
See previous entry.

[*Add in line 4 of note 564: page* [1827]]
Booth v Phillips [2004] EWHC 1437 (Comm); [2004] 1 W.L.R. 3292.

(f) *Voluntary Assignments and Subrogation*

Voluntary assignments

30–115 [*Add at the end of note 570: page* [1828]]
Kieninger in Meeusen, Pertegas and Stratmans (eds.), *The Enforcement of International Contracts in the European Union* (2004), pp.363–387.

Assignor and assignee

30–116 [*Add to note 573: page* [1828]]
Waldwiese Stiftung v Lewis [2004] EWHC 2589 (Ch).

Assignability, etc.

[Add at beginning of note 576: page [1829]]   **30–117**
See *Waldwiese Stiftung v Lewis* [2004] EWHC 2589 (Ch). See also *Peer International Corpn v Termidor Music Publishers Ltd* [2003] EWCA Civ 1156; [2004] Ch. 212.

Subrogation

[Add to note 591: page [1830]]   **30–119**
West Tankers Inc v RAS Riunione Adriatica Di Sicurta [2005] EWHC 454 (Comm); [2005] 1 C.L.C. 347.

Applicable law

[Text after note 594: page [1831]]   **30–120**
See *West Tankers Inc v RAS Riunione Adriatica Di Sicurta,* above.

4. SCOPE OF THE APPLICABLE LAW

(c) *Capacity*

Corporations

[Add to notes 675 and 676: page [1840]]   **30–139**
Continental Enterprises Ltd v Shandong Zhucheng Foreign Trade Group Co [2005] EWHC 92 (Comm). See also *Marubeni Hong Kong and South China Ltd v Government of Mongolia* [2004] EWHC 472 (Comm); [2004] 2 Lloyd's Rep. 198, affd. on other grounds, [2005] EWCA Civ 395; [2005] 1 W.L.R. 2497.

(d) *Particular Issues: Article 10*

Reservation of consequences of nullity

[Add in line 7 of note 697: page [1841]]   **30–141**
cf. Caterpillar Financial Services Corporation v SNC Passion [2004] EWHC 569 (Comm); [2004] 2 Lloyd's Rep. 99 at [16].

Interpretation

[Add at end of note 702: page [1842]]   **30–144**
OT Africa Line Ltd v Magic Sportswear Corp [2005] EWCA Civ 710; [2005] 2 Lloyd's Rep. 170.

Damages

30–150 [*Notes 724 and 725 and text thereto: page* [1845]]
Though see now, *Harding v Wealands* [2004] EWCA Civ 1735; [2005] 1 W.L.R. 1735 where a statutory ceiling on recoverable damages in tort under the law of New South Wales was held by a majority of the Court of Appeal to be substantive rather than procedural. An appeal to the House of Lords is pending.

Interest

30–152 [*Note 739: page* [1847]]
The House of Lords allowed an appeal from the decision of the Court of Appeal in *Lesotho Highlands Development Authority v Impregilo SpA* [2005] UKHL 43; [2005] 3 W.L.R. 129. But no clear view was expressed on the point in the text since the House took the view that the arbitrator's power to award interest under s.49(3) of the Arbitration Act 1996 had not been expressly excluded by the parties. For an earlier, but inconclusive, case on the point see *Zebrarise Ltd v De Nieffe* [2005] 1 Lloyd's Rep. 154.

[*Add to note 740: page* [1847]]
The view expressed in the text was preferred and applied in *Rogers v Markel Corp* [2004] EWHC 1375 (QBD); [2004] EWHC 2046 (QBD).

[*Notes 741 and 742: page* [1847]
See entry at n.739: at [1847]].

Exchange losses

30–153 [*Add to note 743: page* [1847]]
Rogers v Markel Corp [2004] EWHC 2046 (QBD).

Extinguishing obligations, etc.

30–158 [*Note 776: page* [1851]]
Wight v Eckhardt Marine GmbH is now reported at [2004] 1 A.C. 147.

Prescription and limitation of actions

30–159 [*Add at end of note 782: page* [1851]]
See also *Zebrarise Ltd v De Nieffe* [2005] 1 Lloyd's Rep. 154.

Other unspecified issues

30–162 [*Add at end of note 792: page* [1853]]
See also *Laemthong International Lines Co Ltd v ARTIS* [2005] EWHC 1595 (Comm) (whether a person is party to a contract is a matter for the applicable law).

(f) *Illegality and Public Policy*

[*Add in line 5 of note 813: page* [1855]]
Peruzzetto in Meeusen, Pertegas and Straetmans (eds.), *The Enforcement of International Contracts in the European Union* (2004), pp.343–361.

[*Add at the end of note 813: page* [1855]]
Tekron Resources Ltd v Guinea Investment Co Ltd [2004] EWHC 2577 (Comm); [2004] 2 Lloyd's Rep. 26; *Barros Mattos Junior v MacDaniels Ltd* [2004] EWHC 1188 (Ch); [2005] 1 W.L.R. 247.

Illegality under applicable law

[*Add in first line of note 815: page* [1856]]
Barros Mattos Junior v MacDaniels Ltd, above.

30–169

Act illegal under law of country where to be performed

[*Add in line 6 of note 823: page* [1857]]
Tekron Resources Ltd v Guinea Investment Co Ltd, above. See also *Continental Enterprises Ltd v Shandong Zhucheng Foreign Trade Group Co* [2005] EWHC 95 (Comm).

30–171

[*Add at end of note 828: page* [1857]]
Tekron Resources Ltd v Guinea Investment Co Ltd, above.

Public policy

[*Add to note 838: page* [1858]]
Continental Enterprises Ltd v Shandong Zhucheng Foreign Trade Group Co, above.

30–173

[*Add to start of note 841: page* [1858]]
Re COLT Telecom Group plc [2002] EWHC 2815 (Ch); [2003] B.P.I.R. 324; *Continental Enterprises Ltd v Shandong Zhucheng Foreign Trade Group,* above.

[*Note 847: page* [1860]]
Peer International Corp v Termidor Music Publishers Ltd is now reported at [2004] Ch. 212.

30–174

[*Add at end of note 847: page* [1860]]
See also *Barros Mattos Junior v MacDaniels Ltd* [2004] EWHC 1188 (Ch); [2005] 1 W.L.R. 247.

[*Add to note 850: page* [1860]]
See also *Tekron Resources Ltd v Guinea Investment Co Ltd* [2003] EWHC 2577 (Comm); [2004] 2 Lloyd's Rep. 26.

30–175 [*Add in first line of note 851: page* [1860]]
Continental Enterprises Ltd v Shandong Zhucheng Foreign Trade Group Co,
above.

[*Add in line last line of note 852: page* [1860]]
Meidanis (2005) 30 Eur. L. Rev. 95.

(g) *Foreign Currency Obligations*

Currency of damages

30–180 [*Add to note 869: page* [1863]]
For an example, see *Rogers v Markel Corp* [2004] EWHC 2046 although in
this case the contract was governed by the law of Virginia, which seems to be the
same on this point as English law.

[*Add to note 870: page* [1863]]
Virani Ltd v Manuel Revert Y Cia SA [2003] EWCA Civ 1651; [2004] 2
Lloyd's Rep. 14.

Judgments in foreign currency

30–183 [*Add in line 7 of note 887: page* [1865]]
Carnegie v Giessen [2005] EWCA Civ 191; [2005] 1 C.L.C. 259 (charging
order may be expressed in foreign currency).

[*Note 895 and text thereto: page* [1865]]
Section 48(4) of the Arbitration Act 1996 provides that unless otherwise
agreed between the parties (which agreement must be in writing, s.5(1)) an
arbitral tribunal may order the payment of a sum of money in any currency. The
effect of this provision was considered by the House of Lords in *Lesotho
Highlands Development Authority v Impregilo SpA* [2005] UKHL 43; [2005] 3
W.L.R. 129. In the preferred view of Lord Steyn, the power of the tribunal under
s.48(4) was unconstrained by the case law pre-dating the 1996 Act which is
referred to in the text: *ibid.* at [22]. In the alternative he held that the fact that the
tribunal had rendered the award in a currency other than that of the contract did
not constitute a serious irregularity in the award pursuant to s.68 of the 1996 Act
which would justify setting the award aside. It was merely an error of law by the
tribunal which could not be challenged: *ibid.* at [23]. Lord Scott of Foscote and
Lord Rodger of Earlsferry preferred the latter view. Lord Hoffman had reservations in respect of Lord Steyn's preferred view but chose not to express an
opinion on the point. Lord Phillips of Worth Matravers dissented. In the light of
these opinions it would seem that Lord Steyn's alternative view commands a
majority.

[*Add at end of note 896: page* [1865]]
Lesotho Highlands Development Authority v Impregilo SpA, above.

VOLUME II

SPECIFIC CONTRACTS

CHAPTER 31

AGENCY

1. Agency in General

Commercial agents

31–005 [*Add to note 24: page* [4]]
See a case on this point, *McAdam v Boxpak Ltd* 2005 S.L.T.(Sh Ct) 47; also *Gailey v Environmental Waste Controls* [2004] Eur. L.R. 423; 2003 GWD 40–1068 (OH).

General and special agents

31–011 [*Add to note 64: page* [8]]
See on this general topic Brown [2004] J.B.L. 391.

2. Examples of Types of Agent

Insurance agents and brokers

31–018 [*Add to note 110: page* [13]]
Goshawk Dedicated Ltd v Tyser & Co Ltd [2005] EWHC 461 (Comm); [2005] 2 All E.R. (Comm.) 115.

3. Creation of Agency

(a) *Express Agreement*

Powers of attorney

31–024 [*Add to end of note 138: page* [15]]
(including the reference in the Supplement, para.31–165, to the Lasting Power of Attorney created by the Mental Capacity Act 2005).

(c) *Ratification*

Limits on ratification

31–032 [*Add to note 189: page* [20]]
See a further useful discussion by Keith J. (in the context of an originating application issued without authority and ratified after expiry of a three month time limit) in *Nottinghamshire Healthcare Trust v Prisons Officers Assn* [2003] I.C.R. 1192, E.A.T.

(e) *Capacity*

Acting for both parties

[*Add to note 228: page* [24]]
But the point can arise in the context of conflict of interest also: see *Marks & Spencer plc v Freshfields Bruckhaus Deringer* [2004] EWCA Civ 741; [2004] P.N.L.R. 4.

31–038

[*Add to note 230: page* [24]]
See also *Goshawk Dedicated Ltd v Tyser & Co Ltd* [2005] EWHC 461 (Comm); [2005] 2 All E.R. (Comm.) 115 (documents held by insurance broker).

(f) *Delegation*

When delegation permissible

[*Add to note 231: page* [25]]
In *Jacques Lichtenstein v Clube Atletico Mineiro* [2005] EWHC 1300; [2005] All E.R. (D) 341 (Jun) Jack J. said that a commercial agreement of a general nature could be performed through the actions of another. This seems a useful dictum in the light of more restrictive formulations elsewhere.

31–039

Effect of delegation

[*Add to note 236: page* [25]]
See also *Heath Lambert Ltd v Sociedad de Corretaje de Seguros* [2003] EWHC 2269 (Comm); [2004] 1 Lloyd's Rep. 495; affd. [2004] EWCA Civ 792; [2004] 1 W.L.R. 2820.

31–040

4. AUTHORITY

(a) *General Principles*

Express and implied authority

[*Add to note 258: page* [27]]
On the agent's lack of authority to act contrary to the principal's interest see also *Hopkins v T.L.Dallas Group Ltd* [2004] EWHC 1379 (Ch); [2005] 1 B.C.L.C. 543; *Criterion Properties plc v Stratford UK Properties LLC* [2004] UKHL 28; [2004] 1 W.L.R. 1846.

31–042

Implied authority: incidental authority

31–044   *[Add to note 263: page [28]]*
The word "necessarily" is not to be overstressed in this context: implied authority depends on consent, not on the rules for the implication of terms into contracts: *Targe Towing Ltd v Marine Blast Ltd* [2004] EWCA Civ 346; [2004] 1 Lloyd's Rep. 721 at [22].

Customary authority

31–046   *[Add to note 277: page [29]]*
Goshawk Dedicated Ltd v Tyser & Co Ltd [2005] EWHC 461 (Comm); [2005] 2 All E.R. (Comm.) 115.

5. PRINCIPAL'S RELATIONS WITH THIRD PARTIES

(b) *Apparent Authority*

Apparent authority

31–056   *[Add to note 319: page [34]]*
In *Pacific Carriers Ltd v BNP Paribas* [2004] HCA 35; (2004) 72 A.L.J.R. 1045 the High Court of Australia held a bank liable on a letter of indemnity against delivery without bill of lading which it had signed together with the shipper, its customer. The document had been stamped and signed by the Manager of the Documentary Credit Department of its Sydney office. The Manager intended to authenticate the signature of the shipper but on an objective interpretation of the document it was held that the signature was to an indemnity. The Manager had authority to sign authentications of signature but not promises of indemnity. There was no reason for the third party to know this and to the third party, who had had no direct dealings with the bank at all, there was just a stamp accompanied by an illegible signature without description of the signer. The bank was held liable: its organisational structure and absence of procedures for such signatures meant that it had placed the signer in a position which equipped her to deal with letters of indemnity, and on this the third party had relied. See also *Essington Investments Pty Ltd v Regency Property Ltd* [2004] N.S.W.C.A. 375; and for comments on the surprising decision in *Pacific Carriers* Reynolds, (2005) 121 L.Q.R. 55; Watts, (2005) 26 Aust.Bar Rev. 185.

Apparent authority of Crown agents

31–060   *[Add to note 353: page [38]]*
But see, for an attribution of apparent authority to an agent of a foreign government, *Marubeni Hong Kong v Government of Mongolia* [2004] EWHC 472 (Comm); [2004] 2 Lloyd's Rep. 198.

(c) *Undisclosed Principal*

Undisclosed principal

[*Add to note 356: page* [38]]   31–061
See in general Tan Cheng-Han (2004) 120 L.Q.R. 480.

Meaning of "undisclosed principal"

[*Add to note 374: page* [40]]   31–063
The dangers of finding agency between related corporate structures are
stressed by Langley J. in *Peterson Farms Inc v C & M Farming Ltd* [2004]
EWHC 121 (Comm); [2004] 1 Lloyd's Rep. 603 at [62]; but *cf.* the *Rolls Royce*
case, above.

[*Add to note 373: page* [40]]
Both the above cases were applied in *Rolls Royce Power Engineering plc v
Ricardo Consulting Engineers Ltd* [2004] EWHC 2871; [2004] 2 All E.R.
(Comm.) 129.

Exclusion of undisclosed principals

[*Add to note 392: page* [42]]   31–065
The *Siu Yin Kwan* case was applied in *Rolls Royce Power Engineering plc v
Ricardo Consulting Engineers Ltd* [2004] EWHC 2871; [2004] 2 All E.R.
(Comm.) 129, where it was held that the third party did not intend to deal with
anyone on whose behalf the other party might be acting, and hence Rolls Royce
as undisclosed principal could not intervene.

(d) *Further Rules*

Agent acting in fraud of principal

[*Add to note 398: page* [42]]   31–066
See also *Criterion Properties plc v Stratford UK Properties LLC* [2004]
UKHL 28; [2004] 1 W.L.R. 1846.

6. AGENT'S RELATIONS WITH THIRD PARTIES

(a) *On the Main Contract*

When agent liable and entitled

[*Add to note 528: page* [54]]   31–083
A recent example is *Foxtons Ltd v Thesleff* [2005] EWCA Civ 514; [2005] 21
E.G. 140, where a contract to pay estate agent's commission was held also

binding on the person "to whom the letter overleaf is addressed", who was an agent for the vendor but did not sign "as agent only".

[*Add to text at end of paragraph: page* [54]]
And an agent may be entitled as a third party beneficiary of his principal's contract under the Contracts (Rights of Third Parties) Act 1999.[532a]

[532a] See *Laemthong International Lines Co Ltd v Artis (The Laemthong Glory)* [2005] EWCA Civ 519; [2005] 1 Lloyd's Rep. 688 (letter of indemnity given by receiver of goods to charterer against delivery without bill of lading, expressed to be in favour of "you, your servants and agents": owners held agents of charterers to deliver, hence entitled to sue as third parties. But the context in which the owners were held agents is a specialised one, and the decision was largely based on contractual interpretation).

(c) *Breach of Warranty of Authority*

Liability of agent acting without authority

31–099   [*Add to note 607: page* [62]]
In *SEB Trygg Holding Aktiebolag v Manches* [2005] EWHC 35 (Comm); [2005] All E.R. (D) 307 (Feb) Gloster J. regarded *Nelson v Nelson* as establishing that a solicitor commencing proceedings for a named party warrants that the claimant bears that name and is in existence.

Representation must be of fact and relied on

31–101   [*Add to note 611: page* [63]]
Enterprise Plus Ltd v Wagenmann [2003] EWHC 1827 (Comm).

7. OBLIGATIONS OF PRINCIPAL AND AGENT *INTER SE*

(a) *Duties of Agents*

(ii) *Exercise of Care and Skill*

Gratuitous agents

31–115   [*Add to note 682: page* [69]]
In *OBG Ltd v Allen* [2005] EWCA Civ 106; [2005] 2 W.L.R. 1174 receivers whose appointment was invalid and who settled claims under contracts without negligence but on less good terms than the debtor (through its liquidator) could have done was by a majority held not liable for the tort of interference with contract: but see a persuasive dissent by Mance L.J.

(iii) *Loyalty*

Duty not to have conflicting interest

[*Add to note 717: page* [72]]   **31–120**
   See also *Marks & Spencer Plc v Freshfields Bruckaus Deringer* [2004] EWCA
Civ 741; [2004] P.N.L.R. 4, holding that the conflicting interests can arise from
different transactions with the same party.

(iv) *Remedies*

Equity: duty to account and equitable compensation

[*Add to note 752: page* [76]]   **31–126**
   Att-Gen for Hong Kong v Reid (a Privy Council case) was followed on this
point by Lawrence Collins J. in *Daraydan Holdings Ltd v Solland International
Ltd* [2004] EWHC 622 (Ch); [2005] Ch. 119.

[*Add to note 757: page* [77]]
   Newgate Stud Co v Penfold [2004] EWHC 2993 (Ch); [2005] All E.R. (D) 376
(May) (some self-dealing claims time-barred).

(b) *Rights of Agents*

(i) *Remuneration*

Right to remuneration

[*Insert new note 774a after "the principal" in line 1: page* [79]]   **31–132**
   774a The agent's commission may sometimes be provided by the contract which he makes between
principal and third party as payable to him. This is often held to create a trust in his favour: see *Les
Affreteurs Reunis SA v Leopold Walford (London) Ltd* [1919] A.C. 801; see Main Work, Vol.1, paras
18–074 *et seq*. The agent may now be able to sue directly under the Contracts (Rights of Third
Parties) Act 1999: see *ibid*., paras 18–084 *et seq*. It has been held by Colman J. in such a context that
an arbitration clause in the main contract applied to a claim by the agent as third party: *Nisshin
Shipping Co Ltd v Cleaves & Co Ltd* [2003] EWHC 2602; [2004] 1 Lloyd's Rep. 38.

[*Add to note 777: page* [79]]
   Benhams Ltd v Kythira Investments Ltd [2004] EWHC 2973; [2004] All E.R.
(D) 313 (Dec) (implicit in oral agreement that agent to be remunerated).

Other types of estate agent's agreement

[*Add to note 816: page* [84]]   **31–139**
   Foxtons Ltd v Thesleff [2005] EWCA Civ 514; [2005] 21 E.G. 140 (commission due when unconditional contracts exchanged).

Agent must be effective cause of transaction

[*Add to note 831: page* [85]]   **31–142**
   See also *Favermead Ltd v FPD Savills Ltd* [2005] EWHC 626 (Ch); [2005] All
E.R. (D) 30 (Mar) (winding up petition presented by estate agent in respect of

commission, restrained on the ground that there was a real and substantial dispute as to whether the effective cause requirement applied).

[*Add to note 832: page* [85]]
See also *Jacques Lichtenstein v Clube Atletico Mineiro* [2005] EWHC 1300 (QB); [2005] All E.R. (D) 341 (Jun) (agent authorised to "interest" clubs in footballer: purchasing club already interested before agent acted).

[*Add to note 835: page* [86]]
Christie Owen & Davies v Ryelance [2005] 18 E.G.C.S. 148 (sale after authority revoked—commission due).

Where Commercial Agents Regulations applicable

31–147   [*Add to note 873: page* [90]]
In *Cooper v Pure Fishing (UK) Ltd* [2004] EWCA Civ 375; [2004] 2 Lloyd's Rep. 518 it was held that a principal who had cause for terminating the agency but chose not to renew it at its time of expiry had not "terminated" the contract for the purposes of the Regulations.

8. TERMINATION OF AUTHORITY

How authority terminated

31–160   [*Add to note 968: page* [98]]
Lodgepower Ltd v Taylor [2004] EWCA Civ 1367; [2005] 08 E.G. 192 (notice to remedy served on alleged agent of deceased landlord not valid).

Enduring powers of attorney

31–165   [*Page* [101]]
The Enduring Powers of Attorney Act 1985 will be repealed by the Mental Capacity Act 2005 from a day to be appointed. This Act *inter alia* substitutes a new form of power, a "Lasting Power of Attorney", which covers also the taking of (non-business) decisions regarding the grantor's health and welfare. There are detailed provisions similar to but more extensive than those of the 1985 Act, and the new Act also provides for (in effect) a statutory agency of necessity (see above, paras 31–033 *et seq.*) on behalf of the mentally incapable person, making the person liable for necessaries, and entitling the attorney to pledge the credit of the person as well as to be indemnified. The effect of existing enduring powers of attorney is preserved by Sch.4. It is expected that the Act will not come into effect before 2007 (see Chapter 8 section 4, Mentally Disordered Persons, above) and further comment will be appropriate in the next Supplement.

CHAPTER 32

ARBITRATION

1. STATUTORY REGULATION

Arbitration Act 1996

[Add to note 5: page [104]]   **32–003**
Cited with approval in *Lesotho Highlands Development Authority v Impregilo SpA* [2005] UKHL 43; [2005] 3 W.L.R. 129 at [19].

Scope of application of the Act: seat of arbitration in England

[Add to note 16: page [105]]   **32–007**
Arab National Bank v El-Abdali [2004] EWHC 2381 (Comm); [2005] 1 Lloyd's Rep. 541. See also *Tonicstar Ltd v American Home Assurance Co* [2004] EWHC 1234 (Comm); [2005] Lloyd's Rep. I.R. 32 (which court is to determine seat).

ACAS arbitration

[Add to note 40: page [107]]   **32–014**
But see *Flight Training International Inc v International Fire Training Equipment Ltd* [2004] EWHC 721; [2004] 2 All E.R. (Comm.) 568 (ACAS deals only with employment disputes, not commercial).

Human Rights Act 1998

32–015
[*Add to note 41: page* [108]]
Sandy (2004) 20 *Arbitration International* 305.

[*Add to note 43: page* [108]]
BLCT (13096) Ltd v J Sainsbury plc [2003] EWCA Civ 884; [2004] 2
P.&.C.R. 3; *Department of Economic Policy and Development of the City of
Moscow v Bankers Trust Co* [2004] EWCA Civ 314; [2005] Q.B. 207 at [27].

32–016
[*Add at end of note 49: page* [109]]
Ghaidan v Godin-Mendoza [2004] UKHL 30; [2004] 2 A.C. 557 at [37]–[52]
(Lord Steyn); Sandy (2004) 20 *Arbitration International* 305.

[*Add to note 51: page* [109]]
Contrast *BLCT (13096) Ltd v J Sainsbury plc* [2003] EWCA Civ 884; [2004]
2 P.&.C.R. 3 (no right to oral hearing on s.69 application); *Department of
Economic Policy and Development of the City of Moscow v Bankers Trust Co*
[2004] EWCA Civ 314; [2005] Q.B. 207 (confidentiality of judgment on s.68
application).

2. THE ARBITRATION AGREEMENT

Definition of "arbitration agreement"

32–018
[*Add at end of note 66: page* [111]]
Flight Training International Inc v International Fire Training Equipment Ltd
[2004] EWHC 721; [2004] 2 All E.R. (Comm.) 568 (reference to ACAS mediation not arbitration agreement).

[*Add to note 67: page* [111]]
NB Three Shipping Ltd v Harebell Shipping Ltd [2004] EWHC 2001; [2005]
1 Lloyd's Rep. 509; noted (2005) 71 *Arbitration*(1) 201, criticised Mulcahy
(2004) 70 *Arbitration* (3) 172.

Agreements to be in writing

32–019
[*Add to note 75: page* [112]]
Quaere whether an agreement is in "writing" if concluded by electronic means
and whether such an agreement could be enforced under the New York Convention on the Recognition and Enforcement of Foreign Arbitral Awards 1958 (see
para.32–160) having regard to Art.IV.1 of the Convention.

Separability of arbitration agreement

32–023
[*Add to note 85: page* [113]]
Vee Networks Ltd v Econet Wireless International Ltd [2004] EWHC 2909
(Comm); [2005] 1 Lloyd's Rep. 192 at [20]; *Lesotho Highlands Development
Authority v Impregilo SpA* [2005] UKHL 43; [2005] 3 W.L.R. 129 at [21].

[*Add to note 86: page* [114]]
Vee Networks Ltd v Econet Wireless International Ltd, above, at [21].

[*Add to note 89: page* [114]]
Vee Networks Ltd v Econet Wireless International Ltd, above, at [21].

[*Add to note 93: page* [114]]
See s.48(5)(c) (power to order rectification unless parties agree otherwise).

Scope of the arbitration agreement

[*Page* [114]]   **32–025**
The words "in relation to" a contract include disputes which are related to or
connected with it and cover a dispute concerning an alleged variation of the
contract: *El Nasharty v J Sainsbury plc* [2003] EWHC 2195 (Comm); [2004] 1
Lloyd's Rep. 308.

[*Add to note 96: page* [114]]
Benford Ltd v Lopecan SL [2004] EWHC 1897 (Comm); [2004] 2 Lloyd's
Rep. 618 at [26].

[*Add to note 98: page* [114]]
See also *Amec Civil Engineering Ltd v Secretary of State for Transport* [2005]
EWCA Civ 291; [2005] 1 W.L.R. 2339 ("difference" less hard edged than
"dispute").

[*Add in penultimate line of note 102, after reference to Capital Thrush Investments
Ltd v Radio Design TJAB: page* [115]]
Asghar v Legal Services Commission [2004] EWHC 1803, noted (2005) 71
Arbitration (1) 91.

[*Add new paragraph 32–026A: page* [116]]   **32–026A**
Set-off and counterclaim. Subject to the terms of the arbitration clause, a
counterclaim by way of set-off arising out of the same or a closely related
contract will be within the scope of the clause but not a counterclaim by way of
set-off arising out of a separate and unconnected contract.[108a]

[108a] *Metal Distributors (UK) Ltd v ZCCM Investment Holdings plc* [2005] EWHC 156 (Comm);
[2005] 2 Lloyd's Rep. 37. See also *ED&F Man v Société Anonyme Tripolitaine des Usines* [1970] 2
Lloyd's Rep. 416; *Ronly Holdings v JSC Zestafoni Nikoladze Ferroalloy Plant* [2004] EWHC 1354
(Comm); *Benford Ltd v Lopecan SL* [2004] EWHC 1897 (Comm); [2004] 2 Lloyd's Rep. 618.

Third parties

[*Page* [117]]   **32–035**
In *Peterson Farms Inc v C&M Farming Ltd* [2004] EWHC 121 (Comm);
[2004] 1 Lloyd's Rep. 602 at [59]. Langley J. rejected the "group of companies"
doctrine applied in ICC arbitrations.

Confidentiality

[*Add at end of note 137: page* [119]]   **32–040**
Tweeddale (2005) 21 *Arbitration International* 59.

[*Note 142: page* [119]]

Department of Economics, Policy and Development of the City of Moscow v Bankers Trust Co was affirmed in part and reversed in part by the Court of Appeal: [2004] EWCA Civ 314; [2005] Q.B. 307.

3. STAY OF LEGAL PROCEEDINGS

Foreign proceedings

32–042 [*Add to note 150 in line 10, after reference to The Epsilon Rosa (No. 2): page* [120]]
Through Transport Mutual Insurance Association (Eurasia) Ltd v New India Assurance Co Ltd [2004] EWCA Civ 1598; [2005] 1 Lloyd's Rep. 67; *Atlanska Plovibda v Consignaciones Asturianas SA* [2004] EWHC 1273 (Comm); [2004] 2 Lloyd's Rep. 109 at [25].

[*Add after reference to Toepfer International GmbH v Société Cargill France in note 150, line 3 on page* [121]]
Navigation Maritime Bulgare v Rustal Trading Ltd [2002] 1 Lloyd's Rep. 107; *Through Transport Mutual Insurance Association (Eurasia) Ltd v New India Assurance Co Ltd*, above.

[*Add at end of note 152: page* [121]]
See also *Through Transport Mutual Insurance Association (Eurasia) Ltd v New India Assurance Co Ltd*, above (which court is to decide?).

Stay of legal proceedings

32–043 [*Add to note 156: page* [121]]
Contrast *Exeter City Association Football Club Ltd v Football Conference Ltd* [2004] EWHC 2304 (Ch); [2004] 1 W.L.R. 291 (no stay of petition under s.459 of Companies Act 1985).

Mandatory stay

32–046 [*Note 174: page* [123]]
The reference to *Ahmad Al-Naimi v Islamic Press Agency* should be [2000] 1 Lloyd's Rep. 522.

[*Add to Note 174: page* [123]]
On an application for a stay, a cross-application may also be made under s.72 of the Act (see para.32–133, below) by a person who contests the jurisdiction of the arbitrator: *Law Debenture Trust Corp v Elektrim Finance BV* [2005] EWHC 1412 (Ch); *The Times*, August 4, 2005.

Discretionary stay

[*Page* [123]]

The court also has jurisdiction under CPR, r.11, to direct alternative dispute resolution notwithstanding the unwillingness of one party, but it will not order a stay of proceedings pending the attendance at mediation of a named non-party: *Shirayama Shokusan Co Ltd v Danovo Ltd* [2003] EWHC (Ch); [2004] B.L.R. 207.

32–048

[*Note 176: page* [123]]

The reference to *Ahmad Al-Naimi v Islamic Press Agency* should be [2000] 1 Lloyd's Rep. 522.

[*Add at end of note 176*]

Contrast *El Nasharty v J Sainsbury plc* [2003] EWHC 2195 (Comm); [2004] 1 Lloyd's Rep. 309 at [29] (court must be "virtually certain" that there is an arbitration agreement before it grants a stay).

Claims indisputably due

[*Delete note 178 and substitute: page* [124]]

Now CPR, Pt 24.

32–049

[*Add to note 180: page* [124]]

Collins (Contractors) Ltd v Baltic Quay Management (1994) Ltd [2004] EWCA Civ 1757; *The Times*, January 3, 2005.

4. Commencement of Arbitral Proceedings

Power of the court to extend time for beginning arbitral proceedings

[*Add to note 203: page* [127]]

See also *Thompson Monella v Pizza Express (Restaurants) Ltd* [2003] EWHC 2966 (Ch); [2004] 12 E.G. 172 (change in the law not outside the reasonable contemplation of the parties and in any event did not contribute to the failure to observe the time-limit).

32–054

Commencement of arbitral proceedings

[*Page* [128]]

In *Atlanska Plovidba v Consignaciones Asturianas SA* [2004] EWHC 1273 (Comm); [2004] 2 Lloyd's Rep. 109 at [17] Moore-Bick J. said:

32–059

> "If a notice of arbitration is to be effective, it must identify the dispute to which it relates with sufficient particularity and must also make it clear that the person giving it is intending to refer the dispute to arbitration, not merely threatening to do so if his demands are not met. Apart from that, however, I see no need for any further requirements. Whether any particular document meets those requirements will depend on its terms which must be understood in the context in which it was written.

The weight of authority supports a broad and flexible approach to this question . . ."

5. The Arbitral Tribunal

Appointment of arbitrators

32–061   [*Page* [129]]
See *Atlanska Plovidba v Consignaciones Asturianas SA* [2004] EWHC 1273 (Comm); [2004] 2 Lloyd's Rep. 109 at [17]; para.32–059, above.

Power in case of default to appoint sole arbitrator

32–063   [*Add to note 233: page* [130]]
cf. Minermet SpA Milan v Luckyfield Shipping Corp SA [2004] EWHC 729 (Comm); [2004] 2 Lloyd's Rep. 348 (no need for notice where parties otherwise agree).

Failure of appointment procedure

32–064   [*Page* [131]]
In *Vale do Rio Doce Navegacao SA v Shanghai Bao Steel Ocean Shipping Co Ltd* [2000] 2 Lloyd's Rep. 1 at [11], Thomas J. suggested that, on an application under s.18, the court could not intervene to determine whether or not there is an arbitration agreement. The respondent in an application under s.18 could (it is submitted) nevertheless make a cross-application under s.72(1) for a declaration that he is not a party to the arbitration agreement: *Sinochem International Oil (London) Co Ltd v Fortune Oil Co Ltd* [2000] 1 Lloyd's Rep. 682.

32–065   [*Note 243: page* [131]]
The reference for *Durtnell (R) & Sons Ltd v Secretary of State for Trade and Industry* should be [2001] 1 Lloyd's Rep. 275.

[*Add at end of note 243*]
See also *Atlanska Plovidba v Consignaciones Asturianas SA* [2004] EWHC 1273 (Comm); [2004] 2 Lloyd's Rep. 109 (existence of concurrent judicial proceedings in Spain not a ground for refusing appointment).

Removal of arbitrator

32–073   [*Add at end of note 270: page* [134]]
IBA Guidelines on Conflicts of Interest in International Arbitration 2004; Chartered Institute of Arbitrators: Code of Professional and Ethical Conduct (2001, revised 2004); AAA/ABA Code of Ethics for Arbitrators in Commercial Disputes (2004 revision).

[*Add at end of note 272: page* [134]]
Contrast *Home of Homes Ltd v Hammersmith Fulham LBC* [2003] EWHC 807; [2003] 92 Const.L.R. 48 (arbitrator takes leading counsel's opinion on

issues of costs and jurisdiction). On the question of reliance by the arbitrator on his own expertise, see now *Checkpoint Ltd v Strathclyde Pension Fund* [2003] EWCA Civ 84; *Warborough Investment Ltd v S Robinson & Sons (Holdings) Ltd* [2003] EWCA 751; *St George's Investment Co Ltd v Gemini Consulting Ltd* [2004] EWHC 2353 (Ch), noted (2005) 71 *Arbitration* (1) 96; Altaras (2003) 69 *Arbitration* (3) 216.

6. Jurisdiction of the Arbitral Tribunal

Tribunal can rule on its own jurisdiction

[*Add to note 300: page* [137]]
See below, para.32–132 (inherent jurisdiction of court).

32–078

Objection to substantive jurisdiction of tribunal

[*Add to note 307: page* [137]]
See *Vee Networks Ltd v Econet Wireless International Ltd* [2004] EWHC 2909 (Comm); [2005] 1 Lloyd's Rep. 192; Yang (2004) 70 *Arbitration* (4) 279.

32–079

[*Add to note 311, after Athletic Union of Constantinople v National Basketball Association: page* [138]]
; *JSC Zestafoni G Nikoladz Ferroalloy Plant v Ronly Holdings Ltd* [2004] EWHC 245 (Comm); [2004] 2 Lloyd's Rep. 335 at [64]; *Westland Helicopters Ltd v Sheikh Salah al-Hejailan (No.1)* [2004] EWHC 1625 (Comm); [2004] 2 Lloyd's Rep. 523; *Vee Networks Ltd v Econet Wireless International Ltd*, above.

Determination of preliminary point of jurisdiction

[*Add to note 320 after "s.32(2)": page* [139]]
Belgravia Property Ltd v S&R Ltd [2001] Build L.R. 424

32–081

[*Note 320, delete Vale Do Rio Doce Navegacao SA v Shanghai Bao Steel Ocean Shipping Co.* [1999] 2 Lloyd's Rep. 159, 161 *and substitute: page* [139]]
Azov Shipping Co v Baltic Shipping Co, above, at [161]; *Vale Do Rio Doce Navegacao SA v Shanghai Bao Steel Ocean Shipping Co* [2000] 2 Lloyd's Rep. 1, 10.

7. The Arbitral Proceedings

Procedural and evidential matters

[*Page* [140]]
See the IBA rules on the taking of evidence in International Commercial Arbitration 1999.

32–085

Power to appoint experts etc

32–089
[Add to note 354: page [142]]
See the Chartered Institute of Arbitrators' guidelines on the use of tribunal-appointed experts, legal advisers and assessors: (2004) *Arbitration* 70(1), 45–50.

Provisional relief with agreement of parties

32–093
[Add to note 369: page [144]]
Kastner v Jason [2004] EWCA Civ 1599; [2005] 1 Lloyd's Rep. 397 (Lightman J.) (freezing order).

8. POWERS OF THE COURT

Court powers in support of arbitral proceedings

32–100
[Add to note 396: page [146]]
Assimina Maritime Ltd v Pakistan Shipping Corp [2004] EWHC 3005 (Comm); [2005] 1 Lloyd's Rep. 525 (witness summons). But see *ibid.* and *BNP Paribas v Deloitte and Touche LLP* [2003] EWHC 2874 (Comm); [2004] 1 Lloyd's Rep. 233 (no power to order disclosure by non-party).

32–101
[Add to note 400: page [147]]
Hiscox Underwriting Ltd v Dickson Manchester & Co Ltd [2004] EWHC 479; [2004] 2 Lloyd's Rep. 438, noted (2005) 71 *Arbitration* (1) 96 (interim order for disclosure). *Assimina Maritime Ltd v Pakistan Shipping Corp*, above (no power to order disclosure by non-party but power to order preservation of documents by non-party); *Lauritzencool AB v Lady Navigation Inc* [2005] EWCA Civ 579; [2005] 2 Lloyd's Rep. 63 (interim injunction pending arbitration).

[Add to note 401: page [147]]
For the power of the court under s.37 of the Supreme Court Act 1981 to intervene outside of s.44 of the 1996 Act, see *Hiscox Underwriting Ltd v Dickson Manchester & Co*, above.

[Add to note 402]
Hiscox Underwriting Ltd v Dickson Manchester & Co Ltd, above (arbitrator newly appointed and unfamiliar with case and so, in effect, unable to act).

[Add to note 403]
National Insurance and Guarantee Corp Ltd v M Young Legal Services Ltd [2004] EWHC 2972 (QB); [2005] 2 Lloyd's Rep. 46.

[Add to note 405]
Assimina Maritime Ltd v Pakistan Shipping Corp, above.

Power of court to extend time-limits

[Add to note 418, after "s.79(3)": page [148]]
Minermet SpA Milan v Luckyfield Shipping Corp SA [2004] EWHC 729 (Comm); [2004] 2 Lloyd's Rep. 348.

32–106

9. THE AWARD

Conflict of laws

[Add to note 428: page [149]]
See *Peterson Farms Inc v C&M Farming Ltd* [2004] EWHC 121 (Comm); [2004] 1 Lloyd's Rep. 603 at [46].

32–109

Remedies

[Add at end of note 436: page [150]]
a freezing order (*Kastner v Jason* [2004] EWCA Civ 1599; [2005] 1 Lloyd's Rep. 397.

32–111

[Note 438: page [150]]
The decision of the Court of Appeal in *Lesotho Highlands Development Authority v Impregilo SpA* was reversed by the House of Lords [2005] UKHL 43; [2005] 3 W.L.R. 129. But there was a difference of opinion in that case as to the ambit of s.48(4): see paras [22]–[23], [42], [49], [55] and [56].

[Add to note 441: page [151]]
Bath and North East Somerset DC v Mowlem [2004] EWCA Civ 115; [2004] C.I.L.L. 2081; noted (2005) 71 *Arbitration* (2) 161.

Interest

[Add to note 445: page [151]]
The provisions of a foreign law applicable to the matrix contract is not such a contrary agreement: *Lesotho Highlands Development Authority v Impregilo SpA* [2005] UKHL 43; [2005] 3 W.L.R. 129 at [37].

32–112

[Add to note 446: page [151]]
Lesotho Highlands Development Authority v Impregilo SpA [2005] UKHL 43; [2005] 3 W.L.R. 129. *cf. Durham CC v Darlington BC* [2003] EWHC 2598; [2004] B.L.G.R. 311 (no power to award interest for the period before the principal sum became payable). See Chartered Institute of Arbitrators' Guidelines on the Award of Interest (2004); Altaras (2004) 70 *Arbitration* (2) 108.

[Note 452]

The decision of the Court of Appeal in *Lesotho Highlands Development Authority v Impregilo SpA* was reversed by the House of Lords [2005] UKHL 43; [2005] 3 W.L.R. 129.

[Add at end of note 452]

But see *Westland Helicopters Ltd v Sheikh Salah al-Hejailan (No.1)* [2004] EWHC 1625 (Comm); [2004] 2 Lloyd's Rep. 523 (challenge to arbitrator's award of interest under s.67 (lack of jurisdiction) and s.68 (serious irregularity)).

Form of award

32–115 *[Add to note 459: page [152]]*

cf. Tame Shipping Ltd v Easy Navigation Ltd [2004] EWHC 1862 (Comm); [2004] 2 Lloyd's Rep. 626 (reasons can be set out in separate "confidential" document); see below, para.32–145.

Correction of award or additional award

32–119 *[Add to note 476: page [153]]*

Contrast *World Trade Corp v C Czarnikow Sugar Ltd* [2004] EWHC 787 (Comm); [2004] 2 Lloyd's Rep. 446 at [27] ("claim" only applies to a claim which has been presented to the tribunal but has not been dealt with as opposed to an issue which remains undetermined as part of a claim); *World Trade Corp v C Czarnikow Sugar Ltd*, above, at [14] ("claim" does not mean a submission in support of a relevant question of fact as opposed to a claim for relief such as would have to be pleaded).

Award as a defence

32–123 *[Add to note 493: page [154]]*

Contrast *Sun Life Assurance Co of Canada v Lincoln National Life Insurance Co* [2004] EWCA Civ 1660; [2005] 1 Lloyd's Rep. 606 (no estoppel where arbitration between one of the parties and a stranger).

10. Costs of the Arbitration

Costs

32–124 *[Add at end of paragraph: page [155]]*

An agreement in the parties' submission letter that they will share equally the arbitrators' hourly charges does not imply that the costs of the arbitration between the parties are to be similarly allocated.[499a]

[499a] *Carter v Harold Simpson Associates* [2004] UKPC 29; [2005] 1 W.L.R. 919.

[Add at end of note 502: page [155]] **32–125**
Henchie (2004) 70 *Arbitration* 77.

[Add to note 515: page [156]] **32–126**
See *Rotary Watches Ltd v Rotary Watches (USA) Inc*, unreported, noted (2005)
71 *Arbitration* (2) 172.

[Add to note 521: page [157]] **32–127**
But it might be argued, in certain circumstances, that costs could be awarded
on the basis of an estoppel or on the grounds that a party who initiates arbitration
impliedly consents to an order for costs being made against him if the tribunal
rules that it has no jurisdiction.

11. Powers of the Court in relation to the Award

Challenging the award: substantive jurisdiction

[Page [158]] **32–132**
Having regard to s.1(c) of the Act, the question arises whether the court still
retains in addition its inherent powers to rule on jurisdiction: see *ABB Lummus
Global Ltd v Keppel Fils Ltd* [1999] 2 Lloyds Rep. 24; *Vale do Rio Doce
Navegacao SA v Shanghai Bao Steel Ocean Shipping Co Ltd* [2000] 2 Lloyd's
Rep. 1; *J T Mackley & Co Ltd v Gosport Marina Ltd* [2002] EWHC 1315
(TCC); [2002] Build L.R. 367.

[Add to note 536: page [158]]
Zaporozhyve Production Society v Ashly Ltd [2002] EWHC 1410 (Comm);
Peoples Insurance Co of China v Vysanthi Shipping Co Ltd [2003] EWHC 1655
(Comm); [2003] 2 Lloyd's Rep. 617; *Peterson Farms Inc v C&M Farming Ltd*
[2004] EWHC 121 (Comm). [2004] 1 Lloyd's Rep. 603 at [18]; *Metal Distributors UK Ltd v ZCCM Investment Holdings plc* [2005] EWHC 156 (Comm);
[2005] 2 Lloyd's Rep. 37 at [16].

[Add to note 540] **32–133**
Law Debenture Trust Corp v Elektrim Finance BV, The Times, August 4, 2005.
It may be appropriate in some cases for the court to grant an injunction under this
sub-section to prevent the arbitration from going ahead rather than leaving it to
the tribunal to decide: *Zaporozhyve Production Society v Ashly Ltd* [2002]
EWHC 1410 (Comm). See also *Arab National Bank v El-Abdali* [2004] EWHC
238 (Comm); [2005] 1 Lloyd's Rep. 541. cf. *Zaporozozhye Production etc.
Society v Ashly Ltd* [2002] EWHC 1410 (injunction refused).

[Add to note 541 after Athletic Union of Constantinople v National Basketball **32–134**
Association: page [159]].
; *JSC Zestafoni G Nikoladz Ferroalloy Plant v Ronly Holdings Ltd* [2004]
EWHC 245 (Comm); [2004] 2 Lloyd's Rep. 335; *Westland Helicopters Ltd v
Sheikh Salah al-Hejailan (No.1)* [2004] EWHC 1625 (Comm); [2004] 2 Lloyd's
Rep. 523; *Vee Networks Ltd v Econet Wireless International Ltd* [2004] EWHC
2909 (Comm); [2005] 1 Lloyd's Rep. 192.

Challenging the award: serious irregularity

32–137   *[Add to note 554: page* [160]]
Bulfracht (Cyprus) Ltd v Boneset Shipping Co Ltd [2002] EWHC 2292
(Comm); [2002] 2 Lloyd's Rep. 681; *Minermet SpA Milan v Luckyfield Shipping
Corp SA* [2004] EWHC 729 (Comm); [2004] 2 Lloyd's Rep. 348, *Westland
Helicopters Ltd v Sheikh Salah al-Hejailan (No.1)* [2004] EWHC 1625 (Comm);
[2004] 2 Lloyd's Rep. 523; *Tame Shipping Ltd v Easy Navigation Ltd* [2004]
EWHC 1862 (Comm), [2004] 2 Lloyd's Rep. 626; *Alphapoint Shipping Ltd v
Rotem Amfert Negev* [2004] EWHC 2232 (Comm); [2005] 1 Lloyd's Rep. 23;
Vee Networks Ltd v Econet Wireless International Ltd [2004] EWHC 2909
(Comm); [2005] 1 Lloyd's Rep. 192; *Margulead Ltd v Exide Technologies* [2004]
EWHC 1019 (Comm); [2005] 1 Lloyd's Rep. 324; *Home of Homes Ltd v
Hammersmith & Fulham LBC* [2003] EWHC 807; (2003) 92 Const. L.R. 48;
Ronly Holdings Ltd v JSC Zestafoni G Nicoladze Ferroalloy Plant [2004] EWHC
1354 (Comm); [2004] 1 C.L.C. 1168; *St George's Investment Co Ltd v Gemini
Consulting Ltd* [2004] EWHC 2358 (Ch); *Bottiglieri di Navigazione SpA v Cosco
Qingdao Ocean Shipping Co* [2005] EWHC 244 (Comm); [2005] 2 Lloyd's
Rep. 1.

[Add to note 555: page [160]]
Westland Helicopters Ltd v Sheikh Salah al-Hejailan, above. In *Lesotho
Highlands Development Authority v Impregilo SpA* [2005] UKHL 43; [2005] 3
W.L.R. 129, the House of Lords held that a mere error of law by the arbitrators
did not amount to an excess of power under s.68(2)(b).

[At the end of sub-paragraph (c) in paragraph 32–137: page [160], *insert new note
555a]*
[555a] *Westland Helicopters Ltd v Sheikh Salah al-Hejailan,* above.

[Add to note 556: page [160]]
Torch Offshore LLS v Cable Shipping Inc [2004] EWHC 787 (Comm); [2004]
2 Lloyd's Rep. 446; *Tame Shipping Ltd v Easy Navigation Ltd,* above; *Alphapoint Shipping Ltd v Rolem Amfert Negev Ltd,* above; *Margulead Ltd v Exide
Technologies,* above; *World Trade Corp v C Czarnikow Sugar Ltd* [2004] EWHC
2332 (Comm); [2005] 1 Lloyd's Rep. 422; *Marklands Ltd v Virgin Retail Ltd*
[2003] EWHC 3428; [2004] 27 E.G. 130.

[Note 556a]
Delete this note.

[Add to note 558: page [160]]
Thyssen Canada Ltd v Mariana Maritime SA [2005] EWHC 219 (Comm);
[2005] 1 Lloyd's Rep. 640.

[Add to note 562: page [161]]
See also *World Trade Corp v C Czarnikow Sugar Ltd,* above (weight of
evidence); *Lesotho Highlands Development Authority v Impregilo SpA* [2005]
UKHL 43; [2005] 3 W.L.R. 129 at [28].

[Add at end of paragraph: page [161]]   **32–138**
The element of serious injustice does not depend on the arbitrator having come
to the wrong conclusion as a matter of law or fact but whether he was caused by
adopting inappropriate means to reach one conclusion whereas had he adopted
appropriate means he might well have reached another conclusion favourable to
the applicant.[565a]

[565a] *Vee Networks Ltd v Econet Wireless International Ltd* [2004] EWHC 2909 (Comm); [2005] 1
Lloyd's Rep. 192 at [88]–[90]; *St George's Investment Co Ltd v Gemini Consulting Ltd* [2004]
EWHC 2353 (Ch).

[Add to note 564: page [161]]
Torch Offshore LLS v Cable Shipping Inc [2004] EWHC 787 (Comm); [2004]
2 Lloyd's Rep. 446; *Alphapoint Shipping Ltd v Rotem Amfert Negev Ltd* [2004]
EWHC 2232 (Comm); [2005] 1 Lloyd's Rep. 23; *Newfield Construction Ltd v
Tomlinson* [2004] EWHC 3051; (2004) 97 Const. L.R. 148.

Appeal on point of law

[Add to note 577: page [162]]   **32–141**
JSC Zestafoni G Nikoladz Ferroalley Plant v Ronly Holdings Ltd [2004]
EWHC 245 (Comm), [2004] 2 Lloyd's Rep. 335; *Vrinera Marine Co Ltd v
Eastern Rich Operations Inc* [2004] EWHC 1752 (Comm); [2004] 2 Lloyd's
Rep. 465; *Alphapoint Shipping Ltd v Rotem Amfert Negev Ltd* [2004] EWHC
2232 (Comm); [2005] 1 Lloyd's Rep. 23; *Newfield Construction Ltd v Tomlinson*
[2004] EWHC 3051 (Comm); (2004) 97 Const. L.R. 148; *Bottiglieri di Navigazione SpA v Cosco Quindao Ocean Shipping Co* [2005] EWHC 244 (Comm);
[2005] 2 Lloyd's Rep. 1.

[After sub-paragraph (b) in paragraph 32–141: page [162] *insert new note 577a]*
[577a] *Marklands Ltd v Virgin Retail Ltd* [2003] EWHC 3428; (2004) 27 E.G. 130.

[Add to note 582: page [163]]   **32–142**
Alphapoint Shipping Ltd v Rotem Amfert Negev Ltd [2004] HC 2232 (Comm);
[2005] 1 Lloyd's Rep 23 at [7] (conjoined applications under ss.68, 69). Refusal
of an oral hearing is not contrary to Art.6 of the European Convention on Human
Rights: *BLCT (13096) Ltd v J Sainsbury plc* [2003] EWCA Civ 884; [2004] 2
P.&C.R. 3.

[Add at end of note 589: page [164]]   **32–143**
Vrinera Marine Co Ltd v Eastern Rich Operations Inc [2004] EWHC 1752
(Comm); [2004] 2 Lloyd's Rep. 465 at [15].

[Add new paragraph 32–143A: page [164]]
Combined applications. Applications under s.68 (challenge on the ground of   **32–143A**
serious irregularity) and s.69 (for leave to appeal on a point of law) may be
combined in one hearing[589a] but they involve two quite distinct processes of
judicial analysis.[589b] In many cases determination of the s.69 application before
that of the s.68 application may be logically preferable, but in each case it is a
matter for the court whether the application for leave to appeal should be tried
first.[589c]

589a *Bulfracht (Cyprus) Ltd v Boneset Shipping Co Ltd* [2002] EWHC 2292 (Comm); [2002] 2 Lloyd's Rep. 681; *Newfield Construction Ltd v Tomlinson* [2004] EWHC 3051; (2004) 97 Const. L.R. 148; *Alphapoint Shipping Ltd v Rotem Amfert Negev Ltd* [2004] EWHC 2232; [2005] 1 Lloyd's Rep. 23.
589b *Alphapoint Shipping Ltd v Rotem Amfert Negev Ltd*, above, at [5]–[7].
589c *ibid.*, at [7].

Challenge or appeal: reasons for award

32–145   [*Page* [164]]
Where, by agreement of the parties, the arbitral tribunal makes an award without stating its reasons for the award but sets out its reasons in a separate "confidential" document, this does not preclude the court from looking at those reasons for the purpose of an application under s.68 of the Act: *Tame Shipping Ltd v Easy Navigation Ltd* [2004] EWHC 1862 (Comm); [2004] 2 Lloyd's Rep. 626; noted (2005) 71 *Arbitration* (1) 98.

[*Add to note 595: page* [164]]
Alphapoint Shipping Ltd v Rotem Amfert Negev Ltd [2004] EWHC 2232 (Comm); [2005] 1 Lloyd's Rep. 23 at [5]; *Margulead Ltd v Exide Technologies* [2004] EWHC 1019 (Comm); [2005] 1 Lloyd's Rep. 324 at [41]–[42].

Challenge or appeal: restrictions and time-limits

32–148   [*Add at end of note 602: page* [165]]
Torch Offshore LLS v Cable Shipping Inc [2004] EWHC 787 (Comm); [2004] 2 Lloyd's Rep. 446; *World Trade Corp v C Czarnikow Sugar Ltd* [2004] EWHC 2332 (Comm); [2005] 1 Lloyd's Rep. 422 (see para.32–119, n.476, above).

[*Add to note 603*]
See also *Westland Helicopters Ltd v Sheikh Salah al-Hejailan (No.1)* [2004] EWHC 1625 (Comm); [2004] 2 Lloyd's Rep. 523; *Thyssen Canada Ltd v Mariana Maritime SA* [2005] EWHC 219 (Comm); [2005] 1 Lloyd's Rep. 640.

[*Add to note 604: page* [166]]
Thyssen Canada Ltd v Mariana Maritime SA, above.

32–149   [*Add to note 607: page* [166]]
Peterson Farms Inc v C&M Farming Ltd [2004] EWHC 121 (Comm); [2004] 1 Lloyd's Rep. 603; *JSC Zestafoni G Nikoladz Ferroalloy Plant v Ronly Holdings Ltd* [2004] EWHC 245 (Comm) 2004; [2004] 2 Lloyd's Rep. 335; *Westland Helicopters Ltd v Sheikh Salah al-Hejailan (No.1)* [2004] EWHC 1625 (Comm); [2004] 2 Lloyd's Rep. 523; *Vee Networks Ltd v Econet Wireless International Ltd* [2004] EWHC 2909 (Comm); [2005] 1 Lloyd's Rep. 192; *Margulead Ltd v Exide Technologies* [2004] EWHC 1019 (Comm); [2005] 1 Lloyd's Rep. 324; *Thyssen Canada Ltd v Mariana Maritime SA* [2005] EWHC 219 (Comm); [2005] 1 Lloyd's Rep. 640.

[*Add to note 608*]
JSC Zestafoni G Nikoladz Ferroalloy Plant v Ronly Holdings Ltd, above, at [63]–[64].

Challenge or appeal: supplementary orders

[*Add to note 609: page* [166]]   **32–150**
cf., *Peterson Farms Inc v C&M Farming Ltd* [2003] EWHC 2298; [2004] 1
Lloyd's Rep. 614 (Tomlinson J.) (s.68 application).

Foreign awards

[*Add after the first reference to Dardana Ltd v Yukos Oil Co in note 658: page*   **32–160**
[170]]
; *Svenska Petroleum Exploration AB v Government of the Republic of Lithuania* [2005] EWHC 9 (Comm); [2005] 1 Lloyd's Rep. 515; Shone (2005) 71
Arbitration (1) 46.

Civil Jurisdiction and Judgments Act 1982

[*Add to note 660: page* [170]]   **32–162**
Shone (2005) 71 *Arbitration* (1) 46.

Limitation

[*Add to end of note 664: page* [171]]   **32–164**
Good Challenger Navegante SA v Metalexportimport SA [2003] EWCA Civ
1668; [2004] 1 Lloyd's Rep. 67 (acknowledgement).

12. MISCELLANEOUS

Valuers, experts, etc

[*Add to note 674: page* [172]]   **32–166**
Bernhard Schulte GmbH & Co KG v Nile Holdings Ltd [2004] EWHC 977
(Comm); [2004] 2 Lloyd's Rep. 352 at [68], [92]–[95] (apparent bias or unfair-
ness not grounds for resisting determination by expert). cf. *Amec Civil Engineer-
ing Ltd v Secretary of State for Transport* [2005] EWCA Civ 291; [2005] 1
W.L.R. 2339 (adjudication).

Adjudication

[*Add to note 683: page* [173]]   **32–169**
Pegram Shopfitters Ltd v Tally Weijl (UK) Ltd [2003] EWCA Civ 1750 at
[8]

[*Add to note 684: page* [173]]
But see *Amec Civil Engineering Ltd v Secretary of State for Transport*, above
(duty to act independently, honestly and fairly).

[*Add to note 685*]
But see *Pegram Shopfitters Ltd v Tally Weijl (UK) Ltd*, above (challenge to the
jurisdiction of the adjudicator).

Chapter 33

BAILMENT

1. In General

Definition of bailment

33–001   [*Note 7: page* [176]]
Marcq v Christie, Manson & Woods Ltd has been reported at [2004] Q.B. 286.

No one unifying theory

33–006   [*Note 37: page* [179]]
Marcq v Christie, Manson & Woods Ltd has been reported at [2004] Q.B. 286.

2. POSSESSION AND RELATED MATTERS

Conversion of the chattel by the bailee

[*Note 72: page* [183]]
    Marcq v Christie, Manson & Woods Ltd has been reported at [2004] Q.B. 286.

33–014

Entitlement to sue

[*Add to note 99 after first sentence: page* [186]]
    The bailor's rights of recovery are not, however, co-extensive with the rights of the bailee. Claims founded on a reversionary proprietary interest require proof of actual and permanent injury to the interest: *HSBC Rail (UK) Ltd v Network Rail Infrastructure Ltd (formerly Railtrack plc)* [2005] EWHC 403 (Comm); [2005] 1 All E.R. (Comm.) 689 at [27]. Whether the injury is sufficiently permanent to constitute injury to a reversion is a question of fact. Where the subject of the complaint is in fact remedied or removed no cause of action accrues based on the reversionary interest (*ibid.*, at [34]).

33–021

Insurable interest

[*Insert new footnote 113a after "full value" in line two of the text: page* [188]]
[113a] The extent of the bailee's insurance cover is a question of construction of the particular policy and it is not the case that the bailee will in all cases be entitled to recover the full value of the goods lost or damaged. In particular, the policy may be held to cover only the legal liabilities of the bailee towards the bailor or a third party: see *Ramco (UK) Ltd v International Insurance Company of Hanover* [2004] EWCA Civ 675; [2004] All E.R. (Comm.) 866. See further para.41–008.

33–025

Sub-bailment

[*Add to note 122: page* [189]]
    It is, however, necessary to distinguish between consent to a sub-bailment and consent to the creation of a direct contractual relationship between the bailor and the sub-bailee. The two are "conceptually different": see *Targe Towing Ltd v Marine Blast Ltd* [2004] EWCA Civ 346; [2004] 1 Lloyd's Rep. 721.

33–026

4. BAILMENTS FOR VALUABLE CONSIDERATION

(b) *Custody for Reward*

(i) *In General*

Custody for reward

[*Add to note 255: page* [202]]
    While it is not necessary as a matter of law for a bailee to show what the cause of the damage was, the identification of the cause may be a "significant pointer

33–049

as to whether or not the bailee has exercised reasonable care": *Coopers Payne Ltd v Southampton Container Terminal Ltd* [2003] EWCA Civ 1223; [2004] 1 Lloyd's Rep. 331 at [29].

[Add to note 258 after reference to Levison case: page [203]]
 Euro Cellular (Distribution) plc v Danzas Ltd t/a Danzas AEI Intercontinental [2003] EWHC 3161 (Comm); [2004] 1 Lloyd's Rep. 521 at [60]–[66].

Damages

33–050   *[Add to note 263: page* [203]]
The extent of the bailee's insurance cover is a question of construction of the particular policy and it is not the case that the bailee will in all cases be entitled to recover the full value of the goods lost or damaged. In particular, the policy may be held to cover only the legal liabilities of the bailee towards the bailor or a third party: see *Ramco (UK) Ltd v International Insurance Company of Hanover* [2004] EWCA Civ 675; [2004] All E.R. (Comm.) 866. See further para.41–008.

(e) Innkeepers

Defences: negligence of the guest

33–109   *[Note 654: page* [235]]
Update reference to *Cross and Tapper on Evidence* to (10th ed., 2005), p.140 n.49.

(f) Pledge

(i) Pledge at Common Law

Definition of pledge

33–118   *[Note 723: page* [240]]
Marcq v Christie, Manson & Woods Ltd has been reported at [2004] Q.B. 286.

CHAPTER 34

BILLS OF EXCHANGE AND BANKING

1. Negotiable Instruments

(b) *Bills of Exchange*

(ii) *Capacity and Authority of Parties*

Personal liability of company's director

34–046   *[Delete ", if the bill is dishonoured," in second sentence of paragraph and add at end of that sentence: page* [276]*]*

, unless it is duly paid by the company. Where a bill is presented for payment and dishonoured, the bill is not "duly paid" for the purposes of s.349(4).[167a]

[167a] It may not even be necessary to present the bill for payment for s.349(4) to apply. A bill is dishonoured by non-payment when presentment is excused and the bill is overdue and unpaid (Bills of Exchange Act 1882, s.47(1)(b)). Presentment is excused where the drawee is not bound, as between himself and the drawer, to pay the bill and the drawer had no reason to believe that it would be paid if presented (Bills of Exchange Act 1882, s.46(2)(c), as applied in *Fiorentino Comm Giuseppe Srl v Farnesi* [2005] EWHC 160 (Ch) (director held personally liable under s.349(4) despite fact cheque not presented for payment)).

(vii) *Discharge of Bill*

Present scope of doctrine

34–136   *[Add new note 435a at the end of the first sentence: page* [319]*]*

[435a] The defence of change of position is available against restitutionary claims based on unjust enrichment, but even then it is not open to a wrongdoer (*Lipkin Gorman (a firm) v Karpnale Ltd* [1991] 2 A.C. 548, 580). There is some doubt as to whether it is available against a restitutionary claim based on the vindication of property rights, where the action is subject to the bona fide

purchaser for value defence (*Foskett v McKeown* [2001] 1 A.C. 102, 129; *Papamichael v National Westminster Bank* [2003] 1 Lloyd's Rep. 341, 376).

[*Add to note 436 at the end*]
   Commerzbank AG v Gareth Price-Jones [2003] EWCA Civ 1663 (noted by Birks, (2004) 120 L.Q.R. 373).

Assessment

[*Delete note 438: page* [320] *and substitute*]   **34–137**
   Important recent cases on the availability of the change of position defence include: *Scottish Equitable plc v Derby* [2001] EWCA Civ 369; [2001] 2 All E.R. (Comm.) 274 and *Credit Suisse (Monaco) SA v Attar* [2004] EWHC 374 (Comm) (on the need for a causal link between the mistaken receipt and the change of position); *Dextra Bank & Trust Co Ltd v Bank of Jamaica* [2002] 1 All E.R. (Comm.) 193 and *Commerzbank AG v Gareth Price-Jones* [2003] EWCA Civ 1663 (on anticipatory change of position); *Niru Battery Manufacturing Co v Milestone Trading Ltd* [2002] EWHC 1425 (Comm); [2002] 2 All E.R. (Comm.) 705, 741, approved [2003] EWCA Civ 1446; [2004] 4 All E.R. (Comm.) 193 (on what constitutes "bad faith"); *Barros Mattos Junior v MacDaniels Ltd* [2004] EWHC 1188 (Ch); [2004] 3 All E.R. 299 (on a change of position which constitutes an illegal action). See, generally, Vol. I, paras 29–179 *et seq.*

Tracing order

[*Add to note 440 at the end: page* [320]]   **34–138**
   See also *Bank of America v Arnell* [1999] Lloyd's Rep. Bank. 399.

[*Add to note 441 at the end*]
   Bishopsgate Investment Management Ltd v Homan [1995] Ch. 211, C.A.; *Box v Barclays Bank plc* [1998] Lloyd's Rep. Bank. 185, 203; *Shalson v Russo* [2003] EWHC 1637 (Ch); [2005] Ch. 281 at [140]–[141]. See also Smith, [1995] C.L.J. 290.

(c) *Cheques*

(ii) *Crossed Cheques*

Negligence issue

[*Amend note 515: page* [332]]   **34–171**
   Delete "*Linklaters v HKSB* [2003] 1 Lloyd's Rep. 545" and replace with "*Linklaters (a firm) v HSBC Bank plc* [2003] EWHC 1113 (Comm); [2003] 1 Lloyd's Rep. 545 (noted by Ellinger, (2004) 120 L.Q.R. 226)."

2. Aspects of Banking Law

(a) Bank Regulation

(i) Overview

Other legislative controls

34–222   *[Add new note 621a after "by October 9, 2004", 22 lines from the start of this paragraph: page* [351]]
621a EC Directive 2002/65 was implemented in the United Kingdom through the Financial Services (Distance Marketing) Regulations 2004, (SI 2004/2095), which came into force on October 31, 2004.

34–224   *[Delete first two sentences of note 624 and substitute: page* [352]]
The Money Laundering Regulations 2003 (SI 2003/3075) came into force, for the most part, on March 1, 2004. These Regulations repeal and replace the Money Laundering Regulations 1993 (SI 1993/1933) as amended and the Money Laundering Regulations 2001 (SI 2001/3641).

Banking Codes

34–225   *[Page* [352]]
New editions of the *Banking Code* and the *Business Banking Code* came into effect on March 1, 2005.

(ii) The Regulation of Deposit-taking

Sanctions for unauthorised acceptance of deposits

34–236   *[Add to note 655 at end: page* [357]]
The court has jurisdiction under the Supreme Court Act 1981, s.37, to make an order freezing the bank accounts of third parties over which the person who has contravened the authorisation requirements of the 2000 Act has control. See *Financial Services Authority v Fitt* [2004] EWHC 1669 (Ch).

(b) The Relationship of Banker and Customer

(ii) Definition of a Customer

Account in nominee's name

34–249   *[Delete the first sentence of note 693 and substitute: page* [363]]
Money Laundering Regulations 2003 (SI 2003/3075), which came into force, for the most part, on March 1, 2004, and which repeal and replace the Money Laundering Regulations 1993 (SI 1993/1933) as amended and the Money Laundering Regulations 2001 (SI 2001/3641) (see para.34–224 above).

(iv) *Fiduciary Relationship and Duty of Care*

Every day transactions

[*Add to note 708 at the end: page* [367]]
(noted by Ellinger, (2004) 120 L.Q.R. 226).

34–255

[*Add to note 711 at the end*]
Customs and Excise Comrs v Barclays Bank plc [2004] EWCA Civ 1555; [2005] 1 W.L.R. 2082, CA (a bank given notice of the grant of a freezing injunction against its customer was held to owe the claimant a duty to take care to prevent disposal of its customer's funds in breach of that injunction).

Information respecting new products

[*Amend note 713: page* [367]]
Delete "2003 editions" and replace with "2005 editions".

34–256

(v) *Banks and Undue Influence*

O'Brien guidelines in practice

[*Amend note 729: page* [370]]
Replace references to the 2003 editions of the *Banking Code* and *Business Banking Code* with references to the 2005 editions of both codes. Citation of paragraph numbers for each code remains unchanged.

34–262

Nature of the transaction

[*Add to note 743 at the end: page* [372]]
Mortgage Agency Services Number Two Ltd v Chater [2003] EWCA Civ 490; [2004] 1 P. & C.R. 4 (joint loan to mother and son).

34–266

Rescission

[*Add to note 762 at the end: page* [375]]
If the property subject to the security is jointly owned by a husband and wife then, even though the security may not be enforceable against the wife, it may be against the husband, and so the court may still order the property to be sold, under the Trusts of Land and Appointment of Trustees Act 1996, s.14, in order to realise the husband's share: see *First National Bank plc v Achampong* [2003] EWCA Civ 487; [2004] 1 F.C.R. 18, noted by Thompson, [2003] Conv. 314.

34–271

[*Amend note 767: page* [375]]
Delete "recission" at end of first sentence and replace with "rescission".

34–272

[*Add to note 768 at the end: page* [376]]
Applied in *UCB Group Ltd v Hedworth* [2003] EWCA Civ 1717 (a case of sub-subrogation). By contrast, where an earlier charge is voidable for undue influence as against the husband and the bank, a replacement charge, taken out as a condition of discharging that earlier charge, will itself be voidable, even if undue influence was not operative at the time of such replacement: *Yorkshire*

Bank plc v Tinsley [2004] EWCA Civ 816; [2004] 1 W.L.R. 2380 (see this Supplement, para.7–106A, above).

(vi) *Banks as Constructive Trustees*

Dishonest assistance

34–279   [*Add to note 795 at the end: page* [379]]
The nature of the accountability of the accessory or assister in equity, and the remedies available against him, are usefully examined by Elliott and Mitchell, (2004) 67 M.L.R. 16 (arguing that the assister is jointly and severally liable along with the trustee whom he has assisted).

Combined test of dishonesty

34–288   [*Delete "to Y without ensuring that the funds were utilised for the acquisition of the property." in fourth sentence of paragraph and substitute: page* [383]]
"to L. L, who knew of the undertaking given by S, did not take steps to ensure that it was utilised for the acquisition of property by Y. L simply paid out the money on Y's instructions."

[*Add to note 815 at the end: page* [383]]
The Court of Appeal of New Zealand had also expressed (*obiter*) reservations about the subjective element of the combined test of dishonesty, see *US International Marketing Ltd v National Bank of New Zealand Ltd*, C.A. 144/02, October 28, 2003, at [62] and [78]–[79], noted by Yeo, (2004) 120 L.Q.R. 208.

Unconscionability as the test of liability

34–301   [*Delete the ninth, tenth and eleventh sentences of paragraph and substitute: pages* [387]–[388]]
In *Criterion Properties plc v Stratford Properties LLC*,[838] the Court of Appeal held that an assessment of unconscionability based merely on whether the recipient had actual knowledge of the circumstances which gave rise to the breach of duty "was too narrow and one-sided a view of the matter".[839] The court was to have regard to the recipient's actions and knowledge in the context of the commercial relationship as a whole to determine whether the test of unconscionability was satisfied.

[838] [2002] EWCA Civ 1883; [2003] 1 W.L.R. 2108 at [38]; affd. on different grounds: [2004] UKHL 28; [2004] 1 W.L.R. 1846.
[839] In *Papamichael v National Westminister Bank plc* [2003] EWHC 164 (Comm); [2003] 1 Lloyd's Rep. 341 at [247], Judge Chambers Q.C. treated actual knowledge as a necessary condition for liability. More recently, in *Crown Dilmun v Sutton* [2004] EWHC 52 (Ch); [2004] 1 B.C.L.C. 468 at [200], Peter Smith J., reluctantly applying the Court of Appeal decision in *Criterion Properties*, held that "attribution of knowledge is not enough. It must be unconscionable for the . . . defendant to retain the benefit".

[*Delete "however," from the twelfth sentence of paragraph 34–301*]

(vii) *Duty of Secrecy*

Duty of Secrecy

[Amend note 847: page [389]]   **34–304**
Replace references to the 2003 editions of the *Banking Code* and *Business
Banking Code* with references to the 2005 editions of both codes. Citation of
paragraph numbers for each code remains unchanged.

[Amend note 851: page [389]]
Delete "Process" in third sentence of n.851 and replace with "Proceeds".

[Delete "2003 eds" in final sentence of paragraph 34–304 and substitute: page
[390]]
"2005 eds."

[Add to note 851 at end: page [390]]
In general terms, a customer who opens an account at a bank in the UK must
be taken to have accepted and be entitled to assume that the bank will act in
accordance with applicable anti-money laundering and terrorism legislation
(*Tayeb v HSBC Bank plc* [2004] EWHC 1529 (Comm); [2004] 4 All E.R. 1024
at [57], *per* Colman J.).

[Add to note 852 at the end]
See also *Rodaro v Royal Bank of Canada* (2002) 59 O.R. (3d) 74 (Ont. C.A.),
noted by Ogilvie, (2004) 19 B.F.L.R. 103.

[Amend note 853: page [390]]
Replace reference to the 2003 edition of the *Business Banking Code* with
reference to the 2005 edition. Citation of paragraph numbers for the code remain
unchanged.

(viii) *Termination of Relationship*

Termination of relationship by consent

[Amend note 864: page [392]]   **34–308**
Replace references to the 2003 editions of the *Banking Code* and *Business
Banking Code* with references to the 2005 editions of both codes. Citation of
paragraph numbers for each code remains unchanged.

(c) *The Current Account*

(i) *Rights and Duties of the Banker*

Overdrafts

[Add to note 878 at the end: page [394]]   **34–312**
References to the bank's "usual rate of interest" or "usual terms" in standard
form account opening agreements are not necessarily insufficiently certain to be

enforceable as contract terms: whether such a provision fails for uncertainty depends on the evidence placed before the court: *Financial Institutions Services Ltd v Negril Negril Holdings Ltd* [2004] UKPC 40.

[*Add to note 880 at the end*]
affd. [2004] EWCA Civ 64 (but stating that the position would be otherwise where the bank had notice of the agreed limitation as between the account holders).

Combining accounts

34–313   [*Insert new paragraph at the end of note 884: page* [395]]
The new administration regime introduced into the Insolvency Act 1986 by the Enterprise Act 2002 includes a mandatory set-off rule in similar form to r.4.90: see r.2.85 of the Insolvency Rules 1986. Revised versions of r.2.85 and r.4.90 came into force on April 1, 2005 (see the Insolvency (Amendment) Rules 2005 (SI 2005 No. 527)).

Effect of agreement

34–314   [*Add to note 891 at the end: page* [396]]
[2004] 2 Lloyd's Rep. 19, affd. [2004] EWCA Civ 1074; [2005] 1 Lloyd's Rep. 12.

Mandate and third parties

34–317   [*Add to note 907: page* [398]]
To similar effect, see *Tayeb v HSBC Bank plc* [2004] EWHC 1529 (Comm); [2004] 4 All E.R. 1024 at [75]–[77], *per* Colman J.

[*Add to note 908*]
In *Tayeb v HSBC Bank plc* [2004] EWHC 1529 (Comm); [2004] 4 All E.R. 1024, Colman J. held that mere suspicion as to the origin of funds transferred into a customer's bank account by a third party using the CHAPS electronic funds transfer system—as to which, see para.34–380 below—did not present the bank with a justifiable reason for returning those funds to the transferor without the customer's consent. A bank may have to freeze a customer's account where it knows or suspects that the account contains the proceeds of crime or risk committing a criminal offence under the Proceeds of Crime Act 2002, s 328 (see *Squirrell Ltd v National Westminster Bank plc* [2005] EWHC 664 (Ch); [2005] 1 All E.R. (Comm.) 749).

(ii) *Termination of Duty to Pay*

Third party debt orders

34–324   [*Add to note 933 at the end: page* [402]]
Kuwait Oil Tanker Co SAK v Qabazard is now reported at [2004] 1 A.C. 300 and is noted by Rogerson, [2003] C.L.J. 576; Briggs, [2003] L.M.C.L.Q. 418; Dickinson, (2004) 120 L.Q.R. 16.

(iii) *Protection of Paying Banker in Cases of Unauthorised Payment*

Pass books and periodic statement

[*Add to note 957 in line 5, after reference to Royal Bank of Scotland plc v Fielding:*   **34–334**
page [406]]
affd. [2004] EWCA Civ 64.

[*Add to note 960: page* [407]]
See also *Financial Institutions Services Ltd v Negril Negril Holdings Ltd*
[2004] UKPC 40 (conclusive evidence clause was not clear and unambiguous
and so was construed narrowly against the bank).

(iv) *Special Types of Current Accounts*

Survivorship

[*Add to note 1003 at the end: page* [414]]   **34–348**
; *Crill v Wood* (2003–04) 6 ITELR 590 (Royal Court, Jersey).

Trust accounts

[*Insert new note 1008a at the end of first sentence: page* [415]]   **34–350**
[1008a] For the nature of a trust account, see *Mann v Coutts & Co* [2003] EWHC 2138 (Comm);
[2004] 1 All E.R. (Comm.) 1 at [154]–[165].

[*Amend note 1010: page* [415]]
Replace reference to *Hanbury and Martin's Modern Equity* (16th ed., 2001),
p.582 with one to *Hanbury and Martin's Modern Equity* (17th ed., 2005),
para.20–019.

(d) *Discount and Collection*

Non-transferable cheques

[*Add to note 1021 at the end: page* [417]]   **34–353**
noted by Ellinger, (2004) 120 L.Q.R. 226.

Causes of action

[*Add to note 1031 at the end: page* [418]]   **34–354**
noted by Ellinger, (2004) 120 L.Q.R. 226.

Instances of negligence

[*Delete note 1042 and substitute: page* [420]]   **34–356**
[1042] Money Laundering Regulations 2003 (SI 2003/3075) which came into force, for the most part,
on March 1, 2004. These new Regulations repeal and replace the Money Laundering Regulations
1993 (SI 1993/1933) as amended and the Money Laundering Regulations 2001 (SI 2001/3641) (see
para.34–224 above).

34–357   [*Add to note 1047 at the end: page* [421]]
noted by Ellinger, (2004) 120 L.Q.R. 226.

(e) *The Giro System and Electronic Transfer of Funds*

Paper-based and electronic system

34–374   [*Insert in the tenth line of the text after "BACS Ltd" and before "("BACS")": page* [428]]
and, since December 1, 2003, BACS Payment Schemes Ltd,

Clearing house rules

34–379   [*Add to note 1096 at end: page [430]*]
See also *Tayeb v HSBC Bank plc* [2004] EWHC 1529 (Comm); [2004] 4 All
E.R. 1024 at [57].

[*Amend note 1098*]
Update reference to New CHAPS Rules to Version 1.3, r.10.1.1.

UK clearing systems

34–380   [*Insert in the seventh line of the text after "BACS Ltd" and before "which provides": page* [431]]
and, since December 1, 2003, BACS Payment Schemes Ltd,

Cases where payee claims payment is complete

34–402   [*Add to text at end of paragraph: page* [440]]
Similarly, in *Tayeb v HSBC Bank plc*,[1137a] where the payee's bank became
suspicious of the origin of funds transferred into the payee's account using the
CHAPS electronic transfer system and returned those funds to the payer's bank,
Colman J. held that a CHAPS transfer was ordinarily irreversible once the
payee's bank had authenticated the transfer, sent an acknowledgement message
informing the payer's bank that the transfer had been received and credited the
funds to the payee's account.[1137b]

[1137a] [2004] EWHC 1529 (Comm); [2004] 4 All E.R. 1024 (noted by Ellinger, (2005) 121 L.Q.R. 48).

[1137b] At [60] and [85]. However, the judge stated (at [60]) that there was an appropriate analogy with the practice in relation to documentary credits where, at the time of presentation of documents, a bank with cogent evidence of fraud can decline to make payment (*United Trading Corporation v Allied Arab Bank Ltd* [1985] 2 Lloyd's Rep. 554). He added (at [61]) that the same exception was likely to apply in respect of illegal transactions (see *Mahonia Ltd v JP Morgan Chase Bank* [2003] 2 Lloyd's Rep. 911).

Availability as if cash

34–406   [*Add to note 1142 at end: page* [442]]
See also *Tayeb v HSBC Bank plc* [2004] EWHC 1529 (Comm); [2004] 4 All
E.R. 1024 at [88].

(g) *Giving Information on Financial Transactions*

Banking references

[*Amend note 1165: page* [446]]
Replace references to the 2003 editions of the *Banking Code* and the *Business Banking Code* with reference to the 2005 editions. Citations of paragraph numbers for each code remain unchanged.

(i) *Bankers' Commercial Credits*

(ii) *Types of Documentary Credits*

Transfer and assignment of credits

[*Insert new footnote 1230a at the end of paragraph: page* [464]]
1230a The first beneficiary will usually want to keep information about his transaction with the second beneficiary away from the applicant for fear that the applicant will cut him out of the picture and deal directly with the second beneficiary. In *Jackson v Royal Bank of Scotland* [2005] UKHL 3; [2005] 1 W.L.R. 377 at [20]–[24], the House of Lords confirmed that an issuing bank owes the first beneficiary of a transferable letter of credit a duty of confidentiality with regard to this information (breach of duty of confidentiality when issuing bank reveals to applicant the extent of first beneficiary's "mark-up" on price charged).

(iii) *The Contract between Seller and Buyer*

The documentary credit clause

[*Add to note 1241 at the end: page* [467]]
Provision of a letter of credit is a condition precedent to any obligation on the part of the seller to perform any aspect of the loading operation which is the seller's responsibility (*Kronos Worldwide Ltd v Sempra Oil Trading Sarl* [2004] EWCA Civ 3; [2004] C.L.C. 136 at [19], *per* Mance L.J.).

(v) *The Relationship of Banker and Seller*

The autonomy of an irrevocable credit

[*Insert in line 6 of note 1307, after reference to Bank of Credit and Commerce v Somali Bank: page* [478]]
Marconi Communications International Ltd v Pt Pan Indonesia Bank Ltd TBK [2004] EWHC 129 (Comm), affd. [2005] EWCA Civ 422.

[*Amend note 1308:*]
Delete the second sentence of this note.

Illegality

[*Add to the text at the end of paragraph: page* [478]]
The illegality exception to the autonomy doctrine is not confined to cases where payment of the credit infringes exchange control provisions. In *Group Josi*

Re v Walbrook Insurance Co Ltd,[1310a] Staughton L.J. expressed the view that a court would restrain a bank from paying under a letter of credit being used as a means of payment of an illegal arms sale, at least where the illegality was clearly established and known to the bank. More recently, in *Mahonia Ltd v JP Morgan Chase Bank*,[1310b] Colman J. refused to strike out an illegality defence to enforcement of a letter of credit where the underlying contract was alleged to have been made for an illegal purpose, namely the contravention of US Securities law.

[1310a] [1996] 1 W.L.R. 1152.
[1310b] [2003] EWHC 1927 (Comm); [2003] 2 Lloyd's Rep. 911. It was later held at the trial of the action that there was no illegality which affected the transaction: *Mahonia Ltd v JP Morgan Chase Bank* [2004] EWHC 1938 (Comm).

Ambit of rule

34–489   *[Insert in note 1315, at end of second sentence, line 5: page [479]]*
Balfour Beatty Civil Engineering v Technical & General Guarantee Co Ltd (1999) 68 Con. L.R. 180, 190–191; *TTI Team Telecom International Ltd v Hutchison 3G UK Ltd* [2003] EWHC 762 (TCC.); [2003] 1 All E.R. (Comm.) 914.

[Add to note 1320 at the end: page [480]]
For a critique, see Hooley, [2002] C.L.J. 279. The Singapore Court of Appeal has since recognised a separate "nullity" defence: *Beam Technology (Mfg) Pte Ltd v Standard Chartered Bank* [2003] 1 S.L.R. 597, noted by Chin and Wong, [2004] L.M.C.L.Q. 14.

Tender by third party

34–490   *[Add to note 1324 at the end: page [480]]*
In *Armlea plc v Gov & Co of the Bank of Scotland* (unreported, June 4, 2004), Lord Mackay (at [39]–[43]), sitting in the Outer House of the Court of Session, rejected a submission by a principal that it did not have to plead fraud when seeking an injunction against the bank to restrain payment under a demand guarantee (as opposed to where the bank wishes to avoid making payment, when fraud must be pleaded). Lord Mackay (at [44]–[46]) also rejected a submission that the fraud exception only applies to demand guarantees involved in international commerce but not to those involved in domestic commerce.

[Add new paragraphs 34–491A and 34–491B: page [481]]
34–491A   **Restrictions on beneficiary's right to call for payment.** In *Sirius International Insurance Corp (Publ) v FAI General Insurance Co Ltd*,[1326a] the Court of Appeal held that the principle of autonomy did not mean that a beneficiary could draw on a letter of credit when he had expressly agreed not to do so unless certain conditions were satisfied and those conditions had not been met. In this case, the restrictions were contained in a separate agreement made between the beneficiary (Sirius) and the applicant (FAI). May L.J. stated that "although those restrictions were not terms of the letter of credit, and although the bank would have been obliged and entitled to honour a request to pay which fulfilled its terms, that does not mean that, as between themselves and FAI, Sirius were

entitled to draw on the letter of credit if the express conditions of this underlying agreement were not fulfilled. They were not so entitled".[1326b] The Court of Appeal was also of the opinion that if draw-down was attempted in these circumstances, a court would be likely to grant an injunction restraining the beneficiary from drawing on the letter of credit in breach of express conditions contained in the underlying agreement. It should be noted that fraud was not alleged against Sirius and so the case does not fall within the fraud exception to the autonomy principle. The Court of Appeal held that an express condition of the separate agreement between the parties had not been met and that Sirius were not entitled to the proceeds of the credit. The House of Lords[1326c] reversed that decision on the ground that the condition had been satisfied. Their Lordships found it unnecessary to examine arguments about the autonomy principle.

[1326a] [2003] EWCA Civ 470; [2003] 1 All E.R. (Comm.) 865, noted by Hare, [2004] C.L.J. 288. For examples of Australian cases to similar effect, see *Selvas Pty Ltd v Hansen Yuncken (SA) Pty Ltd* (1987) 6 Australian Construction Law Rep 36; *Boral Formwork v Action Motors* [2002] N.S.W.S.C. 713.
[1326b] [2003] EWCA Civ 470 at [27].
[1326c] [2004] UKHL 54; [2004] 1 W.L.R. 3251.

The *Sirius* case raises important questions about the extent of the autonomy principle. There must be some concern as to how far it undermines the principle and its consequential benefits of commercial certainty. However, the English courts have not shown themselves willing to embrace the wider principle of "unconscionable demand" which has gained judicial support in Australia[1326d] and Singapore.[1326e] It is not entirely clear what constitutes unconscionablity, although it seems to be something more than unfairness and less than fraud, nor as to the standard of proof required to obtain injunctive relief on this ground.[1326f] The uncertainty that this creates is obvious. Nevertheless, there have been recent dicta which suggests that the current reluctance of the English courts to apply a concept of "unconsionability" may not last forever.[1326g]

34–491B

[1326d] See, *e.g. Olex Focas Pty Ltd v Skodaexport Co Ltd* [1998] 3 V.R. 380, where statute brought the concept into play.
[1326e] See, *e.g. Samwoh Asphalt Premix Pte Ltd v Sum Cheong Piling Pte Ltd* [2002] B.L.R. 459; *McConnell Dowell Construction (Aust) Pty Ltd v Semcorp Engineering and Constructions Pte Ltd* [2002] B.L.R. 450.
[1326f] See Ganotaki, [2004] L.M.C.L.Q. 148 at 152.
[1326g] See, especially, the dicta of Potter L.J. in *Montrod Ltd v Grundkotter Fleischvertriebs* [2001] EWCA Civ 1954; [2002] 1 All E.R. (Comm.) 257 at [59], and also that of Judge Thornton Q.C., sitting as a deputy High Court judge, in *TTI Team Telecom International Ltd v Hutchison 3G UK Ltd* [2003] EWHC 762 (TCC); [2003] 1 All E.R. (Comm.) 914 at [37].

CHAPTER 35

CARRIAGE BY AIR

1. Introduction

The Warsaw Convention 1929

35–002   *[Replace from "When that Act" on line 7 of page* [500] *to end of para.35–002, and notes 5 and 6, with the following]*

The unamended Warsaw Convention continues to have effect as Sch.2 to the Carriage by Air Acts (Application of Provisions) Order 2004.[5] Schedule 3 to the same Order gives effect to Montreal Additional Protocol No. 1 of 1975. The two Schedules differ only in respect of the currency units by reference to which liability limits are prescribed.

[5] SI 2004/1899.

The Montreal Convention 1999

35–006   *[In note 17, delete "(not yet in force)" and substitute: page* [502]]
, which came into force on June 28, 2004

European Council Regulation No.2027/97

35–007—   *[Pages* [502]–[503]]
35–010   The Montreal Convention 1999 came into force for the European Community on June 28, 2004, and Council Regulation No.2027/97 was radically amended, and in effect replaced, by European Parliament and Council Regulation No.889/2002, as to which see paras 35–011 *et seq.* The Air Carrier Liability

Order 1998, giving effect to Council Regulation No.2027/98 was revoked with effect from the same date by the Air Carrier Liability Regulations 2004 (SI 2004/1418).

European Parliament and Council Regulation No.889/2002

[For the second sentence of paragraph substitute: page [503]]   **35–011**
The amending Regulation applied from June 28, 2004, the date on which the Montreal Convention entered into force for the European Community; the necessary changes to the law of the United Kingdom were made by the Air Carrier Liability Regulations 2004[34a] and the Air Carrier Liability (No. 2) Regulations 2004.[34b]

[34a] SI 2004/1418.
[34b] SI 2004/1974.

Removal of financial limits

[Add at end of paragraph: page [504]]   **35–012**
European Parliament and Council Regulation No.785/2004 of April 21, 2004 on insurance requirements for air carriers and aircraft operators[37a] requires all air carriers and aircraft operators flying within, into, out of, or over the territory of a Member State to have specified levels of insurance cover in respect of their aviation-specific liability in respect of passengers (death and personal injury caused by accidents),[37b] for loss or destruction of or damage to baggage and cargo, and third parties (death, personal injury and damage to property caused by accidents). The insured risks must include acts of war, terrorism, hijacking, acts of sabotage, unlawful seizure of aircraft and civil commotion.[37c] In the United Kingdom, an air carrier or aircraft operator (other than a carrier or operator regulated by another Member State) who fails to comply with these requirements commits an offence.[37d] For the purposes of Regulation 785/04, the Civil Aviation Authority is the competent authority, except in cases where a permit under arts 113 or 115 of the Air Navigation Order 2000,[37e] which relate to certain aircraft registered outside the United Kingdom, where the Secretary of State is the competent authority.[37f]

[37a] O.J. No L138/1, 30.04.2004, which came into force on May 1, 2005. The Regulation does not affect the carriage of mail: Regulation, art.1(2).
[37b] The United Kingdom has set the minimum level at 100,000 SDRs per passenger: Civil Aviation (Insurance) Regulations 2005 (SI 2005/1089), reg.5.
[37c] Regulation 785/04, art.4(1).
[37d] Civil Aviation (Insurance) Regulations 2005 (SI 2005/1089), reg.4. For penalties, see reg.12.
[37e] SI 2000/1562.
[37f] Civil Aviation (Insurance) Regulations 2005 (SI 2005/1089), reg.3.

Conditions of carriage

[Add at the end of paragraph: page [504]]   **35–014**
Failure to comply with the requirements of Art.3a or Art.6 of the amended Regulation is made an offence by the Air Carrier Liability Order 2004.[39a]

[39a] SI 2004/1418.

Parties to the Conventions

35–015 *[For the first sentence of note 40 substitute: page [505]]*
s.2(1) as amended by SI 1999/213 and SI 2002/263 (and see the Carriage by Air Acts (Application of Provisions) Order 2004 (SI 2004/1899), Arts 5(2) and 6(2)).

Scope of the Conventions

35–016 *[For note 43 substitute: page [page 505]]*
Carriage by Air Acts (Application of Provisions) Order 2004 (SI 2004/1899), art.8 (excluding, in art.8(2), cases where members of the Armed Forces are carried during a time of actual or imminent hostilities, severe international tension, or great national emergency).

[For the reference to the 1967 Order at the end of paragraph, and note 44, substitute]
Sch.1 to the Carriage by Air Acts (Application of Provisions) Order 2004, under art.2(2) of which the carrier is liable only to the relevant postal administration and in accordance with the rules applicable to the relationship between carriers and postal administrations.[44]

[44] Carriage by Air Acts (Application of Provisions) Order 2004 (SI 2004/1899), art.4.

Interpretation of the Convention

35–020 *[Note 48: page [506]]*
SI 2002/263 is now in force.

[For note 49 substitute:]
[49] Carriage by Air Acts (Application of Provisions) Order 2004 (SI 2004/1899), arts 5(1) and 6(1).

2. INTERNATIONAL CARRIAGE

(a) *General*

Definition

35–021 *[Note 57: page [507]]*
SI 2002/263 is now in force.

[For notes 59 and 60 substitute: page [508]]
[59] Carriage by Air Acts (Application of Provisions) Order 2004 (SI 2004/1899), Sch.2, art.1(2); Carriage by Air Act 1961, Sch.1, art.1(2), Sch.1A as inserted by SI 1999/1312, art.1(2), Sch.1B as inserted by SI 2002/263, art.1(2).
[60] Carriage by Air Acts (Application of Provisions) Order 2004 (SI 2004/1899), Sch.2, art.1(3); Carriage by Air Act 1961, Sch.1, art.1(3), Sch.1A as inserted by SI 1999/1312, art.1(3), Sch.1B as inserted by SI 2002/263, art.1(3).

Conventions provide exclusive cause of action

[*For note 62 substitute: page* [509]]
62 Carriage by Air Acts (Application of Provisions) Order 2004 (SI 2004/1899), Sch.2, art.24(1); Carriage by Air Act 1961, Sch.1, art.24(1)(2), Sch.1A as inserted by SI 1999/1312, art.24(1)(2) (using different language), Sch.1B as inserted by SI 2002/263, art.29.

35–022

Jurisdiction

[*For the first sentence of note 69 substitute: page* [510]]
Carriage by Air Acts (Application of Provisions) Order 2004 (SI 2004/1899), Sch.2, art.28(1); Carriage by Air Act 1961, Sch.1, art.28(1), Sch.1A as inserted by SI 1999/1312, art.28(1).

35–024

[*Note 70*]
SI 2002/263 is now in force.

[*For the citations in the first sentence of note 71 substitute:*]
Carriage by Air Acts (Application of Provisions) Order 2004 (SI 2004/1899), Sch.2, art.28(2); Carriage by Air Act 1961, Sch.1, art.28(2), Sch.1A as inserted by SI 1999/1312, art.28(2), Sch.1B as inserted by SI 2002/263, art.33(4).

35–025

Limitation of actions

[*For note 82 substitute: page* [511]]
82 Carriage by Air Acts (Application of Provisions) Order 2004 (SI 2004/1899), Sch.2, art.29(1); Carriage by Air Act 1961, Sch.1, art.29(1), Sch.1A as inserted by SI 1999/1312, art.29(1), Sch.1B as inserted by SI 2002/263, art.35(1). English law will, as the *lex fori*, determine the method of calculating the period of limitation: Carriage by Air Acts (Application of Provisions) Order 2004 (SI 2004/1899), Sch.2, art.29(2); Carriage by Air Act 1961, Sch.1, art.29(2), Sch.1A as inserted by SI 1999/1312, art.29(2), Sch.1B as inserted by SI 2002/263, art.35(2).

35–026

(b) *Passengers*

Passenger ticket

[*For note 93 substitute: page* [513]]
93 Carriage by Air Acts (Application of Provisions) Order 2004 (SI 2004/1899), Sch.2, art.3(1).

35–028

[*Note 95*]
SI 2002/263 is now in force.

Absence, irregularity or loss of passenger ticket

[*For the first line of note 103 substitute: page* [514]]
Carriage by Air Acts (Application of Provisions) Order 2004 (SI 2004/1899), Sch.2, art.3(2).

35–030

[*Note 106*]
SI 2002/263 is now in force.

[*For note 107 substitute:*]
[107] Carriage by Air Act 1961, Sch.1, art.34, Sch.1A as inserted by SI 1999/1312, art.34, Sch.1B as inserted by SI 2002/263, art.51. The Warsaw Convention 1929 is wholly excluded in such cases: Carriage by Air Acts (Application of Provisions) Order 2004 (SI 2004/1899), Sch.2, art.34.

Right of refusal

35–031 [*For the first sentence of note 108 substitute: page* [514]]
Carriage by Air Acts (Application of Provisions) Order 2004 (SI 2004/1899), Sch.2, art.33; Carriage by Air Act 1961, Sch.1, art.33, Sch.1A as inserted by SI 1999/1312, art.33, Sch.1B as inserted by SI 2002/263, art.27.

Liability for death and bodily injury

35–032 [*For note 111 substitute: page* 515]]
[111] Carriage by Air Acts (Application of Provisions) Order 2004 (SI 2004/1899), Sch.2, art.17.

[*Note 112*]
SI 2002/263 is now in force.

"Accident"

35–033 [*Page* [516]]
The United States Supreme Court has held that an omission may be treated as an accident; there is no requirement of a positive action on anyone's part: *Olympic Airways v Husain* 124 S Ct 1221 (2004). pet. for rehearing denied 124 S Ct 2065 (2004). See to similar effect, the High Court of Australia in *Povey v Qantas Airways Ltd* [2005] H.C.A. 33. *cf. Deep Vein Thrombosis and Air Travel Group Litigation* [2003] EWCA Civ 1005; [2004] QB 234, where Lord Phillips of Worth Matravers MR advances the contrary view. In *Olympic Airways v Husain*, the deceased passenger had been refused a change of seat to avoid the cigarette smoke to which he was allergic; this was an unusual event external to the passenger and so an "accident".

"Bodily injury"

35–034 [*Page* [516]]
There is no liability for mental injuries which are accompanied by, but not caused by physical injuries: *Ehrlich v American Airlines Inc* 360 F 3d 366 (2nd Cir, 2004).

Defences available to the carrier: "all necessary measures"

35–035 [*For the first line of note 124 substitute: page* [517]]
Carriage by Air Acts (Application of Provisions) Order 2004 (SI 2004/1899), Sch.2, art.20(1);

[*Delete second sentence and note 125: page* [517]]
European Council Regulation No.2027/97 was radically amended, and in effect replaced, by European Parliament and Council Regulation No.889/2002, as

to which see paras 35–011 *et seq*. The Air Carrier Liability Order 1998 was revoked with effect from the same date by the Air Carrier Liability Regulations 2004 (SI 2004/1418). Community air carriers now fall within the regime of the Montreal Convention 1999.

[*Note 126*]
SI 2002/263 is now in force.

Contributory negligence

[*Page* [518]]   **35–036**
European Council Regulation No.2027/97 was radically amended, and in effect replaced, by European Parliament and Council Regulation No.889/2002, as to which see paras 35–011 *et seq*. Community air carriers now fall within the regime of the Montreal Convention 1999.

[*For note 135 substitute:*]
135 Carriage by Air Acts (Application of Provisions) Order 2004 (SI 2004/1899), Sch.2, art.21.

[*Note 138*]
SI 2002/263 is now in force.

Upper financial limit of liability

[*Page* [518]]   **35–037**
European Council Regulation No.2027/97 was radically amended, and in effect replaced, by European Parliament and Council Regulation No.889/2002, as to which see paras 35–011 *et seq*. Community air carriers now fall within the regime of the Montreal Convention 1999.

[*For note 141 substitute:*]
141 Carriage by Air Acts (Application of Provisions) Order 2004 (SI 2004/1899), Sch.2, art.22.

[*Note 145; page* [519]]
SI 2002/263 is now in force.

Misconduct

[*For the first sentence of note 149 substitute: page* [520]]   **35–039**
Carriage by Air Acts (Application of Provisions) Order 2004 (SI 2004/1899), Sch.2, art.25.

[*Note 152*]
SI 2002/263 is now in force.

Fatal accidents

[*Note 161: page* [522]]   **35–045**
SI 2002/263 is now in force.

Several actions by one passenger

35–046   [*Notes 164, 167, 168 and 169: pages* [522]–[523]]
SI 2002/263 is now in force.

[*In line 7: page* [522]]
   The reference in the text to note 165 should now be to the Carriage by Air Acts (Application of Provisions) Order 2004.

[*For note 165 substitute:*]
¹⁶⁵ SI 2004/1899, art.7.

Overbooking

35–047   [*Last sentence, text to note 172: page* [523]]
   Council Regulation 295/91 is with effect from February 17, 2005, repealed and replaced by European Parliament and Council Regulation No.261/2004 of February 11, 2004, for the text of which see OJ 2004 L46/1. In the United Kingdom, the Civil Aviation (Denied Boarding, Compensation and Assistance) Regulations 2005 (SI 2005/975) designate the Civil Aviation Authority as the body responsible for enforcement and the Air Transport Users Council as the body to receive complaints, and also make it an offence, subject to a defence of due diligence, for an operating air carrier to fail to comply with its obligations under Regulation 261/2004.

Successive carriers

35–048   [*For the first sentence of note 173 substitute: page* [524]]
   Carriage by Air Acts (Application of Provisions) Order 2004 (SI 2004/1899), Sch.2, art.1(3); Carriage by Air Act 1961, Sch.1, art.1(3), Sch.1A as inserted by SI 1999/1312, art.1(3), Sch.1B as inserted by SI 2002/263, art.1(3).

[*For the first sentence of note 174 substitute:*]
   Carriage by Air Acts (Application of Provisions) Order 2004 (SI 2004/1899), Sch.2, art.30(1); Carriage by Air Act 1961, Sch.1, art.30(1), Sch.1A as inserted by SI 1999/1312, art.30(1), Sch.1B as inserted by SI 2002/263, art.36(1).

[*For note 175 substitute:*]
   Carriage by Air Acts (Application of Provisions) Order 2004 (SI 2004/1899), Sch.2, art.30(2); Carriage by Air Act 1961, Sch.1, art.30(2), Sch.1A as inserted by SI 1999/1312, art.30(2), Sch.1B as inserted by SI 2002/263, art.36(2).

Contracting carriers and "actual" carriers

35–049   [*Note 178: page* [525]]
SI 2002/263 is now in force.

(c) *Baggage*

Forms of baggage

[For the first line of note 186 substitute: page [526]]
Carriage by Air Acts (Application of Provisions) Order 2004 (SI 2004/1899), Sch.2, art.22(3);

[Note 186, line 4]
SI 2002/263 is now in force.

35–052

Baggage check

[For note 189 substitute: page [526]]
[189] Carriage by Air Acts (Application of Provisions) Order 2004 (SI 2004/1899), Sch.2, art.4.

[For note 191 substitute:]
[191] Carriage by Air Acts (Application of Provisions) Order 2004 (SI 2004/1899), Sch.2, art.4(4).

[Note 195: page [527]]
SI 2002/263 is now in force.

35–053

Liability for damage, destruction or loss

[Page [527]]
Under European Parliament and Council Regulation No.889/2002, Community air carriers now fall within the regime of the Montreal Convention 1999.

[For the first line of note 196 substitute:]
Carriage by Air Acts (Application of Provisions) Order 2004 (SI 2004/1899), Sch.2, art.18(1);

[For the first line of note 197 substitute:]
Carriage by Air Acts (Application of Provisions) Order 2004 (SI 2004/1899), Sch.2, art.18(2);

[Note 198: page [528]]
SI 2002/263 is now in force.

35–054

[Page [528]]
[For note 200 substitute:]
[200] Carriage by Air Acts (Application of Provisions) Order 2004 (SI 2004/1899), Sch.2, art.22(2).

[For note 202 substitute:]
[202] Carriage by Air Acts (Application of Provisions) Order 2004 (SI 2004/1899), Sch.2, art.22(3).

[In note 205, line 1, for the citation of the 1967 Order substitute:]
Carriage by Air Acts (Application of Provisions) Order 2004 (SI 2004/1899), Sch.3, art.22(2)(3).

35–055

[*Note 206*]
SI 2002/263 is now in force.

[*For note 207 substitute: page* [529]]
[207] Carriage by Air Acts (Application of Provisions) Order 2004 (SI 2004/1899), Sch.2, art.22(2); Carriage by Air Act 1961, Sch.1, art.22(2)(*a*), Sch.1A as inserted by SI 1999/1312, art.22(2)(*a*), Sch.1B as inserted by SI 2002/263, art.22(2).

Time for making claims

35–056   [*For notes 208 to 210 substitute: page* [529]]
[208] Carriage by Air Acts (Application of Provisions) Order 2004 (SI 2004/1899), Sch.2, art.26(2); Carriage by Air Act 1961, Sch.1, art.26(2), Sch.1A as inserted by SI 1999/1312, art.26(2), Sch.1B as inserted by SI 2002/263, art.31(2).
[209] Carriage by Air Acts (Application of Provisions) Order 2004 (SI 2004/1899), Sch.2, art.35; Carriage by Air Act 1961, Sch.1, art.35, Sch.1A as inserted by SI 1999/1312, art.35, Sch.1B as inserted by SI 2002/263, art.52.
[210] Carriage by Air Acts (Application of Provisions) Order 2004 (SI 2004/1899), Sch.2, art.26(4); Carriage by Air Act 1961, Sch.1, art.26(4), Sch.1A as inserted by SI 1999/1312, art.26(4), Sch.1B as inserted by SI 2002/263, art.31(4).

(d) *Cargo*

Air waybill

35–057   [*For notes 211 to 215 substitute: page* [529]]
[211] Carriage by Air Acts (Application of Provisions) Order 2004 (SI 2004/1899), Sch.2, art.5(1); Carriage by Air Act 1961, Sch.1, art.5(1).
[212] Carriage by Air Acts (Application of Provisions) Order 2004 (SI 2004/1899), Sch.2, art.10(1); Carriage by Air Act 1961, Sch.1, art.10(1).
[213] Carriage by Air Acts (Application of Provisions) Order 2004 (SI 2004/1899), Sch.2, art.6(5); Carriage by Air Act 1961, Sch.1, art.6(5).
[214] Carriage by Air Acts (Application of Provisions) Order 2004 (SI 2004/1899), Sch.2, art.7; Carriage by Air Act 1961, Sch.1, art.7.
[215] Carriage by Air Acts (Application of Provisions) Order 2004 (SI 2004/1899), Sch.2, art.6(1)(2); Carriage by Air Act 1961, Sch.1, art.6(1)(2).

Statements in waybill

35–058   [*For note 217 substitute: page* [530]]
[217] Carriage by Air Acts (Application of Provisions) Order 2004 (SI 2004/1899), Sch.2, art.11(2); Carriage by Air Act 1961, Sch.1, art.11(2).

Absence of waybill, etc.

35–059   [*For the first line of note 219 substitute: page* [530]]
Carriage by Air Acts (Application of Provisions) Order 2004 (SI 2004/1899), Sch.2, art.9;

Cargo documentation under recent conventions

35–060   [*Notes 223 and 224: page* [530]]
SI 2002/263 is now in force.

Acceptability of goods for carriage

[*Note 226: page [531]*]   **35–061**
Amend the citation to CSC(24)1601.

[*Note 227*]
Amend the citation to art.3.1.1.2.

[*Note 229*]
The Air Navigation (Dangerous Goods) Regulations 2002 are amended by SI 2004/3214.

Liability for damage, destruction or loss

[*For the first line of note 231 substitute: page* [531]]   **35–062**
Carriage by Air Acts (Application of Provisions) Order 2004 (SI 2004/1899), Sch.2, art.18(1);

[*For the first line of note 232 substitute:*]
Carriage by Air Acts (Application of Provisions) Order 2004 (SI 2004/1899), Sch.2, art.18(2);

[*Note 234: page [532]*]
SI 2002/263 is now in force.

Upper financial limit of liability

[*For notes 239 and 240 substitute: page* [532]]   **35–063**
[239] Carriage by Air Acts (Application of Provisions) Order 2004 (SI 2004/1899), Sch.2, art.22(2); Carriage by Air Act 1961, Sch.1, art.22(2)(3) (as amended by the Carriage by Air and Road Act 1979, s.4), Sch.1A as inserted by SI 1999/1312, art.22(2)(*a*), Sch.1B as inserted by SI 2002/263, art.22(2).
[240] Carriage by Air Acts (Application of Provisions) Order 2004 (SI 2004/1899), Sch.2, art.22(2); Carriage by Air Act 1961, Sch.1, art.22(2)(*a*), Sch.1A as inserted by SI 1999/1312, art.22(2)(*a*), Sch.1B as inserted by SI 2002/263, art.22(2).

Stoppage in transit

[*For note 243 substitute: page* [533]]   **35–064**
[243] Carriage by Air Acts (Application of Provisions) Order 2004 (SI 2004/1899), Sch.2, arts 12(4), 13(1); Carriage by Air Act 1961, Sch.1, arts 12(4), 13(1), Sch.1A as inserted by SI 1999/1312, arts 12(4), 13(1), Sch.1B as inserted by SI 2002/263, arts 12(4), 13(1).

[*For the first sentence of note 244 substitute:*]
Carriage by Air Acts (Application of Provisions) Order 2004 (SI 2004/1899), Sch.2, art.12(1); Carriage by Air Act 1961, Sch.1, art.12(1), Sch.1A as inserted by SI 1999/1312, art.12(1), Sch.1B as inserted by SI 2002/263, art.12(1).

[*For the first sentence of note 245 substitute:*]
Carriage by Air Acts (Application of Provisions) Order 2004 (SI 2004/1899), Sch.2, art.12(2); Carriage by Air Act 1961, Sch.1, art.12(2), Sch.1A as inserted by SI 1999/1312, art.12(2), Sch.1B as inserted by SI 2002/263, art.12(2).

[For note 246 substitute]
[246] Carriage by Air Acts (Application of Provisions) Order 2004 (SI 2004/1899), Sch.2, arts 12(4), 13(1); Carriage by Air Act 1961, Sch.1, arts 12(4), 13(1), Sch.1A as inserted by SI 1999/1312, arts 12(4), 13(1), Sch.1B as inserted by SI 2002/263, arts 12(4), 13(1).

Delivery to the consignee

35–065   *[For notes 247 to 249 substitute: page [533]]*
[247] Carriage by Air Acts (Application of Provisions) Order 2004 (SI 2004/1899), Sch.2, art.13(2); Carriage by Air Act 1961, Sch.1, art.13(2), Sch.1A as inserted by SI 1999/1312, art.13(2), Sch.1B as inserted by SI 2002/263, art.13(2). See the I.A.T.A. recommended Conditions of Carriage (CSC(24)1601), art.8.1.
[248] Carriage by Air Acts (Application of Provisions) Order 2004 (SI 2004/1899), Sch.2, art.13(1); Carriage by Air Act 1961, Sch.1, art.13(1), Sch.1A as inserted by SI 1999/1312, art.13(1), Sch.1B as inserted by SI 2002/263, art.13(1).
[249] CSC(24)1601, art.8.3.

Time for making claims: damage or delay

35–067   *[For the first sentence of note 254 substitute: page [534]]*
Carriage by Air Acts (Application of Provisions) Order 2004 (SI 2004/1899), Sch.2, art.26(2); Carriage by Air Act 1961, Sch.1, art.26(2), Sch.1A as inserted by SI 1999/1312, art.26(2), Sch.1B as inserted by SI 2002/263, art.31(2).

[For notes 255 and 256 substitute:]
[255] Carriage by Air Acts (Application of Provisions) Order 2004 (SI 2004/1899), Sch.2, art.35; Carriage by Air Act 1961, Sch.1, art.35, Sch.1A as inserted by SI 1999/1312, art.35, Sch.1B as inserted by SI 2002/263, art.52.
[256] Carriage by Air Acts (Application of Provisions) Order 2004 (SI 2004/1899), Sch.2, art.26(4); Carriage by Air Act 1961, Sch.1, art.26(4), Sch.1A as inserted by SI 1999/1312, art.26(4), Sch.1B as inserted by SI 2002/263, art.31(4).

Loss of cargo

35–068   *[For the first sentence of note 257 substitute: page [535]]*
Carriage by Air Acts (Application of Provisions) Order 2004 (SI 2004/1899), Sch.2, art.23; Carriage by Air Act 1961, Sch.1, art.23, Sch.1A as inserted by SI 1999/1312, art.23, Sch.1B as inserted by SI 2002/263, art.26.

[Note 257, last line]
SI 2002/263 is now in force.

[For the first sentence of note 258 substitute:]
Carriage by Air Acts (Application of Provisions) Order 2004 (SI 2004/1899), Sch.2, art.13(3); Carriage by Air Act 1961, Sch.1, art.13(3), Sch.1A as inserted by SI 1999/1312, art.13(3), Sch.1B as inserted by SI 2002/263, art.13(3).

Who can sue the carrier

35–069   *[For the first sentence of note 264 substitute: page [535]]*
Carriage by Air Acts (Application of Provisions) Order 2004 (SI 2004/1899), Sch.2, arts 13(3) and 24(1); Carriage by Air Act 1961, Sch.1, arts 13(3) and

24(1), Sch.1A as inserted by SI 1999/1312, arts 13(3) and 24(1), Sch.1B as inserted by SI 2002/263, arts 13(3) and 29.

[*For notes 266 and 267 substitute:*]   **35–070**
[266] Carriage by Air Acts (Application of Provisions) Order 2004 (SI 2004/1899), Sch.2, art.24(1); Carriage by Air Act 1961, Sch.1, art.24(1), Sch.1A as inserted by SI 1999/1312, art.24(1), Sch.1B as inserted by SI 2002/263, art.29.

[267] Carriage by Air Acts (Application of Provisions) Order 2004 (SI 2004/1899), Sch.2, art.24(2); Carriage by Air Act 1961, Sch.1, art.24(2), Sch.1A as inserted by SI 1999/1312, art.24(2), Sch.1B as inserted by SI 2002/263, art.29.

(e) *Delay to passengers, baggage or cargo*

Liability for delay

[*For notes 275 to 278 substitute: page* [537]]   **35–072**
[275] Carriage by Air Acts (Application of Provisions) Order 2004 (SI 2004/1899), Sch.2, art.19; Carriage by Air Act 1961, Sch.1, art.19, Sch.1A as inserted by SI 1999/1312, art.19, Sch.1B as inserted by SI 2002/263, art.19.

[276] Carriage by Air Acts (Application of Provisions) Order 2004 (SI 2004/1899), Sch.2, art.20; Carriage by Air Act 1961, Sch.1, art.20, Sch.1A as inserted by SI 1999/1312, art.20, Sch.1B as inserted by SI 2002/263, art.19.

[277] Carriage by Air Acts (Application of Provisions) Order 2004 (SI 2004/1899), Sch.2, art.20(2).

[278] Carriage by Air Acts (Application of Provisions) Order 2004 (SI 2004/1899), Sch.2, art.21; Carriage by Air Act 1961, Sch.1, art.21, Sch.1A as inserted by SI 1999/1312, art.21, Sch.1B as inserted by SI 2002/263, art.20.

[*For note 281 substitute:*]
[281] See I.A.T.A. recommended Conditions (PSC(24) 1724), Art.9.1.1.

3. Non-International carriage

Applicable rules

[*Substitute new paragraph: pages* [537]–[538]]   **35–073**
Applicable rules. The Conventions treated above regulate only international carriage. Carriage which is not international carriage as defined in any of the Conventions falls outside the Convention system. The applicable law is to be found in two sources. Community air carriers engaged in the carriage of persons or baggage are subject to European Parliament and Council Regulation No.889/2002,[282] which applies to national as well as international carriage. The liability of other air carriers, and Community air carriers engaged in the carriage of cargo, is governed by Schedule 1 to the Carriage by Air Acts (Application of Provisions) Order 2004,[283] which applies a modified version of the Montreal Convention 1999. Subject to the Regulation, the 2004 Order applies to all carriage by air other than carriage to which the Warsaw-Hague text, the MP4 Convention or the Montreal Convention 1999 applies, and Sch.1 applies to carriage which is not international carriage as defined in Schs 2 or 3 (applying the

original Warsaw Convention and that Convention as amended by Montreal Additional protocol No.1 of 1975).[283a] To avoid giving too extensive a scope to the predecessor provisions, for it was arguable that the provisions of the United Kingdom Order applied to internal carriage in other countries, the House of Lords held that their application is limited to (a) carriage in which the places of departure and destination and any agreed stopping places are all within the United Kingdom or other British territory; and (b) non-convention carriage involving a place of departure or destination or an agreed stopping place in a foreign state and a place of departure or destination or an agreed stopping place in the United Kingdom or other British territory.[284]

[282] See paras 35–011 et seq.
[283] SI 2004/1899. Note that art.2 is amended by SI 2004/1974.
[283a] Carriage by Air Acts (Application of Provisions) Order 2004 (SI 2004/1899), arts 3(1) and 4.
[284] Holmes v Bangladesh Biman Corp [1989] A.C. 1112.

The modified convention regime under Schedule 1 to the 1967 Order

35–074 [Substitute new paragraph: page [538]]

The modified convention regime under Schedule 1 to the 2004 Order. Only parts of the Montreal Convention 1999 are applied by the 2004 Order.[285] Chapter II (Arts 3–16) dealing with documentation is omitted except for parts of Art.3 requiring the carrier to deliver a baggage identification tag for each piece of checked baggage. Liability for death or injury is unlimited but if the carrier proves an absence of fault there is no liability beyond 100,000 SDRs.[286] There are no provisions regulating the carriage of mail and postal packages save for a provision that in these cases the carrier is liable only to the relevant postal administration and in accordance with the rules applicable to the relationship between carriers and postal administrations.[287]

[285] Carriage by Air Acts (Application of Provisions) Order 2004 (SI 2004/1899).
[286] ibid., Sch.1, art.21.
[287] ibid., Sch.1, art.2(2). See the Postal Services Act 2000, s.90; American Express Co v British Airways Board [1983] 1 W.L.R. 701; Post Office v British World Airlines Ltd [2000] 1 All E.R. (Comm.) 532.

CHAPTER 36

CARRIAGE BY LAND

2. INTERNAL CARRIAGE

(a) *Goods*

(i) *Common and Private Carriers*

The extinction of the common carrier

[*Delete "the Strategic Rail Authority" and the accompanying note from the second sentence: page* [545]]   **36–010**

[*Add note 54a at the end of the fourth sentence: page* [545]]
54a See McBain, "Time to abolish the common carrier" [2005] J.B.L. 545.

(iv) *Contractual Liability*

Construction of contracts

36–028   *[Add to note 133 after second sentence: page [553]]*
In *Frans Maas (UK) Ltd v Samsung Electronics (UK) Ltd* [2004] EWHC 1502 (Comm); [2004] All E.R. (D) 362, the court held that the limitation provision under the BIFA Conditions was reasonable.

(v) *Liability in Tort*

Liability in tort

36–044   *[Add to the end of note 258: page [565]]*
As to the employer's vicarious liability for the acts of his employees, see *Frans Maas (UK) Ltd v Samsung Electronics (UK) Ltd* [2004] EWHC 1502 (Comm); [2004] All E.R. (D) 362.

[Add to the end of note 264: page [566]]
HSBC Rail (UK) Ltd v Network Rail Infrastructure Ltd [2005] EWHC 403 (Comm).

(b) *Passengers*

Common carriers

36–054   *[Delete "the Strategic Rail Authority" from the third sentence: page [571]]*

3. International Carriage

(a) *Introduction*

Modification to COTIF: the Vilnius Protocol

36–080   *[Delete the second and third sentences of the text, and add to text after the fourth sentence: page [585]]*
By the Railways (Convention on International Carriage by Rail) Regulations 2005,[435a] the Vilnius Protocol was implemented as part of the law of the United Kingdom.

[435a] SI 2005/2092.

[Delete the final sentence of the text: page [586]]

Convention for Carriage of Passengers and Luggage by Road

36–082   *[Delete the fourth to eighth sentences and substitute: pages [586]–[587]]*
The possibility of signature and ratification grows remote, however, given that the United Kingdom's implementing legislation in respect of the CVR (the

Carriage of Passengers by Road Act 1974) was repealed by the Statute Law (Repeals) Act 2004, s.1(1) and Sch.1, Pt 14.

(b) *Goods by Rail*

[*Delete these paragraphs and the accompanying notes and substitute: pages* [587]–[602]]

**36–084—
36–119**

Scope of the Uniform Rules (CIM) under Appendix B to COTIF.[452] CIM regulates the form and conditions of the contract of carriage of goods by rail, the performance of the contract, its modification, the disposal of the goods being carried, liability for loss, damage and delay, compensation and enforcement of claims by action.

36–084

[452] See above para.36–078.

Application of CIM. CIM applies to every contract of carriage of goods by rail for reward when the place of taking over of the goods and the place designated for delivery are situated in two different Member States, irrespective of the place of business and the nationality of the parties to the contract of carriage.[453] It follows that CIM will apply even though the carriage is performed through the territory of a non-Member State[454] and that CIM will not apply if the place of taking over and the place of delivery are in the same State even though the carriage is performed through the territory of another State. CIM will also apply to contracts of carriage of goods by rail where only one of the place of taking over or place of delivery are in a Member State provided the parties to the contract agree that CIM will apply.[455] CIM will further apply where the international carriage is the subject of a single contract which contract includes carriage by road or internal inland waterway as a supplement to the trans-frontier carriage by rail or carriage by sea or trans-frontier inland waterway if the latter services are listed in accordance with Art.24 of COTIF.[456] However, CIM will not apply where the carriage is performed between stations situated on the territory of neighbouring States, when the infrastructure of the stations is managed by one or more infrastructure managers subject only to one of those States.[457] Any stipulation in the contract of carriage which, directly or indirectly, derogates from CIM shall be null and void, but such nullity shall not operate to nullify the other provisions of the contract.[457a]

36–085

[453] Art.1(1).
[454] *Azienda Autonoma Ferrovie dello Stato v La Pace* 11 E.T.L. 137 (1976) (Corte di Cassazione Civile, Italy).
[455] Art.1(2).
[456] Art.1(3), 1(4). As to rail-road traffic, see also CMR, Art.2(1) and para.36–122 below.
[457] Art.1(6).
[457a] Art.5.

Interpretation of the Convention. Whilst there have been no English decisions on the interpretation of CIM, some decisions of the courts in the Continental parties to the unmodified Convention have been reported. In view of the

36–086

similarity of the provisions regarding the carrier's liability and the carrier's exemptions from liability between CIM and the Geneva Convention on the Contract for the International Carriage of Goods by Road (CMR),[458] the reported decisions on the interpretation of CMR are often of assistance in the interpretation of CIM.

[458] Some of these decisions have been reported in such periodicals as *European Transport Law* (E.T.L.) and *Lloyds Maritime and Commercial Law Quarterly* (L.M.C.L.Q.).

36–087   **The carrier's role.** Under the contract of carriage, the carrier undertakes to carry the goods consigned for reward to the place of destination and to deliver them at the destination to the consignee.[459] For this service, the carrier is entitled to the payment by the consignor of the carriage charge, customs duties and other costs.[460]

[459] Art.6(1).
[460] Art.10(1).

36–088   **Consignment note.** CIM requires the contract of carriage to be confirmed by a consignment note which accords with a uniform model.[461] The uniform model is to be established by international associations of carriers in agreement with customers' associations and relevant customs authorities.[462] The consignment note is *prima facie* evidence of the conclusion and conditions of the contract and the taking over of the goods being carried.[463] CIM specifies a number of formal requirements for the consignment note, stipulating the particulars which the consignment note must contain (*e.g.* places of issue, taking over and delivery, names of consignor, carrier and consignee, and details of the goods to be carried), the responsibility for which largely falls on the consignor.[464] However, the absence, irregularity or loss of the consignment note shall not affect the existence or validity of the contract which the Convention emphasises shall remain subject to CIM.[465] One consignment note shall be issued for each consignment and, unless the contracting parties agree otherwise, must not relate to more than one wagon load.[466] CIM contemplates that there will be two copies of the consignment note, the duplicate being given to the consignor.[467] CIM provides that the consignment note will not have effect as a bill of lading.[468]

[461] Art.6(2).
[462] Art.6(8).
[463] Art.12(1).
[464] Arts 7, 8.
[465] Art.6(2).
[466] Art.6(6).
[467] Art.6(4).
[468] Art.6(5).

36–089   **Loading, Carriage and Delivery.** CIM contemplates two types of consignments which may be carried by rail, namely packages and full wagon-loads. Unless the parties otherwise agree, the carrier is responsible for the loading and unloading of packages and the consignor is responsible for the loading of a wagon load and the consignee is responsible for the unloading of the wagon load.[469] The consignor is responsible for any defects in the packing of the goods unless the defects were apparent to the carrier on taking them over and the carrier made no reservations concerning the defects.[470] On arrival at the destination, the carrier must deliver the goods to the consignee and hand over the consignment note against the provision of a receipt and the payment of sums outstanding under the carriage contract.[471] Delivery also may be effected by the handing over of the goods to customs authorities, or the deposit of the goods for storage with the railway, with a forwarding agent or in a public warehouse, provided that such delivery is permitted by the provisions in force at the destination station.[472]

[469] Art.13(1).

[470] Art.14.

[471] Art.17(1). In Antwerp, it has been held that the consignee named in the consignment note who acts as agent for the final consignee will become a party to the contract by acceptance of the goods or the consignment note: *Sobelgra NV v Nationale Maatschappij der Belgische Spoorwegen (NMBS)* (1997) 33 E.T.L. 714.

[472] Art.17(2).

Modification of the contract. The consignor shall be entitled to dispose of the   **36–090** goods and to modify the contract of carriage by giving "subsequent orders". Such orders may require the carrier to delay delivery of the goods or to deliver the goods to a consignee or to a destination other than the one identified in the consignment note.[473] The modification of the contract appears to be limited to these matters and must be effected by the consignor producing to the carrier the duplicate consignment note on which the modifications must be entered.[474] Such modifications must be "possible, lawful and reasonable", must not interfere with the normal working of the carrier's undertaking nor prejudice the consignors or consignees of other consignments and must not have the effect of splitting the consignment.[475] The consignee will acquire the right to modify the contract of carriage once the consignment note is drawn up, unless the consignor reserves the right to himself or herself on the consignment note.[476] The consignor will lose the right to modify the contract when the consignee has acquired the right of modification or has accepted from the carrier the consignment note or the goods or has demanded both.[477] Similarly, the consignee will lose the right of modification when he or she has requested or accepted the consignment note or the goods. Additionally, the consignee will lose the right when he or she has instructed the carrier to deliver the goods to another person, who requests the carrier to hand over the consignment note and deliver the goods; that person will not be entitled to modify the contract.[478] The consignor may have a right of stoppage in transit *vis à vis* the consignee pursuant to the Sale of Goods Act 1979 if English law governs the contract between them.[479]

[473] Art.18(1).

[474] Art.19(1). If the carrier accepts the consignor's orders to deliver the goods to some person other than the consignee named in the consignment note without requiring the duplicate consignment note to be produced, it will be liable for any loss or damage arising from that omission: Art.19(7); *SA Nicolas Corman v SNCF* 11 E.T.L. 120 (1976) (Court of Appeal, Paris).

[475] Art.19(3), 19(4).

[476] Art.18(3).

[477] Art.18(2).

478 Art.18(4), 18(5).
479 See below paras 43–353–43–365.

36–091   **Prevention of carriage or delivery.** If the carriage of the goods has been prevented by circumstances,[480] the carrier must decide whether it is preferable (presumably in the interests of the person entitled to dispose of the goods) to modify the route or to ask the person entitled for instructions.[481] If it is impossible to continue the carriage or to effect delivery, the person entitled shall be asked for his or her instructions. If the carrier is unable to obtain instructions, he or she shall take such steps which he or she considers to be in the best interests of the person entitled.[482] If circumstances exist which prevent delivery, the carrier must ask the consignor or (if the consignee has modified the contract) the consignee for instructions.[483] If the consignee refuses delivery, the consignor may give instructions, even if he or she is unable to produce the duplicate consignment note.[484] If circumstances alter permitting delivery before the receipt of instructions, the carrier shall deliver the goods to the consignee.[485] If the goods are of a perishable nature or if the carrier does not receive instructions, the carrier may sell the goods and, after deducting relevant costs, place the proceeds of sale at the disposal of the person entitled.[486]

480 The carrier will not be liable for any loss of or damage to the goods or delay caused by circumstances which are unavoidable by the carrier: Art.23(2).
481 Art.20(1).
482 Art.20(2).
483 Arts 21(1), 21(4).
484 Art.21(3).
485 Art.21(2).
486 Arts 22(3), 22(4).

36–092   **Loss, damage and delay.** The carrier is liable for loss (total or partial) of the goods, damage and delay (*i.e.* for exceeding the transit periods[487]) unless he or she can prove an applicable exception to that liability.[488] The carrier is liable for his or her own employees and for any other persons, including the managers of the railway infrastructure on which the carriage is performed, whose services he or she uses in the performance of the carriage.[489] There are two kinds of exceptions. The first type arises where the relevant loss, damage or delay was caused by (1) the fault of the person entitled; (2) an order given by the person entitled other than as a result of the fault of the carrier; (3) inherent defect in the goods (decay, wastage, etc.)[490]; or (4) circumstances which the carrier could not avoid and the consequences of which he or she was not able to prevent.[491] The burden of proving any of these is on the carrier.[492] Thus far, the exceptions are very similar to those applicable to the common carrier at common law. But the second kind of exception comprises circumstances when loss or damage arises from the special risks inherent in one or more of the following circumstances: (a) carriage in open wagons when that has been agreed; (b) absence or inadequacy of packaging; (c) loading by the consignor or unloading by the consignee; (d) the nature of certain kinds of goods which particularly exposes them to loss or damage, especially through breakage, rust, interior and spontaneous decay, desiccation or wastage; (e) irregular, incorrect or incomplete description or numbering of packages; (f) the carriage of live animals; and (g) the carriage of consignments which, with the parties' agreement, must be accompanied by an attendant.[493] If the carrier establishes that loss or damage could be attributed to one or more of these exceptions, this is rebuttably presumed, unless in (a) above there is an abnormal shortage or a loss of a package.[494] If the goods are not delivered to the consignee or held at his or her disposal within 30 days after the expiry of the transit period, they are presumed to be lost.[495]

[487] The transit period is that which is agreed between the carrier and consignor or, in the absence of agreement, as specified in Art.16.

[488] A failure to comply with the instructions of the person entitled to dispose of the goods during carriage may also render the carrier liable for loss or damage caused thereby: Art.19(6). There is a facility by which the carrier may seek an exception to liability for losses arising by specified causes in respect of rail-sea traffic, provided that the relevant Member State made such provision in the listed services set out in Art.24(1) of COTIF.

[489] Art.40.

[490] Where there is wastage in transit of goods which, by reason of their nature, is caused by the sole fact of carriage, the carrier will be liable only to the extent that the wastage exceeds specified allowances: Art.31.

[491] Art.23(2).

[492] Art.25(1).

[493] Art.23(3). The unmodified Convention included an additional exception in respect of loss caused by a failure to comply with customs formalities. Such matters are now regulated by Art.15. The carrier is under a general duty to maintain its rolling stock put at a customer's disposal in good condition: *NMBS v NV Fonciere Carner* 11 E.T.L. 780 (1976) (Hof van Beroep, Brussels). See also Art.24 which concerns railway vehicles consigned as goods.

[494] Arts 25(2), 25(3).

[495] Art.29(1).

Ascertainment of loss or damage. Upon delivery, the person entitled may ask the carrier for an opportunity to examine the goods to determine the existence of any loss or damage. Any failure by the carrier to permit such an examination will entitle the person entitled to the goods to refuse to accept the goods, even when he or she has accepted the consignment note and/or paid the outstanding charges.[496] In the event of the discovery, presumption or allegation of partial loss of or damage to the goods, the carrier must, without delay prepare, if possible in the presence of the person entitled, a report concerning the condition of the goods and the nature, extent, cause and time of the loss or damage.[497] If the person entitled does not accept the report's findings, he or she can insist upon the circumstances surrounding the loss or damage to be investigated by an expert.[498]

36–093

[496] Art.17(4).

[497] Art.42(1).

[498] Art.42(3).

Upper financial limits of liability. The carrier's liability for loss of the goods, whether total or partial, is limited to 17 units of account[499] per kilogram of gross mass short,[500] unless the consignor and carrier agree that the consignor shall declare in the consignment note a value for the goods exceeding this limit or a

36–094

special interest in delivery by entering an amount in figures on the consignment note, in which case compensation can be claimed up to the value or amount declared.[501] The compensation is calculated by reference to the commodity exchange quoted price or current market price or the usual value of the goods of the same kind and quality at the time and place at which the goods were taken over for the carriage.[502] The carrier must also refund the carriage charges, customs duties and other expenses paid in respect of the missing goods.[503] The carrier's liability for delay (*i.e.* for exceeding the transit periods) depends on whether actual loss or damage was thus caused. If actual loss or damage resulted from the delay, the compensation may not exceed four times the amount of the carriage charges, although the total compensation for the loss or damage caused by delay and otherwise may not exceed the compensation payable for a total loss.[504] The carrier's liability for damage is for the amount by which the goods have been diminished in value, but may not exceed the amount payable in respect of loss.[505] The maximum limits of compensation for loss, damage or delay are removed altogether if it was due to the carrier's wilful misconduct (namely, an act or omission which the carrier has committed either with intent to cause such loss or damage, or recklessly and with knowledge that such loss or damage would probably result).[506] The claimant may recover interest on the compensation payable at the rate of 5 per cent per annum from the time a claim, together with supporting documents, is submitted in accordance with the CIM Uniform Rules,[507] or failing such a claim, from the time of the commencement of legal proceedings in respect of the claim.[508]

[499] However, the carrier is free to assume a greater liability: Art.5. The unit of account is the Special Drawing Right (SDR) defined by the International Monetary Fund (IMF): COTIF, Art.9(1). Its value is expressed in the national currency of a State Member of the IMF in accordance with IMF methods of valuation: Art.9(2). States which are not Members of the IMF shall determine their own methods of calculating the value of the SDR: if their legislation does not permit this, the unit of account is deemed to be the equivalent of three gold francs, each gold franc weighing 1031 of a gramme and of millesimal fineness 900: Arts 9(3), 9(4). In any event the conversion of the gold franc must express in national currency a value approximating closely to the value calculated by reference to the IMF methods of valuation. In the case of judicial proceedings or arbitration in the United Kingdom, the SDR is converted into its sterling equivalent on the day of the judgment or award: Railways (Convention on International Carriage by Rail) Regulations 2005 (SI 2005/2092), reg.7.

[500] Art.30(2).

[501] Arts 34, 35.

[502] Art.30(1).

[503] Art.30(4). The charges do not include charges which would have been incurred in the event that the carriage was performed in accordance with the contract, would have contributed to the value of the goods at the destination, and which were not incurred as a result of the incident giving rise to the claim (*Anon.*, Bundesgerichtshof, June 26, 2003, (2004) 39 E.T.L. 93). The claimant cannot recover any additional duty or VAT payable in respect of the goods which do not find themselves at their destination: *Anon.*, Cass. Paris, January 28, 1975; *cf. James Buchanan & Co Ltd v Babco Forwarding and Shipping (UK) Ltd* [1978] 1 Lloyd's Rep. 119; *contra Anon.*, Supreme Court of Denmark May 4, 1987 (1994) 29 E.T.L. 360 (CMR). See para.36–132, n.729 below.

[504] Arts 33(1), 33(2), 33(3).

[505] Arts 32(1), 32(2). Under the unmodified Convention, in the event of damage by deterioration, the carrier's liability is calculated under the provisions concerning damage not delay: *Anon.* 11 E.T.L. 787 (1976) (Bundesgerichtshof). Under Art.33(4), in the case of damage to goods, not resulting from the transit period being exceeded, the compensation payable under Art.33(1) shall, where appropriate, be payable in addition to that provided for in Art.32.

[506] Art.36.
[507] Art.43. If no supporting documents are provided within a reasonable time so that the amount of the claim can be finally settled, no interest shall accrue between the expiry of the time allotted and the actual submission of such documents: Art.37(3).
[508] Art.37(2).

Successive and substitute carriers. If carriage is governed by a single contract and is performed by several successive carriers, each carrier, by the very act of taking over the goods with the consignment note, shall become a party to the contract of carriage in accordance with the terms of the contract and shall assume the obligations arising therefrom. Each carrier shall be responsible in respect of carriage over the entire route up to delivery.[509] Where the carrier has entrusted all or part of the performance of the carriage to a substitute carrier, the carrier shall remain liable in respect of the entire carriage. The CIM provisions governing the liability of the carrier shall also apply to the liability of the substitute carrier for the carriage performed by him or her.[510] Actions based on the contract of carriage may be brought only against the first carrier, the last carrier or the carrier who performed that part of the carriage on which the event giving rise to the claim occurred.[511] A successive carrier may be sued if that carrier has been named, with his or her consent, in the consignment note as the carrier who must deliver the goods, even if that carrier has not received the goods or the consignment note.[512]

36–095

[509] Art.26.
[510] Arts 27(1), 27(2).
[511] Art.45(1).
[512] Art.45(2).

Claims. Claims against the carrier relating to the contract of carriage must be made in writing only by those persons who have the right to claim.[513] The consignor may bring an action against the carrier until such time as the consignee has taken possession of the consignment note or accepted the goods or demanded that the consignment note be handed over and that the goods be delivered or asserted his or her right to modify the contract.[514] From that time, the consignee may bring an action against the carrier unless and until the person to whom the consignee has ordered the carrier to deliver the goods has accepted the consignment note or the goods or has demanded both.[515] Actions based on CIM may be brought in the Member States designated by the parties' agreement or where the defendant is domiciled or resident or where the goods were taken over by the carrier or where the place designated for delivery is situated.[516]

36–096

[513] Arts 43(1), 43(2). The claim generally has to be supported by the consignment note: see Arts 43(3)–(6).
[514] Art.44(1)(a).
[515] Arts 44(1)(b), 44(2).
[516] Art.46(1).

Extinction of claims. Acceptance of the goods by the person entitled extinguishes all rights of action against the carrier arising from the contract of carriage in case of partial loss, damage or delay,[517] subject to four exceptions. First,

36–097

claims for partial loss or damage can be made if the damage was ascertained by the preparation of a report (unless the report was not prepared solely by reason of the carrier's fault).[518] Secondly, claims for loss or damage which is not apparent and not discovered until after acceptance can still be made, provided the person entitled to claim asks the carrier for a report within seven days of acceptance and proves that the loss or damage occurred between the time of taking over the goods for carriage and the time of delivery.[519] Thirdly, claims for delay in delivery can be made within 60 days of acceptance.[520] Fourthly, the claim is not extinguished if wilful misconduct can be proved.[521]

[517] Art.47(1).
[518] Art.47(2)(a).
[519] Art.47(2)(b). See Clarke, "Non-apparent damage to goods in transit" [1982] L.M.C.L.Q 533.
[520] Art.47(2)(c).
[521] Art.47(2)(d).

36–098   **Limitation of actions.** All actions arising from the contract of carriage are time-barred after one year, or two years in the case of, *inter alia*, wilful misconduct.[522] The period of limitation runs, in the case of partial loss, damage or delay in delivery, from the date of delivery; in the case of total loss, from the 30th day after the expiry of the transit period.[523] A written claim suspends the running of the period of limitation until such date as the carrier rejects the claim in writing.[524]

[522] Art.48(1).
[523] Art.48(2).
[524] Art.48(3).

(c) *Passengers, Luggage and Vehicles by Rail*

(i) *Application and Scope of the Convention*

36–099   **Scope of the Uniform Rules (CIV) under Appendix A to COTIF.** The CIV Uniform Rules regulate the making and performance of the contract of carriage of passengers, luggage and vehicles by rail, the liability of the rail carrier for death of, and personal injury to, passengers, for the failure to keep to the timetable, the liability of the passenger and the relations between carriers.

36–100   **Application of CIV.** CIV provides a unified set of rules to be applied to every contract of carriage of passengers by rail for reward or free of charge, when the place of departure and the place of destination are situated in two different Member States, irrespective of the domicile or the place of business and the nationality of the parties to the contract.[525] CIV applies also to international carriage pursuant to a single contract which includes carriage by road or by internal inland waterway or, provided that the services are provided for in Art.24(1) of COTIF, by sea or trans-frontier inland waterway.[526] CIV also applies, as far as the liability of the carrier in the case of death or personal injury is concerned, to persons accompanying a consignment whose carriage is effected in accordance with the CIM Uniform Rules.[527] As with CIM, CIV will not apply where the carriage is performed between stations situated on the territory of neighbouring States, when the infrastructure of the stations is managed by one or more infrastructure managers subject only to one of those States.[528] Any stipulation in the contract of carriage which, directly or indirectly, derogates from CIV shall be null and void, but such nullity shall not operate to nullify the other provisions of the contract.[529]

[525] Art.1(1).
[526] Arts 1(2), 1(3).
[527] Art.1(4).
[528] Art.1(5).
[529] Art.5.

Rail-sea carriage. As mentioned above, CIV applies to a single contract of international carriage by rail and sea provided that the carriage is performed on services listed pursuant to Art.24(1) of COTIF.[530] It should be noted, however, that, whilst CIV may in certain circumstances cover aspects of rail-sea carriage, legislation in the United Kingdom has provided that as far as English law is concerned, the terms of the Athens Convention relating to the Carriage of Passengers and their Luggage by Sea 1974 are applied to any contract for international carriage by sea under which a place in the United Kingdom is the place of departure or destination.[531] The Athens Convention enables carriers by sea to limit their liability in respect of the death of, or personal injury to, a passenger. The terms of the Athens Convention have also been applied to carriage by sea within the United Kingdom.[532] **36–101**

[530] Art.1(3).
[531] Merchant Shipping Act 1995, s.183. The Athens Convention came into force on April 30, 1987.
[532] Carriage of Passengers and their Luggage by Sea (Domestic Carriage) Order 1987 (SI 1987/670), which now takes effect as if made under the Merchant Shipping Act 1995, s.184. Under s.184(5), the term "contract of carriage" in the context of the Athens Convention excludes a contract which is not for reward.

The carrier's role. Under the contract of carriage, the carrier is obliged to carry the passenger and, where appropriate, the passenger's luggage and vehicle to the place of destination and to deliver the luggage and vehicle at the place of destination.[533] Subject to the terms of the contract, the carrier is entitled to advance payment of the carriage charge.[534] **36–102**

[533] Art.6(1).
[534] Arts 8(1), 19, 25.

(ii) Passengers and Hand Luggage

The passenger's rights. The passenger in possession of a valid ticket is entitled to be carried in accordance with the terms of the contract of carriage. The passenger is also entitled to take with him or her articles which can be handled **36–103**

easily (hand luggage), but it is the passenger's responsibility to supervise such hand luggage.[535] If a passenger is unable to produce a valid ticket, the carrier may require the passenger to pay a surcharge. If the passenger fails to pay the carriage charge or the surcharge, the carrier may require the passenger to discontinue the journey.[536] The carrier may also exclude a passenger from carriage or require a passenger to discontinue his or her journey, without refunding the carriage charge, if that passenger presents a danger for the safety and the good functioning of the operations of the rail operations or for the safety of the other passengers or if that passenger inconveniences other passengers in an intolerable manner.[537]

[535] Arts 12(1), 15.
[536] Art.9(1).
[537] Art.9(2).

36–104   **The ticket.** The contract of carriage must be confirmed by one or more tickets issued to the passenger. However, the absence, irregularity, or loss of the ticket shall not affect the existence or validity of the contract, which remains subject to the application of the CIV Uniform Rules.[538] The ticket is *prima facie* evidence of the making and contents of the contract of carriage.[539] The terms and conditions of the contract are those which are legally in force in each Member State. Such conditions will determine the form and content of tickets.[540] The ticket may be established in the form of electronic data registration, which can be transformed into legible written symbols.[541] However, the ticket must identify the carrier and must state that the carriage is subject to the CIV Uniform Rules.[542] It is incumbent on the passenger to ensure that on receipt of the ticket that it has been made out in accordance with his or her instructions.[543] If the ticket is not made out in the passenger's name, the ticket is transferable, provided that the journey has not yet begun.[544]

[538] Art.6(2). This is subject to the carrier's right, as set out in Art.9, to demand a surcharge in the event of the non-production of the ticket and to require the passenger to discontinue the journey if the carriage charge or surcharge is not paid.
[539] Art.6(3).
[540] Arts 3(c), 7(1).
[541] Art.7(5).
[542] Art.7(2).
[543] Art.7(3).
[544] Art.7(4).

36–105   **Liability for death and personal injury.** In general under CIV the carrier is liable for damage resulting from the death of, or personal injury or any other physical or mental harm to, a passenger, when the damage is caused by an accident arising out of the operation of the railway and happening while the passenger is in, entering or alighting from, railway vehicles.[545] In the event of death, the carrier is liable for damages comprising the necessary costs following the death (including transport and funeral expenses) and is liable to the passenger's dependents, whom the passenger was legally obliged to maintain, for the loss of support.[546] In the case of personal injury (whether or not it leads to death), or other physical or mental harm, the carrier is liable for damage comprising any necessary costs (including medical treatment and transport expenses) and compensation for financial loss due to incapacity to work or increased needs.[547]

[545] Art.26(1).
[546] Arts 27(1), 27(2). National law shall govern the rights of action of those whom the passenger was maintaining without a legal obligation so to do: Art.27(2).
[547] Art.28. National law shall govern the right to claim damages other than those set out in Arts 27 and 28: Art.29.

Fatal accidents. Regulation 5 of the Railways (Convention on International Carriage by Rail) Regulations 2005[548] provides that where under the Convention a person has a right of action in respect of the death of a passenger by virtue of his being a person whom the passenger was under a legally enforceable duty to maintain, no action in respect of the passenger's death may be brought for the benefit of that person under the Fatal Accidents Act 1976, although actions under that Act may be brought for the benefit of any other person. The Regulations further provide that in actions brought under CIV the same benefit shall be excluded in the assessment of damages as would be excluded under s.4 of the Fatal Accidents Act 1976. Where separate proceedings can be brought under CIV and under the Fatal Accidents Act 1976, a court may, in assessing damages under the 1976 Act, take account of any damages awarded in proceedings under the Convention. **36–106**

[548] SI 2005/2092.

Carrier's exemptions from liability for death and personal injury. The carrier is relieved of liability for death or personal injury (a) if the accident was caused by circumstances not connected with the operation of the railway and which the carrier, despite the exercise of the care required in the circumstances, could not avoid and the consequences of which he or she could not prevent[549]; (b) to the extent that the accident was due to the passenger's fault[550]; and (c) if the accident was caused by the behaviour of a third party which the carrier, despite the exercise of the care required in the circumstances, could not avoid and the consequences of which it could not prevent.[551] If the accident is due to the behaviour of a third party and if the carrier is in any event not entirely relieved of liability, he or she shall be liable in full up to the limits imposed by CIV.[552] **36–107**

[549] Art.26(2)(a).
[550] Art.26(2)(b).
[551] Art.26(2)(c). Another undertaking using the same railway infrastructure shall not be considered as a third party for the purposes of this provision.
[552] Art.26(3).

Liability for delay. The carrier is liable to the passenger for loss or damage resulting from the fact that the journey cannot, or could not reasonably, be continued on the same day because of a cancellation, the late running of a train or a missed connection. The damages for which the carrier is liable comprises the reasonable costs of accommodation and the reasonable costs of notifying persons expecting the passenger.[553] The carrier will be exempt from such liability in **36–108**

similar circumstances exempting the carrier from liability for death and personal injury.[554]

[553] Art.32(1). National law shall govern the passenger's right to claim other heads of damage: Art.32(3).
[554] Art.32(2). See para.36–107 above.

36–109   **Liability for hand luggage.** In the event that the passenger dies or sustains a personal injury, the carrier shall also be liable for loss or damage resulting from the total or partial loss of, or damage to, hand luggage.[555] In other cases, the carrier shall not be liable for hand luggage the supervision of which is the responsibility of the passenger, unless the loss or damage was caused by the fault of the carrier.[556]

[555] Art.33(1).
[556] Art.33(2).

36–110   **Upper financial limits of liability.** The amount of damages to be awarded in cases of death or personal injury under CIV are to be determined in accordance with national law. The limit of damages per passenger is fixed, for the purposes of the CIV Uniform Rules, at 175,000 units of account, where national law provides for an upper limit of less than that amount.[557] There is no specified financial limit of liability for delay. Where the carrier is liable for damage to, or loss of, hand luggage, the limit of compensation is 1,400 units of account per passenger.[558] The liability of the carrier is, however, not limited at all if the loss or damage results from an act or omission which the carrier has committed either with intent to cause such loss or damage or recklessly with the knowledge that such loss or damage probably will result.[559]

[557] Art.30(2). As to "units of account", see para.36–094, n.499 above.
[558] Art.34.
[559] Art.48.

(iii) *Registered Luggage and Vehicles*

36–111   **Transport documents.** A passenger may consign articles as registered luggage in accordance with the application general conditions of carriage.[560] The carrier's obligations concerning the forwarding of registered luggage must be established by a luggage registration voucher issued to the passenger. The absence, irregularity or loss of the voucher shall not affect the existence or validity of the contract of carriage, which remains subject to the application of the CIV Uniform Rules.[561] The voucher is *prima facie* evidence of the registration of the luggage and the contents of the contract of carriage.[562] The form and content of the voucher are determined in accordance with the general conditions of carriage.[563] The voucher must identify the carrier and must state that the carriage is subject to the CIV Uniform Rules.[564] It is incumbent on the passenger to ensure that on receipt of the voucher that it has been made out in accordance with his or her instructions.[565] Similar provisions exist in respect of vehicles, for which a carriage voucher must establish the carrier's contractual obligations.[566]

[560] Art.12(2).
[561] Arts 16(1), 16(2). As to the responsibility of successive and substitute carriers, see Arts 38, 39.
[562] Art.16(3).
[563] Art.17(1).
[564] Art.17(2).
[565] Art.17(3).
[566] Arts 24, 25.

Loss, damage and delay. The carrier is liable for loss or damage resulting **36–112** from the total or partial loss of, or damage to, registered luggage or the vehicle carried between the time of taking over by the carrier and the time of delivery as well as from delay in delivery.[567] The carrier will be relieved from this liability to the extent that the loss, damage or delay was caused by a fault of the passenger, an order given by the passenger other than as a result of the carrier's fault, an inherent defect or circumstances which the carrier could not avoid and the consequences of which he or she was unable to prevent.[568] Further, the carrier will be relieved of liability to the extent that the loss or damage arises from the special risks inherent in (a) the absence or inadequacy of packing, (b) the special nature of the luggage or vehicle, and/or (c) the consignment as luggage of articles not acceptable for carriage.[569] The person entitled to the luggage or vehicle may consider the luggage or vehicle lost, without adducing further proof, if has not been delivered within 14 days after a valid request for delivery has been made.[570]

[567] Arts 36(1), 47. It is rebuttably presumed that when the carrier took over the registered luggage that it was apparently in good condition and that the number and mass of the items of luggage corresponded to the entries on the voucher: Art.16(4). Delivery of the luggage or vehicle must be effected on surrender of the voucher: Art.22(1).
[568] Arts 36(2), 47. The carrier bears the relevant burden of proof: Art.37(1).
[569] Arts 36(3), 47. The carrier bears the initial burden of proof, which thereafter falls upon the claimant: Art.37(2).
[570] Art.40(1).

Upper financial limits of liability. The amount of the carrier's liability for **36–113** loss of registered luggage, whether total or partial, depends on whether or not the passenger establishes the amount of loss or damage suffered. If the amount of loss is proved, the loss is limited to 80 units of account per kilogram of gross mass short or 1200 units of account per item of luggage; if not, the carrier must pay liquidated damages of 20 units of account per kilogram of gross mass short or 300 units of account per item of luggage.[571] The carrier must also refund the carriage charges.[572] Liability for damage is for the amount by which the luggage has been diminished in value, but may not exceed the amount payable in respect of loss.[573] As regards delay, if the passenger proves that he or she suffered loss or damage, the maximum amount payable as compensation is 0.80 units of account per kilogram of gross mass of the luggage or 14 units of account per item of luggage delivered late; but if loss or damage is not proved, the measure of damages is liquidated at 0.14 units of account per kilogram of gross mass of the luggage or 2.80 units of account per item of luggage delivered late.[574] The maximum limits of compensation for loss, damage or delay are removed altogether if it was due to the act or omission of the carrier which was done with the intent to cause loss or damage or recklessly with the knowledge that such loss or damage probably will result.[575] As regards vehicles, compensation for loss of or damage to the vehicle shall be calculated on the basis of the usual value of the vehicle subject to a limit of 8,000 units of account[576]; compensation for proven loss or damage resulting from delay is limited to the amount of the carriage charge.[577]

[571] Art.41(1).
[572] Art.41(2).
[573] Art.42.
[574] Art.43(1).
[575] Art.48.
[576] Art.45.
[577] Art.44.

(iv) Claims

36–114   **Claims against carriers.** A claim relating to liability for death or personal injury must be addressed in writing to the carrier against whom an action may be brought. Where successive carriers performed the carriage under a single contract, the claim may also be made against the first or the last carrier as well as the carrier who has his or her principal place of business or whose agency concluded the contract in the State where the passenger is domiciled or resident.[578] An action in respect of death or personal injury may be brought only against the carrier (including substitute carriers) who was bound pursuant to the contract of carriage to provide the service of carriage in the course of which the accident happened.[579] Other claims based on the contract of carriage may be brought only against the first carrier, the last carrier or the carrier who performed that part of the carriage on which the event giving rise to the claim occurred.[580] A successive carrier may be sued if that carrier has been named, with his or her consent, in the voucher as the carrier who must deliver the luggage or vehicle, even if that carrier has not received them or the voucher.[581] Actions based on CIV may be brought before the courts or tribunals as agreed between the parties or in those Member States in which the defendant is domiciled or resident or has his or her principal place of business or agency which concluded the contract.[582]

[578] Art.55(1).
[579] Arts 26(5), 56(1).
[580] Arts 55(2), 56(2).
[581] Art.56(3).
[582] Art.57(1).

36–115   **Extinction of claims.** A claimant loses his right of action based on the carrier's liability for death or personal injury if he or she does not give notice of the accident to one of the carriers to which a claim may be presented within 12 months of his or her becoming aware of the loss or damage.[583] Nonetheless, the right of action is not lost if (a) notice has been given to one of the carriers against a claim brought within the relevant period; (b) the carrier who is liable has learned of the accident within the relevant period in some other way; (c) notice of the accident has not been given, or has been given late, as a result of circumstances for which the claimant is not responsible; or (d) the claimant proves that the accident was caused by fault of the carrier.[584] As regards other claims, acceptance of the luggage by the person entitled extinguishes all rights of action against the carrier arising from the contract of carriage in case of partial loss, damage or delay,[585] subject to four exceptions. First, claims for partial loss or damage can be made if the damage was ascertained in accordance with CIV.[586] Secondly, claims for loss or damage which is not apparent and not discovered until after acceptance can still be made, provided the person entitled to claim asks the carrier for ascertainment within three days of acceptance and proves that the loss or damage occurred between the time of taking over and the time of delivery.[587] Thirdly, claims for delay in delivery can be made within 21 days of acceptance.[588] Fourthly, the claim is not extinguished if the person entitled proves that the loss or damage was caused by fault on the part of the carrier.[589]

[583] Art.58(1).
[584] Art.58(2).
[585] Art.59(1). It is assumed that this provision applies alike to vehicles.
[586] Arts 54, 59(2)(a).
[587] Art.59(2)(b).
[588] Art.59(2)(c).
[589] Art.59(2)(d). *cf.* CIM, Art.47(2)(d).

Limitation of actions. Actions for damages brought under CIV based on the **36–116** carrier's liability for death or personal injury are time-barred in the case of a passenger who has sustained an accident, three years from the day after the accident. In the case of other claimants, actions are barred three years from the day after the death of the passenger or five years from the day after the accident, whichever is the earlier.[590] As regards all other claims, the period of limitation shall be one year (or two years in the case of wilful misconduct) (a) in the case of compensation for loss, from the 14th day after the person entitled calls for delivery, (b) in the case of compensation for partial loss, damage or delay in delivery, from the day when delivery took place, and (c) in all other cases involving the carriage of passengers, from the day of expiry of the validity of the ticket.[591] When a claim is made in writing to the carrier, the limitation period is suspended until the carrier against whom the claim has been made rejects it in writing.[592]

[590] Art.60(1).
[591] Arts 60(2), 60(3).
[592] Art.60(4).

(d) *Goods by Road*

Delivery

36–127   *[Add at the end of note 686: page* [609]]
In *Anon.*, Oberster Gerichtshof-Österreich, May 16, 2002, (2003) 38 E.T.L. 512, it was held that delivery was not prevented if the carrier was able to carry the goods to the destination by alternative means.

The carrier's exemptions from liability: Article 17(2)

36–129   *[Add to the end of note 700: page* [611]]
In *Datec Electronic Holdings Ltd v United Parcels Service Ltd* [2005] EWHC 221 (Comm); [2005] 1 Lloyd's Rep. 470, at [127], the court held that the consignment of a package worth more than U$50,000, pursuant to a contract which provided that the value of a package may not exceed US$50,000, did not constitute a wrongful act for the purposes of art.17(2).

[Add at the end of note 708: page [612]]
Anon., Oberster Gerichtshof-Österreich, February 13, 2003, (2004) 39 E.T.L. 244.

Upper financial limits of liability and measure of damages

36–132   *[Add to note 729, line 11, after "para.98": page* [616]]
Anon., Bundesgerichtshof, June 26, 2003, (2004) 39 E.T.L. 93.

[Add to note 738, line 1, after "Clarke op.cit. para.101": page [617]]
Datec Electronic Holdings Ltd v United Parcels Service Ltd [2005] EWHC 221 (Comm); [2005] 1 Lloyd's Rep. 470, [67]–[68].

Interest

36–134   *[Add to the end of note 742: page* [618]]
Art.27 also applies to claims under Art.37: *Anon.*, Bundesgerichtshof, November 27, 2003, (2004) 39 E.T.L. 517.

Reservations at delivery and extinction of claims

36–144   *[Add note 786a at the end of the third sentence of the text: page* [625]]
Anon., Oberster Gerichtshof-Österreich, September 19, 2002, (2004) 39 E.T.L. 400.

Limitation of actions

36–145   *[Add to the end of note 793: page* [626]]
See also *Frigo Express bvba v Frigo Traffic Company nv* (2004) 39 E.T.L. 521 (Hof van Cassatie van België) (claim by carrier against sub-carrier); *Transports*

Collomb Muret auto SA v Panini France SA (2004) 39 E.T.L. 531 (Cour de Cassation de France) (claim by carrier against consignee).

[Add at the end of note 799: page [627]]
See also *NV Optitrade ea v NV Cat Benelux* (2004) 39 E.T.L. 407 (Hof van Beroep te Antwerpen).

Jurisdiction

[Delete "the Brussels Convention on Jurisdiction . . . 1968" from the second sentence and substitute: page [628]]   **36–147**
Council Regulation (EC) No.44/2001

[Add to the end of note 809: page [629]]
Anon., Oberster Gerichtshof-Österreich, (2003) 38 E.T.L. 656, 658, 661; *DFDS Transport A/S v Dieter Mehrholz Internationale Transporte* (2004) 39 E.T.L. 74 (Supreme Court of Denmark); *Royal & Sun Alliance Insurance Plc v MK Digital Fze (Cyprus) Ltd* [2005] EWHC 1408 (Comm), at [55]–[69].

[Add at the beginning of note 810: page [629]]
Andrea Merzario Ltd v Internationale Spedition Leitner Gesellschaft mbH [2001] EWCA Civ 61; [2001] 1 Lloyd's Rep. 490.

[Add at the end of the second sentence of note 810: page [629]]
Royal & Sun Alliance Insurance Plc v MK Digital Fze (Cyprus) Ltd [2005] EWHC 1408 (Comm), at [55]–[69].

[Add before the final sentence of note 812: page [629]]
In *Blue Water Shipping A/S v Melship Eesti OÜ* (2000) 35 E.T.L. 772, the Supreme Court of Denmark held that Art.39 referred to the residence of the defendant successive carrier and not the claimant successive carrier.

No contracting out

[Add to the end of the second sentence of note 817: page [629]]   **36–149**
Datec Electronic Holdings Ltd v United Parcels Service Ltd [2005] EWHC 221 (Comm); [2005] 1 Lloyd's Rep. 470, at [124].

CHAPTER 37

CONSTRUCTION CONTRACTS

2. FORMATION OF CONTRACT

(a) *General Principles*

General principles

[Add to note 95, page [653]]

37–039

See *Ove Arup & Partners International Ltd v Mirant Asia-Pacific Construction (Hong Kong) Ltd* [2003] EWCA Civ 1729; [2004] B.L.R. 49.

(c) *Tenders*

Good faith

[Add to note 143: page [661]]

37–053

By way of comparison, see the Privy Council treatment of fairness and good faith in an appeal from the New Zealand Court of Appeal in *Pratt Contractors Ltd v Transit New Zealand* [2004] B.L.R. 143.

3. CONTRACT TERMS

(b) *Contract Documents*

Incorporated documents

[Page [666]]

37–064

See the approach of the Court of Appeal in *Aqua Design Ltd v Kier Regional Ltd* [2002] EWCA Civ 797; [2003] B.L.R. 111 to the question of whether certain provisions of the Standard DOM/1 Form of Sub-Contract were incorporated into a negotiated sub-contract.

(c) *Implied Terms*

General principles

37–067 [*Add to note 178:* page [667]]
See the decision of the Court of Appeal in *Ultraframe (UK) Ltd v Tailored Roofing Systems Ltd* [2004] EWCA Civ 585; [2004] B.L.R. 341.

(d) *Statutes Relevant to Construction*

Statutory implied terms

37–077 [*Add to end of note 221: page* [671]]
Contracts for the supply of materials are normally governed by the Sale of Goods Act 1979 (see Main Work, Vol. II, Chap.43); see *Jewsons Ltd v Boykan* [2003] EWCA Civ 1030; [2004] B.L.R. 31 on fitness for purpose under s.14(3) in the building context.

4. PARTICULAR FEATURES

(b) *Instructions, Certificates and Approval*

Final certificate

37–101 [*Add to note 337: page* [684]]
See *Cantrell v Wright and Fuller Ltd* [2003] EWHC 1545 (TCC); [2003] B.L.R. 412

6. SUB-CONTRACTS

(a) *Sub-Contractors*

No right to direct payment

37–169 [*Add at end of paragraph: page* [712]]
In each case, it is a question of construction of the contract as to what rights and obligations have been conferred, or imposed, on the parties.[543a]

[543a] *Actionstrength Ltd v International Glass Engineering IN.GL.EN SpA* [2003] UKHL 17; [2003] 2 A.C. 541 and *Brican Fabrications Ltd v Merchant City Developments Ltd* [2003] B.L.R. 512 (Court of Session).

10. DISPUTES

(a) *Nature of Disputes*

Disputes under construction contracts

[*Page* [743]]
The question of whether a "dispute" or "difference" has in fact arisen may be **37-247**
important in the context of dispute resolution procedures—such as arbitration or
adjudication—which require a "dispute" or "difference" to have arisen before
those procedures can validly be operated. The most recent discussion of this
topic, in the context of arbitration but equally applicable to adjudication, is in
Amec Civil Engineering Ltd v Secretary of State for Transport [2005] EWCA Civ
291; [2005] B.L.R. 227. See also *Collins (Contractors) Ltd v Baltic Quay
Management (1994) Ltd* [2004] EWCA Civ 1757; [2005] B.L.R. 63, where
Clarke L.J. accepted as "broadly correct" the test set out in the form of seven
propositions by Jackson J. in the first instance decision in *Amec* (above).

(d) *Litigation*

Presentation of claims

[*Add to note 772: page* [747]] **37-254**
See the recent review of the decided cases on "global" claims by Lord
Macfayden in *John Doyle Construction Ltd v Laing Management (Scotland) Ltd*
[2002] B.L.R. 393 (Court of Session). Subsequent to the opinion of the Lord
Ordinary, see the opinions of Lords MacLean, Johnston and Drummond Young
in the Extra Division of the Inner House of the Court of Session (following a
reclaiming motion by the management contractor) in *Laing Management (Scotland) Ltd v John Doyle Construction Ltd* [2004] B.L.R. 297.

[*Add new paragraph: page* [747]]
Alternative dispute resolution (ADR). Where a commercial agreement **37-254A**
between parties requires ADR to be undertaken, then the strong tendency of the
courts, especially in the specialist divisions, is to refuse to permit a party to
proceedings without having instituted ADR proceedings first.[778a] On the separate
jurisdiction to stay proceedings in accordance with the principles set out in the
CPR, see *Shirayama Shokusan Company Ltd v Danovo Ltd*,[778b] where Black-
burne J. concluded that the court had jurisdiction to order the parties to mediate
even where one party was opposed to any mediation (although presumably the
prospects for success of such a process must be limited).

[778a] *Cable & Wireless plc v IBM UK Ltd* [2002] EWHC 2059 (Comm); [2003] B.L.R. 89.
[778b] [2003] EWHC 3306 (Ch); [2004] B.L.R. 207.

(e) *Adjudication*

The enforcement of adjudicator's awards

37–260 [*Sub-paragraph (2): page* [750]]
The adjudicator is permitted to take the initiative in ascertaining the facts and the law, but the proper ambit of the dispute will be determined by the notice of adjudication, properly construed, and the adjudicator will ordinarily have no jurisdiction to decide what is the real dispute between the parties: *McAlpine PPS Pipeline Systems Joint Venture v Transco Plc* [2004] EWHC 2030 (TCC); [2004] B.L.R. 352.

[*Sub-paragraph (4)*]
However, in a contract where the obligation upon the employer was to pay certificates issues by the architect, then the contractor was entitled to summary judgment in respect of the sums certified but not paid, with any question of work not having been carried out correctly (or at all) being properly regarded as the subject for a separate claim, rather than a defence to the contractor's claim. The obligation to pay was triggered by the certificate, not by whether the work to which the certificate related had in fact been carried out properly (or at all): *Rupert Morgan Building Services (LLC) Ltd v Jervis* [2003] EWCA Civ 1563; [2004] B.L.R. 18.

[*Sub-paragraph (5)*]
The general law in relation to actual or apparent bias will apply to the conduct of adjudicators, but the courts have indicated that a robust approach will by taken, so that a telephone conversation with one side may not amount to apparent bias (*Amec Capital Projects Ltd v Whitefriars City Estates Ltd* [2004] EWCA Civ 1418; [2005] B.L.R. 1) and where the adjudicator receives privileged material, he may properly continue if he concludes that there can be no legitimate fear that he might not have been impartial (*Specialist Ceiling Services Ltd v ZVI Construction (UK) Ltd* [2004] B.L.R. 403). However, where an adjudicator is very critical of a party for not producing a witness who was never asked to attend, this may amount to bias (*A&S Enterprises Ltd v Kema Holdings Ltd* [2005] EWHC 3365; [2005] B.L.R. 76).

[*Add new sub-paragraph (6)*]

  (6) Although the possibility has been raised that some disputes may be so complex that it is impossible for them to be dealt with fairly within the timescales available in the adjudication process,[804a] such concerns have subsequently not found favour with the courts, particularly in cases where substantial extensions of time have been agreed between the parties.[804b]

[804a] *AWG v Rockingham Motorway Speedway Ltd* [2004] EWHC 888.
[804b] *CIB Properties Ltd v Birse Construction Ltd* [2005] 1 W.L.R. 2252.

CHAPTER 38

CREDIT AND SECURITY

[225]

1. The Consumer Credit Act 1974

38–001A

[*Add new paragraph 38–001A: page* [754]]

Regulation of financial activities. For the Financial Services and Markets Act 2000 and orders made thereunder, see Lomnicka and Powell, *Encyclopedia of Financial Services Law.*

Regulations, orders etc

38–006

[*Add at end of note 18: page* [755]]
SI 2004/1481, 1482, 1483, 1484, 2619, 3237.

Contracting-out

38–008

[*Add to note 25: page* [755]]
See *Wilson v Robertsons (London) Ltd* [2005] EWHC 1425 (Ch); *The Times,* July 28, 2005.

Banks and investment firms authorised in other EEA states

38–011

See also the Electronic Commerce Directive (Financial Services and Markets) (Amendment) Regulations 2004 (SI 2004/3378) amending the Electronic Commerce Directive (Financial Services and Markets) Regulations 2002 (SI 2002/1775). See also SI 2002/682, SI 2002/765.

Banking Code

38–012

[*Page* [757]]
See also the Business Banking Code, March 2005 (para.34–225 of the Main Work).

[*Add to note 39: page* [757]]
The latest revision is March 2005.

Reform of consumer credit law

38–012A

[*Page* [757]]
A Consumer Credit Bill was introduced into Parliament before the general election in May 2005 but lapsed when Parliament was dissolved. The Bill was re-introduced into the House of Commons on May 18, 2005. The most important changes made in the Bill are (1) the removal of the financial limits, (2) a requirement that debtors be given notice of sums in arrears and default sums, (3) the substitution of "unfair relationships between creditors and debtors" for extortionate credit bargains, (4) the tightening of controls over businesses requiring to be licensed, and (5) the application of the financial services ombudsman scheme (in the Financial Services and Markets Act 2000) to cover consumer credit businesses under the 1974 Act.

The following statutory instruments have been made: Consumer Credit (Disclosure of Information) Regulations 2004 (SI 2004/1481) (operative May 31,

2005); Consumer Credit (Agreements) (Amendment) Regulations 2004 (SI 2004/1482) (operative May 31, 2005); Consumer Credit (Early Settlement) Regulations 2004 (SI 2004/1483) (operative May 31, 2005); Consumer Credit (Advertisements) Regulations 2004 (SI 2004/1484) (operative October 31, 2004); Consumer Credit (Miscellaneous Amendments) Regulations 2004 (SI 2004/2619) (operative in part October 31, 2004, and in part May 31, 2005); Consumer Credit Act 1974 (Electronic Communications) Order 2004 (SI 2004/3236) (operative December 31, 2004); Consumer Credit (Enforcement, Default and Termination Notices) (Amendment) Regulations 2004 (SI 2004/3237) (operative December 31, 2004).

(a) *Terminology of the Act*

"Consumer credit agreement"

[Add to note 52: page [759]]
SI 1989/1125 is revoked and replaced by SI 2004/1484 (amended by SI 2004/2619): see below, para.38–061

38–014

"Credit"

[Add to note 62: page [759]]
Nejad v City Index Ltd [2000] C.C.L.R. 7 (C.A.) (allowing a client a "credit allocation" for future gambling did not constitute the provision of credit); *McMillan Williams v Range* [2004] EWCA Civ 294; [2004] 1 W.L.R. 1858 (payment of salary as an advance against commission did not constitute the provision of credit). It would seem that, at the time the agreement is made, it must be certain that credit will be provided: *ibid.*

38–017

"Credit not exceeding £25,000"

[Add in note 72, after Wilson v First County Trust Ltd: page [760]]
Wilson v Robertsons (London) Ltd [2005] EWHC 1425 (Ch); *The Times*, July 28, 2005.

38–020

"Restricted-use credit"

[Add to note 90: page [762]]
See *Office of Fair Trading v Lloyds TSB Bank plc* [2004] EWHC 2600; [2005] 1 All E.R. 843; see paras 38–029 and 38–454, below.

38–025

"Debtor–creditor–supplier" agreement

[Add to note 103: page [763]]
See above para.38–025, n.90.

38–029

[Add to note 107: page [764]]
See *Office of Fair Trading v Lloyds TSB Bank plc* [2004] EWHC 2600; [2005] 1 All E.R. 843, below, para.38–454 (existence of "arrangements" between credit

card issuer and supplier abroad through network schemes such as Visa, Mastercard, etc.)

[*Add to note 109*]
cf., *Office of Fair Trading v Lloyds TSB Bank plc*, above.

"Credit-token agreement"

38–032   [*Add to note 120: page* [765]]
SI 1983/1553 is amended by SI 2004/1482 (amended by SI 2004/2619 and SI 2004/3236); see para.38–071, below. SI 1983/1564 is amended by SI 2004/3236.

"Consumer hire agreement"

38–033   [*Add to note 136: page* [767]]
SI 1989/1125 is revoked and replaced by SI 2004/1484 (amended by SI 2004/2619); see para.38–061 below.

"Exempt agreement"

38–036   [*Page* [767]]
See the amendments of s.16 of the 1974 Act effected in relation to land mortgages by the Financial Services and Markets Act 2000 (Regulated Activities) Order 2001 (SI 2001/544), art.61.

38–037   [*Add after reference to Ketley v Gilbert in note 159: page* [768]]
Thew v Cole [2003] EWCA Civ 1828; *The Times*, January 15, 2004.

38–040   [*Add at end of note 164: page* [769]]
and by Sch.17, para.47 of the Communications Act 2003.

Consequences if part is a separate agreement

38–048   [*Add to note 212: page* [772]]
SI 1983/1553 is amended by SI 2004/1482 (amended by SI 2004/2619 and SI 2004/3236); see para.38–071, below.

"Total charge for credit"

38–055   [*Add to note 234: page* [774]]
SI 2004/1482 (amended by SI 2004/2619 and SI 2004/3236).

[*Insert new paragraph 38–055A: page* [775]]
38–055A   **Service of documents.** Documents required or permitted to be served under the Act may be served as prescribed by ss.176, 176A (inserted by the Consumer Credit Act 1974 (Electronic Communications) Order 2004 (SI 2004/3236) (operative December 31, 2004)).

(b) *Licensing of Credit and Hire Businesses*

Licensing and control

[Add at end of note 271: page [777]]   **38–058**
and by SI 2004/3236.

(c) *Seeking Business*

Advertising and quotations

[Page [778]]   **38–061**
The Consumer Credit (Advertisement) Regulations 1989 are revoked and replaced by the Consumer Credit (Advertisement) Regulations 2004 (SI 2004/1484) (operative October 31, 2004) as amended by SI 2004/2619.

[Delete note 294: page [778] *and substitute]*
SI 1999/2725, as amended by SI 2000/1797. But these regulations are revoked in part by SI 2004/1484 (as amended by SI 2004/2619), above.

(e) *The Agreement*

Pre-contract disclosure

[Page [781]]   **38–070**
The Consumer Credit (Disclosure of Information) Regulations 2004 (SI 2004/1481), have now been made under s.55(1) of the Act (operative May 31, 2005). These regulations do not apply to agreements to which s.58 of the Act applies (see para.38–496 of the Main Work) nor in respect of distance contracts (as defined in reg.1(2)).

Form and content of agreement

[Page [781]]   **38–071**
The Consumer Credit (Agreements) Regulations 1983 are extensively amended by the Consumer Credit (Agreements) (Amendment) Regulations 2004 (SI 2004/1482) (operative May 31, 2005), as amended by SI 2004/2619 and SI 2004/3236.

Signing of agreement

[Add to notes 339 and 341: page [782]]   **38–072**
SI 1983/1553 is amended by SI 2004/1482 (as amended by SI 2004/2619 and SI 2004/3236); see para.38–071, above.

[Add at end of note 347]
as amended by SI 2004/1482 (as amended by SI 2004/2619 and SI 2004/3236).

Supply of copies

38–075   [*Text to note 362: page* [783]]
The copy may now be transmitted electronically: SI 2004/3236, art.2(3).

38–077   [*Page* [783]]
The Consumer Credit (Cancellation Notices and Copies of Documents) Regulations 1983 have been amended by the Consumer Credit (Miscellaneous Amendments) Regulations 2004 (SI 2004/2619) and by the Consumer Credit Act 1974 (Electronic Communications) Order 2004 (SI 2004/3236).

Notice of cancellation rights

38–079   [*Page* [784]]
The Consumer Credit (Cancellation Notices and Copies of Documents) Regulations 1983 have been amended by the Consumer Credit (Miscellaneous Amendments) Regulations 2004 (SI 2004/2619) (operative May 31, 2005) and by the Consumer Credit Act 1974 (Electronic Communications) Order 2004 (SI 2004/3236) (operative December 31, 2004).

38–080   [*Text to note 377: page* [784]]
The notice may now be transmitted electronically: SI 2004/3236, art.2(4).

Failure to comply

38–083   [*Add to note 391: page* [785]]
SI 1983/1553 is amended by SI 2004/1482 (as amended by SI 2004/2619 and SI 2004/3236): see para.38–071, above.

(f) *Withdrawal and Cancellation*

Cancellable agreements

38–091   [*Page* [788]]
For a discussion of the various statutory provisions conferring rights of cancellation (and considered in paras 38–091–38–095) see Hellwege (2004) Camb. L.J. 712.

Consumer Protection (Cancellation of Contracts Concluded away from Business Premises) Regulations 1987

38–093   [*Add to note 450: page* [789]]
See also *Heininger v Bayerische Hypo-und Vereinsbank AG* (C481/99) [2004] All E.R. (EC) 1 (mortgage transaction).

Consumer Protection (Distance Selling) Regulations 2000

38–094   [*Page* [790]]
These Regulations have been amended by the Consumer Protection (Distance Selling) (Amendment) Regulations 2005 (SI 2005/689). See also the amendments effected by SI 2004/2095, reg.25.
In *easyCar (UK) Ltd v Office of Fair Trading* (2005) (Case C–336/03), *The Times*, March 15, 2005, the European Court of Justice held that a car hire

company which took bookings only via the internet did not come within Directive 97/7/EC.

[Insert new paragraph 38–094A: page [790]]
Financial Services (Distance Marketing) Regulations 2004. These Regulations give effect in the United Kingdom to Directive 2002/65/EC of the European Parliament and of the Council and give consumers a right to cancel most distance contracts for financial services during a set period after commencement of the contract.

38–094A

Notice of cancellation

[Note 482: page [792]]
A new s.69(7) was substituted by SI 2004/3236, dealing with deemed service in the case of electronic communication.

38–098

Cancellation: repayment of credit

[Add to note 531: page [795]]
amended by SI 2004/3236, art.7.

38–106

(g) *Supply of Information*

Information to debtor under running-account credit agreement

[Notes 603 and 607: page [800]]
SI 1983/1577 has been amended by SI 2004/2619 and SI 2004/3236.

38–118

Periodic statements

[Add to note 613: page [800]]
amended by SI 2004/3236, art.12.

38–119

Information to "surety"

[Add at end of note 626: page [801]]
amended by SI 2004/2619 and SI 2004/3236.

38–120

Copy of security instrument

[Add to note 634: page [802]]
SI 1983/1533 has been amended by SI 2004/1482 (as amended by SI 2004/2619).

38–122

Information as to settlement figure

[Amend the text to note 642: page [802]]
The period of 12 days prescribed by SI 1983/1564 is reduced to seven days by SI 2004/1483, reg.9, as from May 31, 2005.

38–124

[*Add to note 643*]

SI 1983/1564 is amended and SI 1983/1562 revoked and replaced by SI 2004/1483 (as amended by SI 2004/2619); see para.38–139, below.

(h) *Variation of Agreements*

Mutual variation by subsequent agreement

38–131 [*Add to note 676: page* [806]]

SI 1983/1553 is amended by SI 2004/1482 (as amended by SI 2004/2619 and SI 2004/3236); see para.38–071, above.

Form, etc., of modifying agreement

38–135 [*Add to note 688: page* [807]]

SI 1983/1553 is amended by SI 2004/1482 (as amended by SI 2004/2619): see para.38–071, above.

(i) *Appropriation of Payments and Early Settlement*

Rebate on early settlement etc

38–139—
38–140

[*Page* [808]]

The Consumer Credit (Rebate on Early Settlement) Regulations 1983 are revoked and replaced by the Consumer Credit (Rebate on Early Settlement) Regulations 2004 (SI 2004/1483) (amended by SI 2004/2619), but the 1983 Regulations continue to apply for a limited period to regulated consumer credit agreements entered into before the date on which the 2004 Regulations come into force (May 31, 2005). The 2004 Regulations incorporate an actuarial formula for the calculation of the rebate in place of the various formulae provided for in the 1983 Regulations. Regulation 6 provides for the settlement date to be deferred by a month (or, at the option of the creditor, 30 days) in the case of agreements for a term of more than one year, and is thus less generous to the creditor than the 1983 Regulations.

(j) *Restrictions on Enforcement or Termination of Agreement*

Enforcement notice (non-default cases)

38–144 [*Add to note 722: page* [810]]

The notice must be in writing and given to the debtor in paper form: SI 2004/3237.

Form and content of default notice

38–148 [*Add to note 741: page* [811]]

The notice must be in writing and given to the debtor in paper form: SI 2004/3237.

Notice of termination (non-default cases)

[*Add to note 759: page* [813]]
The notice must be in writing and given to the debtor in paper form: SI 2004/3237.

38–153

Copy of notices to "surety"

[*Add to note 771: page* [813]]
amended by SI 2004/2619 and SI 2004/3236.

38–154

(k) *Security*

"Security" defined

[*Add to note 795: page* [816]]
SI 1989/1125 is revoked and replaced by SI 2004/1484 (as amended by SI 2004/2619); see para.38–061, above.

38–161

Form and content of security instrument

[*Page* [817]]
The Consumer Credit (Guarantees and Indemnities) Regulations 1983 have been amended by the Consumer Credit Act (Electronic Communications) Order 2004 (SI 2004/3236), art.5.

38–164

Supply of copies to surety

[*Add to note 806: page* [817]]
SI 1983/1557 has been amended by SI 2004/2619 and SI 2004/3236.

38–166

Security provided by debtor or hirer

[*Add at end of note 814: page* [818]]
SI 2004/1482 (amended by SI 2004/2619 and SI 2004/3236).

38–168

Pledges

[*Add to note 843: page* [820]]
SI 2004/3236.

38–176

(m) *Extortionate Credit Bargains*

Rate of interest

[*Add to note 979: page* [830]]
Batooneh v Asombang [2003] EWHC 2111 (QB) (interest rate of 100 per cent on informal commercial loan reduced to 25 per cent).

38–198

(n) *Ancillary Credit Businesses*

Seeking business

38–220 *[Add to note 1076: page [839]]*
SI 1989/1125 is entirely revoked, and SI 1999/2725 and SI 2000/1797 partially revoked, by SI 2004/1484 (operative October 31, 2004) (amended by SI 2004/2619): see para.38–061, above.

2. Loans and Interest

(a) *Loans of Money*

[Insert next paragraph 38–222A: page [840]]
38–222A   **Regulatory provisions**. For the Financial Services and Markets Act 2000 and orders made thereunder: see Lomnicka and Powell, *Encyclopedia of Financial Services Law*.

Events of default

38–238 *[Page [847]]*
A notice of acceleration purporting to have been given under an "events of default" clause when no event of default has arisen will normally be merely ineffective and will not, in the absence of any contractual obligation (express or implied) between the person giving the notice and the borrower, give rise to any liability on the part of that person to the borrower: *Concord Trust v Law Debenture Trust Corp plc* [2005] UKHL 27; [2005] 1 W.L.R. 1591 at [30]–[45].

Student loans

38–247 *[Add to note 1202: page [851]]*
SI 2004/1175, SI 2004/2752.

(b) *Interest*

Default interest

38–258 *[Add to note 1250: page [856]]*
Contrast *Jeancharm Ltd v Barnet Football Club Ltd* [2003] EWCA Civ 58; [2003] 92 Const. L.R. 26 (default interest of 5 per cent per week held penal).

(c) *Effect of the Consumer Credit Act 1974*

Consumer Credit Act

38–263 *[Add to note 1273: page [858]]*
But see para. 38–012A above (proposed removal of financial limit).

3. Hire-Purchase Agreements

(b) *At Common Law*

Relief from forfeiture

[Add after reference to Sport International Bussum BV v Inter-Footwear Ltd in note 1448: page [873]]
The Jotunheim [2004] EWHC 671 (Comm); [2005] 1 Lloyd's Rep. 181.

38–308

(c) *Effect of the Consumer Credit Act 1974*

Scope of 1974 Act

[Page [880]]
But see para.38–012A, above (proposed removal of financial limit).

38–321

(d) *Defective Goods*

Exclusion of implied terms: consumer agreements

[Note 1644: page [891]]
SI 1976/1813 was further amended by SI 2005/871.

38–354

(e) *Rights and Liabilities of Third Parties*

(v) *Execution and Distress*

Execution

[Amend the text to note 1758: page [903]]
s.138B(1) of the Supreme Court Act 1981 has been repealed by s.109(3) and Sch.10 of the Courts Act 2003 and replaced by Sch.7, para.11, of that Act.

38–390

4. Conditional Sale Agreements

Scope of 1974 Act

[Add to note 1827: page [909]]
But see para.38–012A, above (proposed removal of financial limit).

38–410

Title to goods

[Note 1861: page [911]]
SI 1976/1813 was further amended by SI 2005/871.

38–423

Defective goods

38–424   [*Note 1863: page* [912]]
SI 1976/1813 was further amended by SI 2005/871.

5. CREDIT SALE AGREEMENTS

Scope of Consumer Credit Act

38–432   [*Add to note 1896: page* [914]]
But see para.38–012A, above (proposed removal of financial limit).

Implied terms

38–435   [*Note 1910: page* [915]]
SI 1976/1813 was further amended by SI 2005/871.

6. CREDIT AND OTHER PAYMENT CARDS AND CHECKS

Consumer Credit Act 1974

38–454   [*Add to note 1958: page* [921]]
On the use of a credit card abroad, see *Office of Fair Trading v Lloyds TSB Bank plc* [2004] EWHC 2600; [2005] 1 All E.R. 843, where it was held that s.75 had no extra territorial effect and that the creditor was not liable in respect of a transaction effected by the debtor outside the UK, governed by a foreign law and where the goods were delivered (or services supplied) outside the UK. See also above paras 38–025, 38–029.

"Credit-token" and "credit-token agreements"

38–462   [*Add to note 2003: page* [924]]
SI 1983/1553 is amended by SI 2004/1482 (amended by SI 2004/2619 and SI 2004/3236): see para.38–071, above.

[*Add to note 2004: page* [924]]
SI 1983/1557 is amended by SI 2004/2619 and SI 2004/3236.

Misuse of credit-token

[*Page* [927]]
38–475   The Consumer Protection (Distance Selling) Regulations 2000 have been amended by the Consumer Protection (Distance Selling) (Amendment) Regulations 2005 (SI 2005/689).
Regulation 14 of the Financial Services (Distance Marketing) Regulations 2004 (SI 2004/2095) makes similar provision with respect to the fraudulent use

of a consumer's payment card in connection with a distance contract within the meaning of those Regulations. Again the protection is stated not to apply to an agreement to which s.83(1) of the Consumer Credit Act 1974 applies, but again the same result is achieved by removing the potential liability of the debtor for the first £50 of loss to the creditor in respect of any use of a card which is a credit-token and his liability for misuse of such a card by a person who acquired possession of it with his consent.

It is submitted that, in both the Regulations mentioned in this paragraph, the words "fraudulent use is made . . . of [that] card" will include fraudulent use of the details on the card which are supplied by the consumer to the supplier when entering into a transaction where the consumer is not physically present.

7. MORTGAGES OF PERSONAL PROPERTY

Mortgage or charge of choses in action

[*Page* [931]]   **38–489**
See para.38–012A, above (proposed removal of financial limit).

8. MORTGAGES OF LAND

Consumer credit

[*Text to note 2104a: page* [932]]   **38–491**
See now the Financial Services and Markets Act 2000 (Regulated Activities) Order 2001 (SI 2001/544), regs. 61, 90, 91 and the Financial Services Authority (FSA) rules contained in the Mortgage Conduct of Business source book (operative October 31, 2004). See also Lomnicka and Powell, *Encyclopedia of Financial Services Law.*

Form, etc

[*Page* [932]]   **38–494**
The Consumer Credit (Disclosure of Information) Regulations 2004 (SI 2004/1481) (see para.38–070, above) do not apply to agreements to which s.58 of the Act applies.

Special "pause" provisions

[*Add to note 2116: page* [933]]   **38–496**
SI 1983/1557 has been amended by SI 2004/2619 and SI 2004/3236.

[*Add to note 2118*]
SI 1983/1557 has been amended by SI 2004/2619 and SI 2004/3236.

[*Text to note 2119*]

The unexecuted agreement may now be transmitted in electronic form: SI 2004/3236, art.2(2).

[*Add at end of note 2124*]

and by SI 2004/2619, SI 2004/3236.

CHAPTER 39

EMPLOYMENT

1. Introduction

The Employment Act 2002

39–002   *[Add to note 11: page* [937]]
These provisions, which make significant changes to the costs regime for the Employment Appeal Tribunal and for employment tribunals, and which make various other changes designed to increase the efficiency of the management of applications to employment tribunals, were brought into effect from July 9, 2004.

The contract of service or personally to execute any work or labour: "workers" and "persons employed"

39–009   *[Add to note 54: page* [941]]
See *Wright v Redrow Homes (North West) Ltd* [2004] EWCA Civ 469; [2004] I.C.R. 1126 where the contracts of independent individual bricklaying contractors were construed as intended to require them to work "personally" so as to constitute them as "workers"; see also Main Work and Supplement, para. 39–009, nn 60, 64; compare Main Work and Supplement para.39–022, nn 143–147.

[Add to notes 60, 64: pages [942] *and* [943]]
See also Main Work and Supplement, para.39–009, n.54; compare Main Work and Supplement para.39–022 nn 143–147.

[Add to note 65: page [943]]
See *Mingeley v Pennock and Ivory* [2004] EWCA Civ 328; [2004] I.C.R. 727, where the relationship between a taxi-driver and the organisation co-ordinating his work was held not to amount to a contract personally to execute any work or labour; see also Supplement, para.39–023, n.150.

[Add to note 66]
See *South East Sheffield Citizens Advice Bureau v Grayson* [2004] I.R.L.R. 353, E.A.T., where an unpaid volunteer worker was held to fall outside this definition.

2. The Factors identifying a Contract of Employment

Personal performance

[Add to note 145: page [950]] **39–022**
The requirement of personal performance was strictly maintained and applied in *Staffordshire Sentinel Newspapers Ltd v Potter* [2004] I.R.L.R. 752, EAT, so that an express power for the worker to substitute another worker was treated as negating a contract of employment although the power was subject to the approval of the employer. Compare also Main Work and Supplement, para. 39–009, nn 50, 60, 64.

The extent of the obligation to work or to employ

[Add to note 150: page [951]] **39–023**
Compare now *Mingeley v Pennock and Ivory* [2004] EWCA Civ 328; [2004] I.C.R. 727, where the relationship between a taxi-driver and the organisation co-ordinating his work was held not to amount to a contract personally to execute any work or labour.

[Add to note 152]
Compare the decision in *Dacas v Brook Street Bureau (UK) Ltd* [2004] EWCA Civ 217; [2004] I.R.L.R. 358, regarding the relationship between the employment agency and the temporary agency worker—see further, Main Work and Supplement para.39–027, n.184.

The intention of the parties

[Page [952]] **39–025**
In *Smith v Reliance Water Controls Ltd* [2003] EWCA Civ 1153, Arden L.J. stressed the importance, in cases where there was an express change of status from employee to self-employed worker, of nevertheless weighing all the objective factors according to the test laid down in the *Market Investigations* case to assess whether the contract was a contract of employment.

Special cases: (2) agency workers

[Add to note 184: page [954]] **39–027**
However, the Court of Appeal in *Dacas v Brook Street Bureau (UK) Ltd* [2004] EWCA Civ 217; [2004] I.R.L.R. 358, held that the temporary agency worker was not an "employee" of the agency, though she might be an employee of the end-user of her services.

3. FORMATION OF THE CONTRACT

Public policy, restraint of trade, and illegality

39–032   *[Page* [957]]
The Gangmasters Licensing Act 2004, the essential provisions of which were brought into effect from April 1, 2005, requires individuals to be licensed as gangmasters if they are to engage in the supplying of workers for the use of their services in agricultural work and various kinds of gathering, harvesting, processing or packaging of foodstuffs. Sections 12–14 of that Act create a series of criminal offences involving the disregarding of these licensing requirements, including an offence of acting as a gangmaster without a licence, and an offence of entering into arrangements with gangmasters who are not licensed. The principles discussed in this paragraph of the Main Work will apply to determine whether and when contracts of employment will be rendered unenforceable because their formation or performance involves the commission of one or more of those offences.

[Add to note 221: page [958]]
The decision of the EAT was upheld by the Court of Appeal in *Vakante v Addey & Stanhope School* [2004] EWCA Civ 1065; [2004] 4 All E.R. 1056.

[Add to note 228]
The approach in the *Woolston Hall Leisure* case was reiterated and applied in *Colen v Cebrian (UK) Ltd* [2003] EWCA Civ 1676; [2004] I.C.R. 568, and in *Wheeler v Qualitydeep Ltd (t/a Thai Royale Restaurant)* [2004] EWCA Civ 1085; [2005] I.C.R. 265, where the requirement of active participation by the employee in the illegality as to performance was insisted upon.

4. COLLECTIVE AGREEMENTS AND STATUTORY AWARDS OF TERMS

(b) *Incorporation of Collective Agreements into Individual Contracts of Employment*

Express incorporation

39–046   *[Add to note 333: page* [969]]
Compare, however, *Ackinclose v Gateshead MBC* [2005] I.R.L.R. 79, EAT, where it was held that when a contract of employment only made reference to a national agreement as the relevant collective agreement without any further reference or incorporation, a successor agreement would not thereby be incorporated so as to take effect following transfer of the employment in question from a local authority employer party to the national bargaining structure to a private employer not party to that structure. Contrast, however, *Griffiths v Salisbury DC* [2004] EWCA Civ 162, where an agreement implementing the national agreement was held to be incorporated in the individual contract and where therefore a backdated pay freeze imposed under that agreement was effective.

Incorporation by implication

[*Add to note 346: page* [970]] **39–048**
Compare *Kaur v MG Rover Group Ltd* [2004] EWCA Civ 1507; [2005]
I.R.L.R. 40, where a set of provisions concerning job security in a collective
agreement were held to be inappropriate for incorporation into individual contracts of employment, as to certain of them because they were aspirational in
character, and as to certain others because they were essentially collective
undertakings rather than undertakings to individuals.

5. RIGHTS AND DUTIES UNDER AND ASSOCIATED WITH A CONTRACT OF
EMPLOYMENT

(a) *Duties of the Employee*

Duties to disclose information

[*Add to notes 408–411: page* [976]] **39–060**
The decision in *Tesco Stores Ltd v Pook* [2003] EWHC 823; [2004] I.R.L.R.
618, ChD, suggests that a sufficiently senior employee may in certain circumstances come under a generally implied duty to disclose his own breaches of trust
as well as those of other employees.

(b) *Duties of the Employer*

(i) *Remuneration*

The national minimum wage

[*Page* [986]] **39–076**
Sections 44–46 of the Employment Relations Act 2004 make extensive additions and amendments to the regime for the enforcement of the national minimum wage, with effect from April 6, 2005.

General restrictions on deductions made, or payments received, by employers

[*Add to note 716: page* [1001]] **39–093**
It was held in *Farrell Matthews & Weir v Hansen* [2005] I.C.R. 509 (EAT) that
there was no reason to construe s.27(3) as meaning that non-contractual bonuses
could not come within the definition of wages unless they were actually paid.

(ii) *Other Duties*

Action in tort

[*Add to note 767: page* [1006]] **39–100**
Update reference to *Clerk & Lindsell* to 18th ed., 2004.

[*Add to note 769*]

In *Barber v Somerset County Council* [2004] UKHL 13; [2004] 1 W.L.R. 1089, the House of Lords broadly endorsed the guidelines laid down in *Sutherland v Hatton*, though applying them to somewhat different outcomes in the particular cases which were under appeal.

The Working Time Regulations

39–108 [*Add to note 823: page* [1011]]

Compare, as to collective agreements, *Prison Service v Bewley* [2004] I.C.R. 422, E.A.T.

[*Add to note 824*]

The issue of whether this entitlement can be discharged by the payment of "rolled-up" holiday pay has been referred to the E.C.J. by the Court of Appeal in *Caulfield v Marshalls Clay Products Ltd* [2004] EWCA Civ 422; [2004] 2 C.M.L.R. 45.

The rights of the employee [or worker] in relation to trade union membership and activities

39–111—
39–112 [*Pages* [1012]–[1013]]

The material in these paragraphs is extensively affected by, and should now be read subject to, the provisions of ss.29–32 of the Employment Relations Act 2004, which came into force on October 1, 2004. The Act established new or enhanced rights for workers not to be offered inducements relating to trade union membership and collective bargaining, and extended their rights not to suffer detrimental action in circumstances relating to trade union membership.

Sections 29–32 of the 2004 Act make a series of additions and amendments to ss.146–151 of the Trade Union and Labour Relations (Consolidation) Act 1992; s.29 of the 2004 Act inserts new ss.145A–F into the 1992 Act. In particular it should be noted that s.31 of the 2004 Act amends ss.146–151 of the 1992 Act to extend the existing protections of employees against detrimental action by their employer for being, or not being, a member of a trade union or for taking part in the activities of their union to workers who are not employees. The heading to these two paragraphs is accordingly amended, as shown above, to refer to the larger category of "workers" rather than the more limited category of "employees" (see para.39–009 of the Main Work).

Statutory rights of employees to time off

39–113 [*Page* [1013]]

A new kind of statutory right to time off has been conferred on employees by s.40 of the Employment Relations Act 2004, which by inserting a new s.43M into the Employment Rights Act 1996 protects employees from being subjected to detriment by the employee by reason of being summoned for or being absent from work on jury service, with effect from April 6, 2005.

Equality clauses in contracts of employment

[*Add to note 887: page* [1017]] **39–122**
Compare *Allonby v Accrington & Rossendale College* Case C-256/01 [2004] I.R.L.R. 224, E.C.J., as to the construction of the "same employment" concept in accordance with art.141(1) of the EC Treaty.

Disability discrimination during the period of employment

[*Page* [1033]] **39–131**
The Disability Discrimination Act 2005 amends and extends in various respects the provisions of the Disability Discrimination Act 1995 concerning disability discrimination in employment. Specific amendments of the existing law will be mentioned in this Supplement as and when they are brought into force.

[*Add to note 935: page* [1022]]
See now *Archibald v Fife Council* [2004] UKHL 32; [2004] I.R.L.R. 651 on the meaning of the concept of reasonable adjustment.

References and testimonials

[*Add to note 968: page* [1027]] **39–142**
Compare now also, to comparably restrictive effect, *Aspin v Metric Group Ltd* [2004] EWHC 1265.

Trust and confidence and other implied duties

[*Add to note 993: page* [1029]] **39–145**
Compare the application of the implied obligation in favour of a senior manager in *Horkulak v Cantor Fitzgerald International* [2003] EWHC 1918 (QB) [2004] I.C.R. 697. In *Waltham Forest LBC v Omilaju (No.2)* [2004] EWCA Civ 1493; [2005] I.R.L.R. 35 it was re-asserted that the test of whether an act was capable of breaching the implied obligation was an objective one, so that the employee's subjective loss of trust and confidence was not sufficient in itself. In *Nottinghamshire CC v Meikle* [2004] EWCA Civ 859; [2004] 4 All E.R. 97, the objectivity of the test had been likewise asserted, but to the contrary effect that it was not necessary for the employee subjectively to have lost confidence in her employer in an overall sense.

[*Add to note 1001*]
Compare now *Crossley v Faithful & Gould Holdings Ltd* [2004] EWCA Civ 293; [2004] I.R.L.R. 377, in which it was held that there is no general obligation upon the employer to take reasonable care for the employee's economic well-being, and that the application of the criteria articulated in the *Scally* case did not require disclosure on the present facts. To similar effect has been *Lennon v Commissioner of Police of the Metropolis* [2004] EWCA Civ 130.

The extensions and limits of the implied obligation of trust and confidence

39–146 [*Add to note 1005 : page* [1030]]

Compare also now *Bunning v GT Bunning & Sons Ltd* [2005] EWCA Civ 104 where it was held to be arguable that a failure to conduct a proper risk assessment of the continued employment of the employee as a welder, as required by Regulations when she became pregnant, might constitute a serious breach of the implied obligation as to trust and confidence.

[*Add to note 1006 : page* [1030]]

In *Holladay v East Kent Hospitals NHS Trust* [2003] EWCA Civ 1696 it was held that the breach of the implied obligation must be a material cause of the event (arrest on suspicion of theft) which had caused the employee harm, but that it was not necessary to conclude that the event would not have occurred but for the breach.

[*Add to notes 1008 and 1009: page* [1031]]

See now *Eastwood v Magnox Electric plc, McCabe v Cornwall County Council* [2004] UKHL 35; [2005] 1 A.C. 503, in which the House of Lords seeks authoritatively to draw the boundary between the area of exclusion of liability for breach of the implied term of trust and confidence envisaged in the *Johnson* case, and the area of pre-dismissal conduct on the part of the employer, apparently including conduct capable of being treated as constructive dismissal, within which liability for breach of the implied term may arise.

Duties to avoid less favourable treatment of part-time work and fixed-term work

39–149 [*Page* [1032]]

In *Department for Work and Pensions v Webley* [2004] EWCA Civ 1745; [2005] I.C.R. 577 it was confirmed that the employer's allowing a fixed-term contract to expire by effluxion of time without renewal does not in itself constitute a detriment, or less favourable treatment of a fixed-term employee than of a permanent employee, within reg.3 of the 2002 Regulations.

6. TERMINATION OF THE CONTRACT

(a) *Termination by Notice*

Form of notice

39–152 [*Add to note 1043: page* [1034]]

See, as to contingent or equivocal notice, *Rai v Somerfield Stores Ltd* [2004] I.C.R. 656, E.A.T.

(b) *Termination by Payment in Lieu of Notice*

The statutory and contractual effects of payment in lieu of notice

[*Page* [1042]]   **39–163**
See now *Hardy v Polk Ltd* [2004] I.R.L.R. 420 (EAT), where Burton J. held, in effect, that s.86 did not create an entitlement to payment in lieu of notice, or a claim in debt for failure to give the statutory minimum period of notice or payment in lieu thereof.

(c) *Termination by Agreement or by Expiry of Fixed Period*

Termination by subsequent agreement

[*Add to note 1152: page* [1045]]   **39–166**
Compare *Solectron Scotland Ltd v Roper* [2004] I.R.L.R. 4, E.A.T, as to the validity of a compromise agreement which could be regarded as limiting the application of the TUPE Regulations.

(e) *Assignment, Winding-up and Changes in the Employing Enterprise*

Transfer of employment: (2) the effect of the Transfer Regulations

[*Add to notes 1193 and 1198: page* [1049]]   **39–171**
Compare *Martin v South Bank University*, Case C-4/01 [2004] I.R.L.R. 74, E.C.J., as to the application of the Acquired Rights Directive and the Transfer Regulations to early retirement benefits.

Dissolution of partnership

[*Add to note 1206: page* [1050]]   **39–172**
See now, however, *Stevens v Bower* [2004] EWCA Civ 496; [2004] I.C.R. 1582 where the approach taken in *Harold Fielding Ltd v Mansi* was rejected and it was held that the employees in question had continuity of service despite the change in the status of their employer from that of a partnership of solicitors to that of a sole practitioner.

(h) *Constructive Dismissal*

Termination as the result of constructive dismissal

[*Add to note 1308: page* [1060]]   **39–187**
In *Waltham Forest LBC v Omilaju (No.2)* [2004] EWCA Civ 1493; [2005] I.R.L.R. 35 it was held that the final act or "last straw" in a series of actions which cumulatively amounted to constructive dismissal need not itself be a breach of contract or unreasonable; but it had to be more than very trivial and had

to be capable of contributing, however slightly, to a breach of the implied obligation as to mutual trust and confidence. Compare also now *Bunning v GT Bunning & Sons Ltd* [2005] EWCA Civ 104, in which the judgment of Wall L.J. adds further support to the notion of the "last straw" as articulated in the *Omilaju* case.

7. REMEDIES, AND RIGHTS, INCIDENTAL TO THE TERMINATION OF EMPLOYMENT

(d) *Damages for Wrongful Dismissal*

Damages for loss of earnings following wrongful dismissal

39–193 [*Add to note 1385: page* [1066]]
See now *Harper v Virgin Net Ltd* [2004] EWCA Civ 271, in which it was held that damages for wrongful dismissal should not include compensation for the chance that, if the employee had not been dismissed with insufficient notice, she would have become time-qualified to make a claim for unfair dismissal.

Damages for injury to feelings or reputation

39–196 [*Add to note 1404: page* [1068]]
An appeal to the House of Lords was allowed in *Eastwood v Magnox Electric plc* [2004] UKHL 35; [2005] 1 A.C. 503: see this Supplement, para.39–146, nn.1008 and 1009, above.

Deductions for Social Security contributions and benefits

39–198 [*Note 1412: page* [1068] *Punctuation misplaced; the first three lines should read:-*]
Claims for damages for wrongful dismissal would seem not to be affected by the recoupment provisions either of the Social Security (Recovery of Benefits) Act 1997, which applies to "payments in consequence of any accident, injury or disease" [etc.].

(e) *Equitable Remedies and Declarations*

Declaration and other remedies

39–203 [*Add to note 1441: page* [1072]]
Compare *Kaur v MG Rover Group Ltd* [2004] I.R.L.R. 279, Q.B.D., where a declaration was granted of contractual entitlement not to be made redundant. The decision was reversed on appeal on other, substantive, grounds ([2004] EWCA Civ 1507; [2005] I.R.L.R. 40), but remains of interest as to this remedial point.

(f) *Employment Tribunal Jurisdiction*

Jurisdiction of employment tribunals in relation to contracts of employment

[Add to note 1460: page [1073]]
Compare *Peninsula Business Services Ltd v Sweeney* [2004] I.R.L.R. 49, E.A.T., denying entitlement to commission payments which would normally have accrued due at a date later than that of termination of employment, and where the rules of the commission scheme excluded post-termination accrual.

39–205

8. UNFAIR AND DISCRIMINATORY DISMISSAL

(a) *Unfair Dismissal*

(i) *General Considerations*

Employments covered and employments specifically excluded

[Add to note 1478 : page [1075]]
As to the implicit exclusion of employees working abroad, see *Lawson v Serco Ltd* [2004] EWCA Civ 12.

39–208

[Add to note 1484: page [1076]]
Compare *Wall v British Compressed Air Society* [2003] EWCA Civ 1762; [2004] 2 All E.R. 200 in which it was held that an employee may have a "normal retiring age" although in a unique position within the employing enterprise.

(ii) *Dismissal and Effective Date of Termination*

The effective date of termination

[Add to note 1538: page [1080]]
Compare *Fitzgerald v University of Kent at Canterbury* [2004] EWCA Civ 143; [2004] I.C.R. 737, in which it was held that a retrospective agreement did not validly alter the effective date of termination. But compare also now *Palfrey v Transco plc* [2004] I.R.L.R. 916 (EAT) where a later agreement for payment in lieu of notice was held to have advanced the effective date of termination.

39–213

[Add to note 1540: page [1081]]
In *Harper v Virgin Net Ltd* [2004] EWCA Civ 271; [2004] I.R.L.R. 390 it was held that the legislation did not bring about a further postponement of the effective date of termination to the later date at which a contractual notice period, longer than the statutory minimum notice period, would have expired.

39–214

(iii) *Unfairness*

Introduction

39-215   [*Page* [1081]]
A new specially designated ground of unfair dismissal has been created by s.40 of the Employment Relations Act 2004, which, by inserting a new s.98B into the Employment Rights Act 1996, renders it unfair to dismiss an employee by reason of his or her being summoned for or being absent from work on jury service, unless the employer shows the likelihood of substantial injury to the undertaking being caused by the absence on jury service. This provision was effective from April 6, 2005.

[*Add to note 1547: page* [1081]]
As to the impact of the Human Rights Act 1998 on the adjudication of unfairness, see *X v Y (Employment: Sex Offender)* [2004] EWCA Civ 662; [2004] I.R.L.R. 625.

Reasonableness of dismissal

39-217   [*Add to note 1578: page* [1084]]
This should now be considered in conjunction with the provisions about statutory dispute resolution procedures, detailed in paras 39–258—39–262 of the Main Work. The provisions came into force on October 1, 2004.

Dismissal by reason of trade union membership, non-membership or activity

39-219   [*Page* [1085]]
The reference in the text to s.46 of the Trade Union and Labour Relations (Consolidation) Act 1992 should be to ss.146–151 of that Act.
Section 152 of the 1992 Act has been amended by s.32 of the Employment Relations Act 2004 so as to make the dismissal of an employee unfair where it is for making use of the services of his union or refusing to accept certain specified inducements in respect of trade union membership or collective bargaining. This provision was brought into effect on October 1, 2004.

Dismissal during lock-out, strike or other industrial action

39-220   [*Add to note 1621: page* [1087]]
The provisions of s.238A of the 1992 Act concerning "protected industrial action" have been amended by the Employment Relations Act 2004. Sections 27–28 of the 2004 Act, which, by amending s.238A and adding a new s.238B to the 1992 Act, increase the protections against the dismissal of employees taking official lawfully organised industrial action by extending the "protected period" from 8 to 12 weeks, by exempting days of lock-out from the 12-week protected period, and also defining more closely the actions which employers and unions should undertake by way of recourse to conciliation and mediation with regard

to "protected industrial action". These provisions were brought into effect on April 6, 2005.

(iv) *Remedies*

Compensation for unfair dismissal: the compensatory award

[*Add to note 1706: page* [1094]]   **39–233**
The principle in the *Norton Tool* case was upheld on the appeal to the House of Lords in *Dunnachie v Kingston-upon-Hull City Council* [2004] UKHL 36.

9. Redundancy Payments and Procedure

(b) *Redundancy Procedure*

Consultation with the representatives of recognised trade unions or of employees

[*Add to note 1879: page* [1109]]   **39–256**
See, as to the making of the award, *Susie Radin Ltd v GMB* [2004] EWCA Civ 180; [2004] 2 All E.R. 279.

10. Statutory Dispute Resolution Procedures

Introduction

[*Page* [1111]]   **39–258**
In connection with the statutory dispute resolution procedures, reference should now be made to the right for workers to be accompanied by certain trade union officials or fellow workers at non-trivial disciplinary and grievance hearings. That right was originally conferred by ss.10–12 of the Employment Relations Act 1999. Section 37 of the Employment Relations Act 2004 amended s.10 of the 1999 Act, with effect from October 1, 2004, in order further to clarify the role of the companion at such disciplinary and grievance hearings.

The statutory dispute resolution procedures

[*Note 1902: page* [1111]]   **39–259**
The Employment Act 2002 (Dispute Resolution) Regulations 2004 were duly enacted on March 12, 2004 with the SI number SI 2004/752, to come into force on October 1, 2004.

CHAPTER 40

GAMING AND WAGERING

1A. GAMBLING ACT 2005

40–A001   **Contracts which relate to gambling generally enforceable.** The Gambling Act 2005 will, when it is brought into force,[a1] fundamentally change the law with regard to gaming and wagering contracts as discussed in Ch.40 of the Main Work. So far as the effects of gaming and wagering contracts are concerned, that discussion is mainly concerned with the restrictions on the validity of such contracts and of certain associated transactions which had been imposed by the Gaming Acts 1710, 1835, 1845 and 1892, as interpreted in the cases discussed in Pt 2 of that Chapter (paras 40–018—40–088). Section 334 of the 2005 Act will repeal all those provisions,[a2] though not with retrospective effect,[a3] thus rendering most of that discussion obsolete; s.356 will also repeal the remaining provisions of those Acts, as well as the Gaming Act 1968, s.16 which is discussed in paras 40–057, 40–058 and 40–077—40–080 of the Main Work. Section 335(1) of the 2005 Act marks a fundamental shift in the approach of the law to the legal effects of gambling contracts in laying down the general rule that contracts which relate to gambling are to be legally enforceable. This general rule is, under the Act, subject to two principal exceptions; the general rule and the exceptions to it are discussed in paras 40–A004—40–A007 of this Supplement. By way of introduction, a (necessarily brief) account must be given of the principal elements of the structure of this complex legislation and of its terminology, so far as these matters relate to the legal effect of gambling contracts under the Act.

[a1] By order made under s.358(1); at the time of writing, no order has been made bringing Pt 17 of the Act (ss.334–338), with which the following discussion is mainly concerned, into force.
[a2] s.334(1).
[a3] s.334(2).

General scheme of the Act. The main purpose of the Act is to create a new   **40–A002** scheme for the regulation of gambling in Great Britain, to be supervised by a body (the Gambling Commission) created by the Act.[a4] The scheme does not extend to "spread bets" (such as contracts for differences) which are regulated under the Financial Services and Markets Act 2000,[a5] or to the National Lottery.[a6] The general principle underlying the Act is that commercial gambling which does not fall within either of these exceptions is unlawful, so that the provision of facilities, or the use of premises, for gambling is an offence unless a licence has been obtained from the appropriate local authority[a7] and the conditions of the licence have been complied with.[a8] It is also an offence under the Act to invite or permit a child or young person to take part in commercial gambling[a9] and for a young person to engage in such gambling[a10] or to provide facilities for such gambling.[a11] The licencing requirements described above,[a12] and the offences resulting from failure to comply with them do not extend to "private" gaming or betting or to certain other non-commercial gaming or betting.[a13]

[a4] s.20.
[a5] s.10.
[a6] s.15, except for the purposes of ss.42 and 335 (below, paras 40–A004 and 40–A005).
[a7] s.2.
[a8] ss.33(2), 37(1).
[a9] s.46.
[a10] s.48.
[a11] s.50.
[a12] At nn 7 and 8.
[a13] ss.296, 297–302.

Terminology of the Act. "Gambling" in the Act means gaming, betting and   **40–A003** participating in a lottery.[a14] "Gaming" means playing (*i.e.* participating in) a game of chance (not including a sport) for a prize.[a15] "Betting" means "making or accepting a bet on (a) the outcome of a race, competition or other event or process, (b) the likelihood of anything occurring or not occurring, or (c) whether anything is or is not true."[a16] The events on which the outcome of the bet depends in some important respects resemble those which could be the subject of a wager (an expression which forms no part of the definition of "gambling", "gaming" or "betting" in the 2005 Act) within the definition which had been formulated at common law for the purposes of the earlier Gaming Acts which are to be repealed.[a17] The phrase "making a bet" is not defined, but it can be inferred that the person making the bet must pay or deposit a stake or make some other payment in order to participate in the bet.[a18] "Betting" in the 2005 Act does not include activities regulated under s.22 of the Financial Services & Markets Act[a19]; contracts for differences (Main Work para.40–010) fall into this category,[a20] as do so-called "spread bets". On the other hand, the concept of "gambling" under the 2005 Act is wider than that of a wager under the common law definition in that it includes participating in a lottery[a21] and in that the concept of betting includes pool betting.[a22] It is also not in terms restricted to cases in which the party to whom money is to be paid on the outcome of the bet has no other "interest" in the contract than the sum or stake that he will win or lose.[a23] The existence of such an "interest" was thought to be one reason why contracts of insurance were not wagers where the requirement of the insured's having been an "insurable interest" was satisfied. But, as is pointed out in para.40–005 of the Main Work, a contract of insurance was not necessarily a wager merely because the requirement of insurable interest was not satisfied; and in such cases the contract of insurance was nevertheless void under s.4 of the Marine Insurance Act 1906 and might be illegal under the Marine Insurance (Gambling Policies) Act 1909. Neither of these enactments is repealed or amended by the 2005 Act, in spite of the fact that by s.4 of the 1906 Act a contract of marine insurance is "deemed to be a gaming or wagering contract"[a24] where "the assured has not an insurable interest as defined by this Act"[a25] and that "a contract of marine by way of gaming or wagering is void."[a26] The absence of any reference to these provisions in the 2005 Act seems to indicate a legislative intention not to change the law with regard to insurance without interest, at any rate with regard to marine insurance, and probably with regard to insurance generally since the provisions of the 1906 Act are, where appropriate, regarded as applicable to contracts of insurance generally.[a27] It follows that insurance, even without interest, is not subject to the regulatory provisions which form the bulk of the 2005 Act, and that Pt 17 of that Act, which relates to the legality and enforceability of gambling contracts, does not apply to contracts of insurance which are void for want of insurable interest.

[a14] s.3.

[a15] s.6.

[a16] s.9.

[a17] See Main Work, paras 40–001—40–012.

[a18] See Gambling Act 2005, s.11(1) ("despite the fact that he does not deposit a stake in the normal way of betting"), 11(1)(b) ("required to pay").

[a19] Gambling Act 2005, s.10.

[a20] Financial Services and Markets Act 2000 (Regulated Activities) Order 2001 (SI 2001/544), art.85.

[a21] Gambling Act 2005, s.3(1).

a22 Gambling Act 2005, s.12(1); contrast Main Work para.40–003 for the view that pool betting was not "wagering" under the previous law.

a23 See Main Work, para.40–005 for this requirement under the previous law.

a24 Marine Insurance Act 1906, s.4(2).

a25 *ibid.*, s.4(2)(a); see also s.4(2)(b) ("interest or no interest policy").

a26 *ibid.*, s.4(1).

a27 *cf. Locker & Woolf Ltd v W Australian Insurance Co Ltd* [1936] 1 K.B. 408 at 414.

Enforceability of contracts relating to gambling: s.335(1). At common law, **40–A004** the general rule was that wagering contracts were legally enforceable, though this rule was subject to qualifications stated in para.40–017 of the Main Work. The restrictions on the enforceability of such contracts imposed by the legislative provisions referred to in para.40–A001 of this Supplement are to be removed by the repeal of those provisions by the 2005 Act,a28 but this repeal will not, of itself, restore the common law rule by which wagering contracts were, in general, legally enforceable.a29 It was therefore necessary for that Act to contain a specific provision to this effect. This is made by s.335(1), which provides that "the fact that a contract relates to gambling shall not prevent its enforcement". Four points must here be made about this provision.

The first arises from what is in substance the double negative contained in the phrase "shall not prevent". The subsection does not in terms say that contracts relating to gaming shall be enforceable; it merely says that the fact of a contract's being so related shall not prevent its enforcement. It therefore does not rule out the possibility that enforcement may be refused on some ground other than the fact that the contract relates to gambling. The significance of this point is further considered in the discussion in paras 40–A005 and 40–A006 below of one of the exceptions to the general principle of enforceability laid down by the 2005 Act.a30

Secondly, s.335(1) refers to "the fact that a contract relates to gambling". This phrase is wide enough to cover, not only the gambling contract itself, but also associated transactions. Problems that have in the past arisen (and may continue to arise) out of associated transactions such as agency arrangements related to gambling, partnerships, stakeholders, securities and loans for gambling,a31 would all seem to be covered by the phrase and such related transactions will be enforceable by virtue of s.335(1).

Thirdly, the only direct effect of s.335(1) is to make the contracts covered by it enforceable; but the enforceability of such contracts will also have repercussions on a number of further legal effects of such contracts which had given rise to problems under the previous law. Thus if money is paid or property deposited under a gambling (or related) contracta32 there can no longer be any question of its being recoverable by the payee or depositor merely because that contract was a gambling contract. The payment or deposit would simply have been made under a valid contract and any right to its return would depend on the terms of the contract, or on other rules of law governing the recoverability of payments or deposits made under a contract. The fact that a payment was made under a gambling contract which is now enforceable will also have repercussions on the law relating to gambling with stolen money.a33

Fourthly, the general principle of the enforceability of contracts relating to gambling is, under the 2005 Act, subject to two significant exceptions. Enforcement may be refused on the ground of "unlawfulness"; and the Gambling Commission is given power to "void" certain bets. These exceptions are discussed in paras 40–A005—40–A007 below.

a28 Above, para.40–A001.
a29 See Interpretation Act 1978, s.16.
a30 *cf.* Gambling Act 2005, s.337(1).
a31 See Main Work, paras 40–033—40–080.
a32 See *ibid.*, paras 40–028—40–032.
a33 See *ibid.*, paras 40–081—40–087; below, paras 40–082—40–083 of this Supplement.

40–A005   **Unlawfulness: s.335(2).** Section 335(2) of the 2005 Act provides that "subsection (1) is without prejudice to any rule of law preventing the enforcement of a contract on the ground of unlawfulness (*other than a rule relating specifically to gambling*)." The first question that arises from this provision is its effect on cases in which the unlawfulness is due to failure to comply with the provisions of the Act, outlined above, such as its licensing requirements. In one sense, those requirements might be said to consist of rules of law "relating specifically to gambling" and so not to fall within the restriction on the enforceability of contracts contained in s.335(2). But it is submitted that this reasoning would be contrary to the policy of the Act in that it would allow a party to a gambling contract who had failed to comply with the Act nevertheless to enforce the contract. Such a conclusion can, and should, be avoided by arguing that, in cases of this kind, the "unlawfulness" arises, not "specifically" because the transaction is a bet, but because the making of the contract constitutes a form of activity which is prohibited, with penal sanctions, by law (in this case, by other provisions of the Act itself). The purpose of the words italicised above appears to be to exclude the argument that gambling contracts are "unlawful" *as such* because their enforcement would be contrary to public policy; for if this argument were accepted, s.335(2) would (but for those italicised words) wholly negate the validating effect on gambling contracts of s.335(1). The purpose of subs.(2) is, in the terms of the Explanatory Notes[a34] to the Act, to ensure that subs.(1) "does not . . . override any other rule that prevents enforcement on the ground of unlawfulness. Therefore gambling contracts may be void on the same basis as any other contract (for example, on the basis of lack of intention, mistake or illegality)." The rule that a contract may be void or for illegality because it is one to engage in a form of activity that is prohibited by legislation with penal consequences is of general application in that it applies to all contracts, of whatever nature; and the rule is not excluded, by the words italicised above, from the restriction on enforceability in s.335(2) merely because the activity happens to be gambling.

It follows from the above reasoning that, if a person who provided facilities for gambling did so without the requisite licence, or failed to comply with conditions of the licence, and so committed an offence under the Act,[a35] then that person would, under the law relating to illegal contracts, not be entitled to enforce the contract; the other party's ability to enforce it would depend on the degree of his knowledge of or complicity in the failure. Conversely, if that other party committed the offence of cheating contrary to s.42 of the Act, then that other party would not be entitled to enforce the contract, though the victim of the offence might be able to do so. Where the gambling amounts to an offence because it is between the holder of a licence and a child or young person, any money paid (*e.g.* by way of stake) by the child or young person must be returned to the child or young person,[a36] even (it seems) to a young person who is himself guilty of the offence of gambling[a37]; and the provider of the facilities for gambling "may not give a prize to the child or young person."[a38] It follows from this last provision that the contract is not enforceable by the child or young person. A further possible ground of unlawfulness under the 2005 Act lies in the provision of credit for gambling. In this respect, the Act maintains the policy of some of the earlier gaming legislation,[a39] which it will repeal,[a40] to restrict the giving of such credit. For example, it provides that an operating licence may restrict the giving of credit "in connection with the licensed activities"[a41]; and that certain premises licences shall be subject to the condition that the licensee does not "give credit in connection with gambling authorised by the licence."[a42] Failure to comply with such a condition would be an offence under the Act.[a43] It is also an offence under the Act to supply, install or make available for use a gaming machine which is designed or adapted to permit money to be paid by means of a credit card.[a44] In the first two cases, it follows that the licensee could not enforce the terms of the credit against the person to whom it had been granted; and it is arguable that the illegality of the loan would also infect the gambling transaction itself. The latter argument could also be available in the third case, though it would not affect the legal relations between the cardholder and the issuer of the card (assuming the issuer to be a person other than the licensee). A premises licence must also be subject to the condition that the premises shall not be used for gambling on Christmas Day.[a45] Such gambling would therefore be unlawful and contracts relating to it unenforceable.

Unlawfulness of a contract relating to gambling can also result from rules of law other than those contained in the 2005 Act: *e.g.* where the gambling was prohibited by other rules of law, or where the event on which the outcome of a bet depended involved the commission of an illegal act, whether by one or more of the parties to the bet or by one of the participants in gaming on which the bet was placed. In such cases, the contract would be invalid, not because it related to gambling, but because it could be said to encourage breaches of the law. It is submitted that the same reasoning could apply where the unlawfulness arose because the conduct in question, though not contrary to law, was contrary to public policy on grounds other than the mere fact that it related to gambling. This was the position at common law before the Gaming Acts of 1710, 1835, 1845 and 1892. As explained in para.40–017 of the Main Work, at common law wagers were generally valid but a wager could not be enforced if enforcement was "against sound policy"[a46]: *e.g.* because it tended to cause public disorder.[a47] While the repeal by the Gambling Act 2005 of earlier legislation invalidating wagering contracts has not of itself restored the earlier common law rules,[a48] the wording of s.335(2) has, it is submitted, left it open to the courts to develop grounds of public policy on which they could refuse to enforce contracts relating to gambling; again, the reason for such refusals would be, not that the contract related to gambling, but that its enforcement would be contrary to public policy on some other ground. In relation to the example given above,[a49] of a wager causing public disorder, it should be emphasised that the first of the "licensing objectives" stated in s.1(a) of the 2005 Act is "preventing gambling from being a source of crime or disorder, being associated with crime or disorder or being used to support crime." It is submitted that a contract which tended to subvert any part of this objective should not be enforceable by virtue of s.335(1) but should be denied enforceability by virtue of s.335(2). In the case of most commercial gambling, such a contract would in all probability involve the breach of a condition of the relevant licence and so amount to an offence under the Act. But the scope of s.335 is quite general: it applies not only to commercial gambling, but also to gambling which is not subject to any licensing requirements, such as private and non-commercial gambling.[a50] The court may thus not only enforce contracts relating to such gambling, but also refuse to enforce them on the ground of "unlawfulness" (not relating specifically to gambling).

[a34] See para.829 of the Explanatory Notes; for further discussion of this Note, see below, para.40–A006 of this Supplement.
[a35] Gambling Act 2005, ss.33(2), 37(2).
[a36] *ibid.*, ss.58, 83(1)(a).
[a37] *ibid.*, s.48.
[a38] *ibid.*, s.83(1)(b).
[a39] Especially Gaming Act 1710, s.1 and Gaming Act 1968, s.16.
[a40] Above, para.40–A001 of this Supplement.
[a41] Gambling Act 2005, s.81(2)(a); see also s.81(2)(b).
[a42] *ibid.*, s.177(2)(a).
[a43] *ibid.*, ss.33(1) and (2), 37(1) and (2).
[a44] *ibid.*, s.245.
[a45] *ibid.*, s.183.
[a46] *Good v Elliott* (1790) 3 T.R. 693 at 695.
[a47] *Eltham v Kingsman* (1818) 1 B. & Ald. 683.
[a48] See Interpretation Act 1979, s.16.
[a49] At n.47.
[a50] See Gambling Act 2005, ss.33(1)(b)(v) and (vi), 37(7).

40–A006   **Scope of s.335(2).** The grounds on which the courts may refuse to enforce a contract relating to gambling are by no means exhaustively stated in s.335(2). That subsection states only *one* such ground, *i.e.* unlawfulness (other than a rule relating specifically to gambling). Enforcement may also be refused on other grounds, such as the failure of the parties to reach agreement, lack of contractual intention, invalidating causes such as mistake, misrepresentation or duress, and any other ground on which a contract may be void, voidable or unenforceable irrespective of its being a contract relating to gambling. The Explanatory Note to s.335, indeed, includes among its illustrative list of rules that prevent "enforcement on the grounds of unlawfulness" not only "illegality" but also "lack of intention" and "mistake".[a51] It is, however, respectfully submitted that to regard "lack of intention" or "mistake" as illustrations of "unlawfulness" is, to say the least, unusual; and that it may be misleading when the exact legal effects of such factors fall to be considered. The possibility that enforcement may be refused on account of these factors, and of other factors such as those listed above in this paragraph, follows, not from the exception to enforceability contained in s.335(2), but from the negative language of s.335(1).[a52] The subsection does not say that contracts relating to gambling are enforceable; it says only that the fact of a contract's being so related does not prevent its enforcement. Where the contract is affected by some invalidating cause such as those listed above, it simply does not fall within the scope of s.335(1). The same is, *a fortiori*, true where the alleged contract is impugned for lack of intention, *e.g.* because it contains an "honour" or similar clause, as appears to be common in the case of agreements between football pool promoters and participants in such betting.[a53] In such cases there is simply no "contract" which could be made enforceable by virtue of s.335(1).

[a51] Explanatory Note, para.829.
[a52] See above, para.40–A004 of this Supplement.
[a53] See Main Work paras 40–003 and Vol.I, para.2–157.

Voiding a bet. Section 336 of the 2005 Act confers on the Gambling Commission[a54] power, in certain cases,[a55] to make an order to avoid a bet if the commission is "satisfied that the bet was substantially unfair".[a56] The power is exercisable in relation to a bet accepted by or through the holder of (a) a general operating licence, (b) a pool betting licence, or (c) a betting intermediary licence.[a57] It is thus restricted to commercial gambling and so does not, for example, extend to private and non-commercial gaming as betting.[a58] The effects of an order under s.336 are that (a) any contract or other arrangement in relation to the bet is void, and (b) that any money paid in relation to the bet (whether by way of stake, winnings, commission or otherwise) must be repaid to the payor.[a59] In deciding whether a bet is "unfair" the Commission is required to take account of any of a list of factors (set out in s.336(4)) that applies to the case in question. The list is not intended to be exhaustive[a60]; it includes "the fact that either party to the bet supplied insufficient, false or misleading information in connection with it".[a61] An order under s.336 can be made only within six months of the beginning of the day on which the bet is determined[a62]; but where the circumstance which makes the bet unfair would also amount to a factor vitiating the contract under general principles of law, a party to the contract could rely on that circumstance even after the expiry of the six month period by way of defence to an action on the bet under s.335. This follows from the discussion in paras 40–A005 and 40–A006 of "unlawfulness" and other grounds on which the court may refuse to enforce a contract relating to gambling. This reasoning would also apply where the contract was one in respect of which no order under s.336 would be made: *e.g.* because the contract related to private gaming or betting. An order under s.336 may relate to the whole or any part of a betting transaction[a63] and may make incidental provisions about other parts of a transaction one part of

40–A007

which is made void by the order,[a64] and about related bets.[a65] Any order made by the Commission under s.336 is subject to appeal to the Gambling Appeals Tribunal[a66] from which a further appeal lies on a point of law to the High Court with leave of the Tribunal or the court.[a67]

An order under s.336 will no doubt normally be sought by the party to the contract who is prejudiced by the unfairness of the bet. But nothing in the section limits the power of the Commission to cases in which the order is sought by that person. On the contrary, s.338 suggests that the Commission may act on its own initiative in this respect. That section applies "where the Commission has reason to suspect that it may wish to make an order under section 336(1) in respect of a bet"[a68] and empowers the Commission in such a case to make an "interim moratorium" order by which an obligation to pay money in relation to the bet ceases to have effect for 14 days.[a69] It seems also to be possible for an order under s.336 to be made on the application of a third party who might be prejudiced by the enforcement of, or the retention of money paid under, the bet.[a70]

[a54] Created by Gambling Act 2005, s.20.
[a55] See below, after n.56.
[a56] *ibid.*, s.336(3).
[a57] *ibid.*, s.336(1).
[a58] Within Pt 14 of the 2005 Act (ss.295–302).
[a59] *ibid.*, s.336(2).
[a60] See the words "in particular" in the opening phrase of s.336(4).
[a61] s.336(4)(a).
[a62] s.336(5).
[a63] s.337(2).
[a64] s.337(3)(a).
[a65] s.337(3)(b).
[a66] Established by s.140.
[a67] s.143.
[a68] s.338(1).
[a69] ss.338(2), (3); the time can be extended: s.338(4).
[a70] *e.g.* by the victim of a theft of money used by the thief for gambling: see below, para.40–083 of this Supplement.

1. DEFINITIONS

(a) *Wagering Contracts*

Wagering contract defined

40–001   *[Add to note 1: page [1115]]*
The definition of "wagering contract" quoted in para.40–001 of the Main Work was formulated for the purposes of s.18 of the Gaming Act 1845. This definition will be made obsolete by the repeal of s.18 by the Gambling Act 2005: see above, para.40–A001 of this Supplement. The 2005 Act does not use the expressions "wagering contract" or wager. For the meaning of "gambling" in the 2005 Act, see above, para.40–A003.

Future uncertain event

[Add to note 3: page [1116]]
Some of the elements of the common law definition of a wagering contract are reflected in the definition of "betting" in s.9 of the Gambling Act 2005.

No other interest

[Add to note 18: page [1117]]
The rules stated in s.4(2) of the Marine Insurance Act 1906 and in the Marine Insurance (Gambling Policies) Act 1909 appear not to be affected by the Gambling Act 2005: see above, para.40–A003.

(b) *Gaming Contracts*

Statutory definitions

[Add to note 56: page [1121]]
The Gaming Act 1968 will be repealed by the Gambling Act 2005: above, para.40–A001. Elements of the definition quoted in the Main Work at n.56 are reflected in the definitions of "gaming" and "game of chance" in s.6 of the 2005 Act. The basic concept of "gaming" remains "playing a game of chance for a prize" (s.6(1)). The other legislation cited in para.40–014 of the Main Work is also (except for the National Lottery Act 1993) repealed by the 2005 Act.

Lawful and unlawful gaming

[Add at end of paragraph: page [1121]]
For the repeal of the Gaming Act 1968, see above, para.40–A001 of this Supplement; for the principal categories of cases in which gambling will be unlawful under the Gambling Act 2005, see *ibid.*, para.40–A002.

2. Effects of Gaming and Wagering Contracts

(a) *Enforcement*

Under the Gaming Act 1845, s.18

[Add new text after note 76: page [1123]]
The repeal of s.18 of the Gaming Act 1845 by the Gambling Act 2005 will make the discussion in paras 40–018—40–024 of the Main Work obsolete: see above, para.40–A001.

Excepted transactions

40–025   *[Add to note 96: page* [1125]]
The reference in s.412 of the Financial Services and Markets Act 2000 to s.18 of the Gaming Act 1845 is to be deleted by ss.334(1)(e) and 356 and Sch.17 of the Gambling Act 2005 but without change of substance since under s.335(1) contracts which relate to gambling will, in general, be enforceable: see above, para.40–A004 of this Supplement.

Distance contracts

40–026   *[Add to note 97: page* [1125]]
For amendments of the Consumer Protection (Distance Selling) Regulations 2000, see above, Vol.I, para.2–026.

(b) *Recovery Back Money Paid*

Gaming Act 1845 s.18

40–029   *[Add to note 107: page* [1126]]
The repeal of s.18 of the Gaming Act 1845 by the Gambling Act 2005 (see above, para.40–A001) will make the reasoning of para.4–029 of the Main Work obsolete. Money paid under a contract relating to gambling will continue to be irrecoverable, but on the different ground that the payment was made under a valid contract. Where the gambling contract is illegal or defective in some other way, the right (if any) to recover money paid under it will be governed by the general rules of law relating to the recovery of money under illegal or otherwise defective contracts.

Overpayment

40–030   *[Add to note 113: page* [1127]]
The reasoning of *Morgan v Ashcroft* [1938] 1 K.B. 49 (Main Work, Vol.I, para.29–038) will be undermined by the repeal of s.18 of the Gambling Act 1845 by the Gambling Act 2005 (see above para.40–A001) and by the enforceability (in general) of contracts relating to gambling by virtue of s.335(1) of the 2005 Act (see above, para.40–A004). After these developments, there seems to be no reason why the normal rules relating to the recovery of overpayments made under valid contracts (*e.g.* under a mistake) should not apply to overpayments made under gambling contracts.

(c) *Recovering Back Money or Property Deposited*

Lawful wagers

40–032   *[Add to note 122: page* [1127]]
The reasoning of *Universal Stock Exchange v Strachan* [1896] A.C. 166, in so far as it is based on the voidness of the debt, will become obsolete when contracts

relating to gaming become generally enforceable by virtue of s.335(1) of the Gambling Act 2005 (above, para.40–A004). The same is true of other parts of the reasoning of para.40–032 of the Main Work so far as they are based on the assumption that the wagering contract is void.

(d) *Principal and Agent*

[Add new paragraph 40–032A before paragraph 40–033: page [1128]]

Gambling Act 2005. The agency situations discussed in Main Work paras **40–032A** 40–033—40–039 will generally give rise to enforceable contracts as contracts related to gambling by virtue of the Gambling Act 2005, s.335(1), above para.40–A004 of this Supplement. The provisions of the Gaming Acts 1845 and 1892 discussed in the above paragraphs of the Main Work are to be repealed by the Gambling Act 2005: see above, para.40–A001.

Excepted transactions

[Add to note 143: page [1130]]
Section 412 of the Financial Services and Markets Act 2000 is to be amended, **40–041** but without change of substance, by the Gambling Act 2005, ss.334(1)(e) and 356 and Sch.17: see above, para.40–025 of this Supplement.

(e) *Partnership*

Partnership for betting

[Add to note 147: page [1130]]
A partnership for betting will generally be an enforceable contract as a contract **40–042** related to gambling by virtue of the Gambling Act, 2005, s.335(1), above para.40–A004 of this Supplement. Section 1 of the Gaming Act 1892 is to be repealed by the 2005 Act (see above, para.40–A001).

(f) *Stakeholders*

Gaming Act 1845, s.18

[Page [1131]]
A contract with a stakeholder for the purposes of gambling will generally be **40–044** enforceable as a contract related to gambling by virtue of the Gambling Act 2005, s.335(1), above, para.40–A004 of this Supplement. Section 18 of the Gaming Act 1845 is to be repealed by the 2005 Act, above, para.40–A001 of this Supplement.

Gaming Act 1892, s.1

40–045 [*Page* [1131]]
Section 1 of the Gaming Act 1892 is to be repealed by the Gambling Act 2005, above para.40–001A of this Supplement.

(g) *Prizes for Lawful Games*

Gaming Act 1845, s.18

40–047 [*Page* [1132]]
Section 18 of the Gaming Act 1845 is to be repealed by Gambling Act 2005, see above, para.40–A001 of this Supplement; but the policy of the third limb of s.18 of the 1845 Act is maintained by s.339 of the 2005 Act. This section provides that "participating in a competition or other arrangement under which a person may win a prize is not gambling for the purposes of this Act unless it is" gaming, participating in a lottery, or betting within specified other provisions of the Act. Such prize *competitions* are to be distinguished from prize *gaming*, which is regulated by Pt 13 (ss.288–294) of the 2005 Act.

(h) *Securities*

In general

40–048 [*Add to note 161: page* [1132]]
By virtue of s.335(1) of the Gambling Act 2005 contracts relating to gambling will, as a general rule, be enforceable (see above, para.40–A004 of this Supplement). It follows that if the loser gives the winner a cheque in payment, an action can be brought on the cheque no less than on the bet. If, however, a debt is incurred in relation to gambling in violation of the restrictions on the giving of credit imposed by the terms of a licence (see s.81 of the 2005 Act) or by virtue of the Act itself (see *ibid.*, s.177), then the contract by which credit was given would not be enforceable on the ground of unlawfulness (see s.335(2), above para.40–A005 of this Supplement) and the creditor would not be able to enforce the security any more than the contract under or in respect of which it was given.

Excepted transactions

40–050 [*Add to note 166: page* [1133]]
For amendment of the legislation referred to in n.166, see above, paras 40–025 and 40–041 of this Supplement. In line 3 of the text of para.40–050, substitute "1845" for "1945"; for the repeal of s.18 of the Gaming Act 1845, see above, para.40–A001 of this Supplement.

Gaming wagers and wagers on games

[Page [1133]]
For the repeal of the Gaming Acts 1710, 1835 and 1968, see above, para. **40–051**
40–A001 of this Supplement.

Gaming Acts 1710 and 1835

[Page [1133]]
For the repeal of the Gaming Acts 1710 and 1835, see above, para.40–A001 **40–052**
of this Supplement. It should be noted that the Act of 1710 referred not only to
securities given for money won by gaming, etc., but also to securities for
repaying money lent in connection with gaming. Where the loan contravenes the
restrictions on the giving of credit imposed by or under the Gambling Act 2005
(see ss.81, 177) the reasoning in para.40–048 of this Supplement will apply, so
that neither the loan nor the security will be enforceable: see s.335(2) of the 2005
Act (above, para.40–A005 of this Supplement). This reasoning would not apply
to the gambling contract itself or to a security given in respect of losses incurred
under it, so that these would be enforceable by virtue of s.335(1) of the 2005 Act
(above, para.40–A004 of this Supplement).

Securities for loans to pay debts already lost

[Page [1134]]
For "debts" in the heading to this paragraph, substitute "bets". For the repeal **40–053**
of the Gaming Acts 1710, 1835 and 1892, see above para.40–A001 of this
Supplement. These repeals will make the reasoning of para.40–053 of the Main
Work obsolete; but neither the contract of loan nor the security could be enforced
if the loan contravened the restrictions on the giving of credit imposed by the
Gambling Act 2005: see above, para.40–052 of this Supplement.

Securities for loans of gaming chips

[Page [1134]]
For the repeal of the Gaming Acts 1710, 1835, 1845 and 1968, see above **40–054**
para.40–A001 of this Supplement, making the reasoning of para.40–054 of the
Main Work obsolete; the reasoning of para.40–053 of this Supplement will,
mutatis mutandis, apply.

New promise to pay

[Page [1135]]
The repeal of the Gaming Acts 1710, 1835 and 1845 (see above, para. **40–056**
40–A001 of this Supplement) will make the reasoning of para.40–056 of the
Main Work obsolete.

Gaming Act 1968, s.16

40–057 [*Add new text after note 192: page* [1135]]
For the repeal of the Gaming Act 1968, see above, para.40–A001 of this Supplement.

(i) *Loans in General*

Introductory

40–059 [*Page* [1136]]
The discussion of loans related to gaming in paras 40–059—40–076 is largely based on cases concerned with the effects on such loans of the Gaming Acts 1710, 1835, 1845 and 1892. The repeal of those Acts (above, para.40–A001 of this Supplement) will make most of that discussion obsolete. Under s.335(1) of the Gambling Act 2005, contracts relating to gambling are, in general, enforceable (see above, para.40–A004 of this Supplement); but under s.335(2) enforcement of such contracts may be refused on the ground of "unlawfulness" (see above, para.40–A005 of this Supplement). Thus if the gambling itself is carried on in contravention of the Act and amounts to an offence under it, the common law principle, that a loan made to enable a person to play an illegal game is irrecoverable, will continue to apply (see Main Work, para.40–059 at n.201). Where the loan itself amounts to the giving of credit in contravention of the 2005 Act (see ss.81, 177), the unlawfulness of the loan will be a ground for refusing its enforcement. Where the loan is not affected by such (or any other) unlawfulness, the giving of a security in respect of it will no longer affect the enforceability of the loan.

[*Add to note 202: page* [1136]]
For amendment of this legislation (Financial Services and Markets Act 2000, s.412), but without change of substance, see above paras 40–025 and 40–041 of this Supplement.

(j) *Loans for Gaming on Licensed Premises*

Gaming Act 1968, s.16

40–077 [*Add new text: page* [1142]]
For the repeal of the Gaming Act 1968, s.16 by the Gambling Act 2005, see above, para.40–A001 of this Supplement; this repeal will make the discussion in Main Work, paras 40–077—40–080 obsolete. For restrictions on credit for gambling under the Gambling Act 2005, see above, paras 40–048 and 40–052 of this Supplement.

(k) *Gambling with Stolen Money*

(i) *Illegal Wagers*

Stolen money used to pay losses under illegal wagers

[*Add to note 248: page* [1144]]

In so far as the outcome of *Clarke v Shee and Johnson* (1774) 1 Cowp. 197 was based on the ground that the recipient of the stolen money had provided no consideration for the payment of it to him because his promise to the thief was void on the ground of illegality, that reasoning is not affected by the Gambling Act 2005; see further below, para.40–083 of this Supplement.

40–082

(ii) *Lawful Wagers*

Stolen money used to pay losses under lawful wagers

[*Add at end: page* [1144]]

The reasoning of *Lipkin Gorman v Karpnale Ltd*[250a] will be undermined by the repeal of s.18 of the Gaming Act 1845 by the Gambling Act 2005[250b] and by the provision of s.335(1) of the latter Act that "the fact that a contract relates to gambling shall not prevent its enforcement".[250c] Since on such facts the club will be bound by its promise to pay his winnings to Cass (the thief of the money) that promise would, unless defective for some reason other than that it was contained in a contract relating to gambling, bind the club; it would therefore constitute consideration for the payment of the money to the club. The assumption on which this view is based is that the gambling was lawful. If it was unlawful, *e.g.* because the club lacked a requisite licence or had failed to comply with a condition of its licence, then its promise would be illegal and void,[250d] so that in such a case the reasoning of the *Lipkin Gorman* case would still apply.

40–083

The further question arises whether that reasoning would also still apply where it was arguable that the bet was "unfair" so that an order could be made under s.336 of the 2005 Act, making the bet void and ordering money paid under it to be repaid.[250e] It is submitted that the possibility of such an order's being made would not deprive the club's promise of its potential of constituting consideration for the payment. The power to make the order is discretionary[250f] so that there can be no certainty of its being exercised. The club's promise may then be of doubtful value but this is not sufficient to negative the possibility of its amounting to consideration.[250g] Moreover, the power to make an order under s.336 is exercisable only for six months after the determination of the bet[250h]; and if no attempt were made during that time to obtain such an order there would be no doubt that the club's promise (unless it were otherwise defective) would then constitute consideration for the payment to it of the stolen money. Where the bet is indeed unfair, there may, however, be a mechanism under the Act by which the victim of the theft can indirectly secure the return of the stolen money, or at least of part of it. It has been suggested in para.40–A007 of this Supplement that there is nothing in s.336 which expressly restricts the power to apply for an order under the section to the parties of the bet. If this is right, an application for such an order could be made by the victim of the theft. The effect of the order (in cases of the present kind) would be that any money paid in relation to the bet "shall be repaid to the person who paid it and repayment may be enforced as a debt by that person.[250i] The person entitled to repayment would indeed be the thief, but the victim of the theft would then have a civil claim against the thief for the restitution of the stolen money. It is an open question whether such a claim would be a proprietary claim or a personal one (under which the victim of the theft would rank equally with the thief's other creditors). In this respect, the claim against the thief could be less advantageous to the victim than the claim against the club was in the *Lipkin Gorman* case.[250j] On the other hand, in a restitution claim against the thief the partial defence of change of position *by the club*, that prevailed in the *Lipkin Gorman* case[250k] would not be available to the thief since that defence is not available to a defendant who has changed his position in bad faith.[250l] Nor would change of position by the club afford it a partial defence to an order to make repayment (if the bet is unfair) under s.336. Such repayment "may be enforced as a debt due to that person"[250m] (*i.e.* the payer of the money). In actions for the recovery of a debt there is no defence of change of position; and even if there were such a defence it would not be available to the recipient of a payment who was responsible for the unfairness of the bet.[250n] In this respect the rights of the victim of the theft against the thief might actually be more favourable to him, if he could invoke s.336, than his rights against the club were in the *Lipkin Gorman* case.

[250a] [1991] 2 A.C. 548.
[250b] See above, para.40–A001 of this Supplement.
[250c] See above, paras 40–A004 and 40–A006 of this Supplement.
[250d] See above, para.40–A005 of this Supplement.
[250e] See above, para.40–A007 of this Supplement.
[250f] s.336(1) begins with the words "The Commission *may* make an order . . . ".
[250g] *cf.* above, Vol.I, para.3–051.
[250h] Gambling Act 2005, s.336(5).
[250i] *ibid.*, s.336(2)(b).
[250j] Above, n.250a.
[250k] Main Work, para.40–087.
[250l] *ibid.*, Vol.I, para.29–183.
[250m] Gambling Act 2005, s.336(2)(b).
[250n] The reasoning at n.250l above would apply by way of analogy.

(1) *Gaming Chips*

Gaming chips treated as money

40–088   *[Page [1147]]*
The discussion in Main Work, para.40–088 will be rendered obsolete by the repeal by the Gambling Act 2005 of the Gaming Acts 1710, 1892 and 1968 (above para.40–A001 of this Supplement) and of other legislation indirectly referred to in that discussion; and by the general principle stated in s.335(1) of the 2005 Act making contracts related to gambling enforceable (above, para. 40–A004 of this Supplement).

INSURANCE

2. INSURABLE INTEREST

Definition of insurable interest

[*Update note 24: page* [1152]]
O'Kane v Jones is now reported at [2004] 1 Lloyd's Rep. 389.

41–004

The relevance of the risk of financial loss

[*Update note 31: page* [1153]]
O'Kane v Jones is now reported at [2004] 1 Lloyd's Rep. 389.

41–005

Types of insurable interest

41–006   *[Delete "but only in the event insured against" from note 46 and substitute: page [1154]]*
but only in the profits or the subject matter lost

Insurance of another's interest

41–008   *[Add to the end of note 88: page [1157]]*
Ramco (UK) Ltd v International Insurance Co of Hannover Ltd [2004] EWCA Civ 675; [2004] 2 Lloyd's Rep. 595 at [8].

[Add to the end of note 89]
Ramco (UK) Ltd v International Insurance Co of Hannover Ltd [2004] EWCA Civ 675; [2004] 2 Lloyd's Rep. 595.

[Add to the end of note 90]
Ramco (UK) Ltd v International Insurance Co of Hannover Ltd [2004] EWCA Civ 675; [2004] 2 Lloyd's Rep. 595.

[Add to the end of note 91]
BP Exploration Operating Co Ltd v Kvaerner Oilfield Products Ltd [2004] EWHC 999 (Comm); [2005] 1 Lloyd's Rep. 307.

Life Assurance Act 1774

41–012   *[Update note 107: page [1159]]*
O'Kane v Jones is now reported at [2004] 1 Lloyd's Rep. 389.

The Marine Insurance Act 1906

41–014   *[Update note 123: page [1160]]*
O'Kane v Jones is now reported at [2004] 1 Lloyd's Rep. 389.

3. THE EVENT INSURED AGAINST

(d) *The Nature of the Loss or Damage*

Nature of loss

41–025   *[Add at the end of note 188: page [1167]]*
Horbury Building Systems Ltd v Hampden Insurance NV [2004] EWCA Civ 418; [2004] 2 C.L.C. 453, at [13]–[27].

[Add at end of note 194: page [1168]]
affd. [2004] EWCA Civ 277; [2004] Lloyd's Rep. I.R. 481.

4. *Uberrima Fides*

Utmost good faith

[*Note 206: page [1169]*]
Update reference to *Good Faith and Insurance Contracts* to (2nd ed., 2004).

The duty to disclose material facts

[*Add at the end of the first sentence of note 220: page [1171]*]
Whitlam v Hazel [2004] EWCA Civ 1600; [2005] Lloyd's Rep. I.R. 168.

[*Update note 222: page [1171]*]
O'Kane v Jones is now reported at [2004] 1 Lloyd's Rep. 389.

[*Add at the end of note 223: page [1171]*]
Doheny v New India Assurance Co Ltd [2004] EWCA Civ 1705; [2005] Lloyd's Rep. I.R. 251, at [16]–[20].

[*Update note 225: page [1171]*]
O'Kane v Jones is now reported at [2004] 1 Lloyd's Rep. 389.

[*Add at the end of the second sentence of note 226: page [1172]*]
North Star Shipping Ltd v Sphere Drake Insurance plc [2005] EWHC 665 (Comm); [2005] 2 Lloyd's Rep. 76; *ERC Frankona Reinsurance v American National Insurance Co* [2005] EWHC 1381 (Comm).

Scope of duty of disclosure

[*Add at end of note 231: page [1172]*]
In order to determine whether a particular person is the assured's agent to know, it is necessary to analyse both the nature of the relationship between that person and the assured and the nature of the information in question: *ERC Frankona Reinsurance v American National Insurance Co* [2005] EWHC 1381 (Comm), at [132].

[*Add to note 238 at end of first sentence: page [1173]*]
WISE (Underwriting Agency) Ltd v Grupo Nacional Provincial SA [2004] EWCA Civ 962; [2004] 2 Lloyd's Rep. 483; *Doheny v New India Assurance Co Ltd* [2004] EWCA Civ 1705; [2005] Lloyd's Rep. I.R. 251 at [16]–[20].

[*Update note 240: page [1174]*]
O'Kane v Jones is now reported at [2004] 1 Lloyd's Rep. 389.

Time of disclosure

41–031   *[Add at end of the first sentence of note 253: page [1175]]*
Swiss Reinsurance Co v United India Insurance Co Ltd [2005] EWHC 237 (Comm); [2005] Lloyd's Rep. I.R. 341 at [35]–[36].

Misrepresentation

41–032   *[Add to note 259, after reference to the Economides case: page [1176]]*
Rendall v Combined Insurance Co of America [2005] EWHC 678 (Comm); [2005] 1 C.L.C. 565.

Honesty

41–034   *[Add to note 265, after reference to Merchants' and Manufacturers' Insurance case: page [1176]]*
Whitlam v Hazel [2004] EWCA Civ 1600; [2005] Lloyd's Rep. I.R. 168 at [28].

Effect of non-disclosure or misrepresentation

41–035   *[Update note 272: page [1177]]*
Drake Insurance plc v Provident Insurance plc [2003] EWCA Civ 1834 is now reported at [2004] Q.B. 601.

Affirmation

41–036   *[Add to the end of note 287: page [1179]]*
As to the affirmatory effect of a contractual notice of cancellation, see *Mint Security Ltd v Blair* [1982] 1 Lloyd's Rep. 188, 198; *WISE (Underwriting Agency) Ltd v Grupo Nacional Provincial SA* [2004] EWCA Civ 962; [2004] 2 Lloyd's Rep. 483.

5. THE PARTIES

The insurer

41–040   *[Add note 310a at end of the first sentence: page [1182]]*
[310a] See McMeel, "The FSA's insurance conduct of business regime: a revolution in (consumer) insurance law?" [2005] L.M.C.L.Q. 186.

Broker

41–042   *[Add to end of note 321: page [1183]]*
As to the broker's entitlement to claim commission from either the insurer or the assured, see *Carvill America Inc v Camperdown UK Ltd* [2005] EWCA Civ 645; [2005] 1 C.L.C. 845.

[Add after the second sentence in note 322: page [1183]]
In so far as custom purports to oblige the broker to disclose documents to the insurer in circumstances which would be contrary to the instructions or the best interests of the assured, the custom is not enforceable: *Goshawk Dedicated Ltd v Tyser & Co Ltd* [2005] EWHC 461 (Comm); [2005] Lloyd's Rep. I.R. 379 at [41].

[Add to note 325 after the reference to Jackson & Powell: page [1183]]
As to the assumption of a duty of care, see *European International Reinsurance Co Ltd v Curzon Insurance Ltd* [2003] EWCA Civ 1074; [2003] 1 Lloyd's Rep. 793.

Lloyd's

[Add to note 329 before the final sentence: page [1184]]   **41–043**
Heath Lambert Ltd v Sociedad de Corretaje de Seguros [2004] EWCA Civ 792; [2004] 1 W.L.R. 2820.

6. The Contract of Insurance

Open covers and declarations

[Add at end of note 351: page [1187]]   **41–045**
As regards the insurer's obligations towards his reinsurer in deciding whether or not to accept a risk which would be ceded to the reinsurer, see *Bonner v Cox Dedicated Corporate Member Ltd* [2004] EWHC 2963 (Comm) at [255].

Payment of premium

[Add before the final sentence of note 373: page [1189]]   **41–050**
Heath Lambert Ltd v Sociedad de Corretaje de Seguros [2004] EWCA Civ 792; [2004] 1 W.L.R. 2820.

[Add to the end of note 378: page [1190]]
As regards the position in respect of marine insurance, see *Heath Lambert Ltd v Sociedad de Corretaje de Seguros* [2004] EWCA Civ 792; [2004] 1 W.L.R. 2820; see above, para.41–043, n.329.

Repayment

[Add at the end of note 402: page [1192]]   **41–051**
cf. Swiss Reinsurance Co v United India Insurance Co Ltd [2005] EWHC 237 (Comm); [2005] Lloyd's Rep. I.R. 341.

[Add at the end of the first sentence of note 403: page [1192]]
Swiss Reinsurance Co v United India Insurance Co Ltd [2005] EWHC 237 (Comm); [2005] Lloyd's Rep. I.R. 341.

41–051A   [*Add new paragraph: page [1192]*]

Construction of insurance contracts. Insurance contracts are subject to the same approach to contractual construction as other commercial contracts, namely that the words of the contract will be interpreted to divine their contextual meaning consistently with the commercial sense and purpose of the policy, even if that is at odds with the literal meaning of the contract.[404a] Therefore, where a word is used in an insurance policy which has a technical, legal connotation, the court will not necessarily infer that the parties intended that meaning and will inquire into the ordinary, commercial meaning to be ascribed to the word.[404b] There is one rule of construction applicable to ordinary contracts which applies with particular force in the context of insurance contracts, namely that *verba chartarum fortius accipiuntur contra proferentem*: *i.e.* where the contractual provision is ambiguous, the provision will be construed against the person who drafts or puts forward the provision, which in many cases will be the insurer.[404c] The construction of contractual terms "against the insurer" is not limited to cases where the insurer has produced the wording. If the insurer seeks to rely on a provision, such as a condition precedent, warranty or an exclusion, so as to extinguish or reduce his or her basic obligations, the court will resist such a construction unless the contractual terms are especially clear.[404d]

[404a] *Sirius International Insurance Co (Publ) v FAI General Insurance Ltd* [2004] UKHL 54; [2004] 1 W.L.R. 3251, at [18]–[19]; *Blackburn Rovers Football & Athletic Club Plc v Avon Insurance Plc* [2005] EWCA Civ 423; [2005] Lloyd's Rep. I.R. 447 at [9].

[404b] *Wooldridge v Canelhas Comercio Importacao e Exportacao Ltda* [2004] EWCA Civ 984; [2005] 1 All E.R. (Comm.) 43 ("robbery"); *cf. Dobson v General Accident Fire & Life Assurance Corp plc* [1990] 1 Q.B. 274 ("theft").

[404c] *Tektrol Ltd v International Insurance Co of Hanover Ltd* [2005] EWCA Civ 845; [2005] 1 All E.R. (Comm.) 132.

[404d] *Tektrol Ltd v International Insurance Co of Hanover Ltd* [2005] EWCA Civ 845; [2005] 1 All E.R. (Comm.) 132; *Royal & Sun Alliance Insurance Plc v Dornoch Ltd* [2005] EWCA Civ 238; [2005] 1 All E.R. (Comm.) 590; *Blackburn Rovers Football & Athletic Club Plc v Avon Insurance Plc* [2005] EWCA Civ 423; [2005] Lloyd's Rep. I.R. 447 at [9].

7. Conditions and Warranties

Construction of terms

41–053   [*Add at the end of note 407: page [1193]*]
affd. [2004] EWCA Civ 622; [2004] Lloyd's Rep. I.R. 354, at [40]–[46].

Conditions precedent

41–054   [*Add to the end of note 412: page [1193]*]
As to a claims control clause in a reinsurance policy, see *Eagle Star Insurance Co Ltd v Cresswell* [2004] EWCA Civ 602; [2004] 2 All E.R. (Comm.) 244.

[*Add to the end of note 415: page [1194]*]
Whether or not there is a class of insurance term as an innominate term, the breach of which will entitle the insurer to decline the claim as opposed to terminate the contract, is now in doubt, given the Court of Appeal's decision in *Sirius International Insurance Corp v Friends Provident Life & Pensions Ltd*

[2005] EWCA Civ 601; [2005] 1 C.L.C. 794, although (putting aside the sense of that decision) it must be questioned whether the Court of Appeal was free to overrule the court's decisions in *Alfred McAlpine v BAI* and *K/S Merc-Scandia v Lloyd's Underwriters*.

[Add to the end of the first sentence of note 416: page [1194]]
   Tektrol Ltd v International Insurance Co of Hanover Ltd [2005] EWCA Civ 845; [2005] 1 All E.R. (Comm.) 132; *Royal & Sun Alliance Insurance Plc v Dornoch Ltd* [2005] EWCA Civ 238; [2005] 1 All E.R. (Comm.) 590.

Waiver

[Add to the end of note 435: page [1196]]   **41–057**
   Fortisbank SA v Trenwick International Ltd [2005] EWHC 399 (Comm); [2005] Lloyd's Rep. I.R. 464.

[Delete "there is prejudice to the assured thereby, or" from the penultimate sentence: page [1196]]

9. CLAIMS

Notice of loss

[Add to the end of note 483: page [1201]]   **41–064**
   In *Tioxide Europe Ltd v Commercial Union Assurance Co Plc* [2005] EWCA Civ 928; [2005] All ER (D) 281 (Jul), the relevant notice was given to the wrong addressee. For an example of a clause which exercised the court's powers of interpretation, see *Royal & Sun Alliance Insurance Plc v Dornoch Ltd* [2005] EWCA Civ 238.

[Add to the end of note 486: page [1201]]
   See also *Sirius International Insurance Corp v Friends Provident Life & Pensions Ltd* [2005] EWCA Civ 601; [2005] 1 C.L.C. 794, where the Court of Appeal disapproved *Alfred McAlpine v BAI* in so far as it recognised that there might be an innominate term of an insurance contract, the breach of which would entitle the insurer to decline the insurance claim, rather than terminate the contract.

Details of loss

[Add to the end of note 491: page [1202]]   **41–065**
   As to the adequacy of particulars provided by the assured, see *Super Chem Products Ltd v American Life and General Insurance Co Ltd* [2004] UKPC 2; [2004] Lloyd's Rep. I.R. 446, at [28]–[30].

Choice of law

41–068 *[Add to the end of the penultimate sentence of note 511: page [1204]]*
Travelers Casualty & Surety Co of Europe Ltd v Sun Life Assurance Co of Canada (UK) Ltd [2004] EWHC 1704 (Comm); [2004] Lloyd's Rep. I.R. 846.

Fraudulent claims

41–069 *[Add to text after the first sentence: page [1204]]*
Beyond that simple axiom, the law is currently in an uncertain state.[512a]

[512a] *Interpart Comerciao e Gestao SA v Lexington Insurance Co* [2004] Lloyd's Rep. I.R. 690; *Marc Rich Agriculture Trading SA v Fortis Corporate Insurance NV* [2004] EWHC 2632 (Comm).

[Add to the end of note 515: page [1204]]
Axa General Insurance Ltd v Gottlieb [2005] EWCA Civ 112; [2005] Lloyd's Rep. I.R. 369.

[Add after the second sentence of note 516: page [1204]]
cf. *Axa General Insurance Ltd v Gottlieb* [2005] EWCA Civ 112; [2005] Lloyd's Rep. I.R. 369.

The burden of proof

41–070 *[Line 5 of note 528: page [1206]]*
The *Kastor Navigation* case was affirmed, [2004] EWCA Civ 277; [2004] Lloyd's Rep I.R. 481.

Multiple Causes

41–073 *[Add to note 557 before reference to Kuwait Airways case: page [1208]]*
Midland Mainline Ltd v Eagle Star Insurance Co Ltd [2004] EWCA Civ 1042; [2004] 2 Lloyd's Rep. 604.

The amount recoverable

41–074 *[Add to the end of note 569: page [1210]]*
Thor Navigation Inc v Ingosstrakh Insurance Co Ltd [2005] EWHC 19 (Comm); [2005] 1 Lloyd's Rep. 547.

Rateable proportion clauses

41–077 *[Update note 584: page [1211]]*
Drake Insurance plc v Provident Insurance plc [2003] EWCA Civ 1834 is now reported at [2004] Q.B. 601.

[Update note 585: page [1211]]
Phillips v Syndicate 992 Gunner is now reported at [2004] Lloyd's Rep. I.R. 426.

10. THE RIGHTS OF THE INSURER UPON PAYMENT

Contribution

[Update note 645: page [1217]]
O'Kane v Jones is now reported at [2004] 1 Lloyd's Rep. 389.

41–086

[Update note 647: page [1217]]
O'Kane v Jones is now reported at [2004] 1 Lloyd's Rep. 389.

11. SPECIFIC TYPES OF INSURANCE CONTRACT

(a) *Liability Insurance*

General characteristics

[Delete "s.310 and Companies Act 1989, s.137(1)" from note 661 and substitute: page [1219]]
ss.309A, 309B and 309C, introduced by the Companies (Audit, Investigations and Community Enterprise) Act 2004, s.19.

41–088

[Add after the first sentence in note 662: page [1219]]
In *Lumbermens Mutual Casualty Co v Bovis Lend Lease Ltd* [2004] EWHC 2197 (Comm); [2005] Lloyd's Rep. 74, the court held that a liability will not be established by a settlement agreement where that settlement agreement does not identify the specific cost of discharging the liability in question. Accordingly, where under a global settlement agreement, the assured agreed to receive, not pay, a single sum in settlement of all claims and counterclaims, the assured's liability for the counterclaims was held not to have been established and extrinsic evidence could not be adduced for that purpose. This proposition is questionable.

[Add to the end of note 663: page [1219]]
cf. Sun Life Assurance Co of Canada v Lincoln National Life Insurance Co [2004] EWCA Civ 1660; [2005] 1 Lloyd's Rep. 606.

Employers' liability

[Delete note 666 and substitute: page [1219]]
Employers' Liability (Compulsory Insurance) Regulations 1998 (SI 1998/2573). As to reg.3, see *R (on the application of Geologistics Ltd) v Financial Services Compensation Scheme* [2003] EWCA Civ 1877; [2004] Lloyd's Rep. I.R. 336, at [20]–[22].

41–089

Statutory assignment

41–090   [*Delete the reference to Tarbuck case from note 669 and substitute: page* [1220]]
   In the matter of OT Computers Ltd (in administration) [2004] EWCA Civ 653;
   [2004] 2 All E.R. (Comm.) 331; *Freakley v Centre Reinsurance International Co*
   [2005] EWCA Civ 115; [2005] Lloyd's Rep. I.R. 303.

   [*Add to note 672 before 2nd sentence: page* [1220]]
   See *Centre Reinsurance International Co v Curzon Insurance Ltd* [2004]
   EWHC 200 (Ch); [2004] 2 All E.R. (Comm.) 28.

(b) *Motor Insurance*

Road Traffic Act 1988

41–091   [*Add to note 681 after first sentence: page* [1221]]
   cf. Slater v Buckinghamshire County Council [2004] Lloyd's Rep. I.R. 432.

   [*Add to the end of note 690: page* [1222]]
   The defendant to a claim for damages for personal injury is not entitled to
   counterclaim for a breach of this statutory duty for purely economic losses in
   connection with the defendant's liability to the claimant, as opposed to the
   defendant's own injuries: *Bretton v Hancock* [2005] EWCA Civ 404; [2005]
   Lloyd's Rep. I.R. 454 at [42]–[50].

Third parties and uninsured drivers

41–093   [*Delete note 703 and substitute: page* [1223]]
   The current agreement dated August 13, 1999 (and called "Compensation of
   Victims of Uninsured Drivers"), is between the M.I.B. and the Secretary of State
   for the Environment, Transport and the Regions, and applies to claims arising on
   or after October 1, 1999. It is effectively based upon the original 1945 agreement,
   with subsequent agreements in 1946, 1971, 1972 and 1988. A more complex
   scheme (first introduced in 1969) covers the position of untraced drivers. This is
   now governed by the Untraced Drivers Agreement dated February 14, 2003, the
   immediate predecessor to which was the 1996 Agreement. The M.I.B.'s liability
   under the 2003 Agreement is dependent on establishing that the untraced driver
   would have been liable to the victim and that that liability is of a kind required
   to be covered by compulsory insurance under the Road Traffic Act 1988.
   Applicants for compensation under these agreements, however, cannot rely on
   the doctrine of direct effect in the event that there is any shortfall in the cover
   provided by them and the cover required to be legislated by the United Kingdom
   by EC Directives 72/166, 84/5 and 90/232: *Evans v Motor Insurers' Bureau*
   [1999] Lloyd's Rep. I.R. 30. However, in *Evans v Secretary of State for the
   Environment, Transport and the Regions* [2001] EWCA Civ 32; [2002] Lloyd's
   Rep. I.R. 1, at [4], the Court of Appeal indicated that the victim might have the

right to enforce the Agreement pursuant to the Contracts (Rights of Third Parties) Act 1999. Clause 31(5) of the Untraced Drivers Agreement dated February 14, 2003, confirms that the Agreement is intended to benefit the victim. As to the level of compensation obtainable under the agreements, see *Evans v Secretary of State for the Environment, Transport and the Regions* (Case C-63/01) [2004] Lloyd's Rep. I.R. 391 (E.C.J.). As to the relationship between the M.I.B. and the Secretary of State, see *Sharp v Pereira* [1999] Lloyd's Rep. I.R. 242.

[Add at end of note 705: page [1224]]
In *Pickett v Motor Insurers Bureau* [2004] EWCA Civ 6; [2004] Lloyd's Rep. I.R. 513, the Court of Appeal considered whether the M.I.B. was liable under the 1988 Agreement where the claimant, who was also the owner of, but a passenger in, the vehicle, knew that the vehicle was uninsured. The court held that the claimant had not withdrawn her consent to be carried in the vehicle because she had not unambiguously required the vehicle to be stopped so that she could get out, thus permitting the M.I.B. to rely on an exception to liability.

(c) *Reinsurance*

General characteristics

[Note 709: page [1224]]   **41–094**
Update reference to *The Law of Reinsurance in England and Bermuda* to (2nd ed., 2004).

[Add at the end of the second sentence of note 713: page [1225]]
American International Marine Agency of New York Inc v Dandridge [2005] EWHC 829 (Comm); [2005] All ER (D) 48 (May) ("follow the leader" clause).

[Add to the end of note 713: page [1225]]
For a case where the terms of the underlying insurance are summarised in the reinsurance contract itself, see *Toomey v Banco Vitalcio De Espana SA de Seguros y Reasseguros* [2004] EWCA Civ 622; [2005] Lloyd's Rep. I.R. 423.

Liability of the reinsurer

[Line 4 of note 722: page [1226]]   **41–095**
Assicurazioni Generali SpA v CGU International Insurance plc was affirmed, [2004] EWCA Civ 429; [2004] 2 Lloyd's Rep. I.R. 457.

(d) *Insurance against Financial Loss*

Types of financial loss insurance

[Add to the end of note 733: page [1227]]   **41–096**
Pilkington United Kingdom Ltd v CGU Insurance plc [2004] EWCA Civ 23; [2004] Lloyd's Rep. I.R. 891.

CHAPTER 42

RESTRICTIVE AGREEMENTS AND COMPETITION

2. COMPETITION RULES UNDER THE EC TREATY

(a) In General

Purpose of this section

42–004 [*Note 10: page* [1233]]
See now Kerse and Khan, *EC Antitrust Procedure* (5th ed., 2005).

Principal sources of law

42–008 [*Note 22: page* [1234]]
See now *Butterworths Competition Law Handbook* (10th ed., 2005).

European Economic Area

[Page [1235]]
For the position on the EEA Enlargement Agreement, see *http://secretariat. efta.int/Web/EuropeanEconomicArea/EEAAgreement/eeaenlargementagreement*

42–010

(b) *Article 81(1)*

Effect on trade between Member States

[Page [1242]]
The Commission has published *Guidelines on the effect on trade concept in Articles 81 and 82 of the Treaty,* OJ 2004 C101/81.

42–027

(c) *Article 81(3)*

Agreements likely to satisfy Article 81(3)

[Page [1243]]
The Commission has published *Guidelines on the application of Article 81(3) of the Treaty,* OJ 2004 C 101/97.

42–032

Block exemptions currently in force

[Note 106: page [1245]]
Regulation 240/96 was replaced, with effect from May 1, 2004, by Regulation 772/2004, OJ 2004 L 123/11.

42–034

(d) *Application of Article 81 to Specific Agreements*

Mergers

[Page [1247]]
Regulation 4064/89 was replaced, with effect from May 1, 2004, by Regulation 139/2004, OJ 2004 L 24/1.

42–037

Technology transfer agreements

[Page [1254]]
Regulation 240/96 was replaced, with effect from May 1, 2004, by Regulation 772/2004, OJ 2004 L 123/11. The European Commission has also published *Guidelines on the application of Article 81 of the EC Treaty to technology transfer agreements*: OJ [2004] C101/2.

42–056

(e) *Article 82*

Examples of abusive contractual provisions

42–063   *[Page* [1258]]
One of the abusive practices for which the European Commission fined Microsoft 497 million in March 2004 was that it had made the availability of its *Windows Client PC Operating System* conditional upon the simultaneous acquisition of *Windows Media Player: Microsoft* Commission Decision of March 24, 2004; the case is on appeal to the Court of First Instance, Case T-201/04, judgment pending.

Refusal to contract as abusive conduct

42–064   *[Page* [1258]]
One of the abusive practices for which the European Commission fined Microsoft 497 million in March 2004 was that it had refused to supply *Interoperability Information* and allow its use for the purpose of developing and distributing work group server operating system products: *Microsoft* Commission Decision of March 24, 2004; the case is on appeal to the Court of First Instance, Case T-201/04, judgment pending.

(f) *Enforcement at the National Level*

Effect of the Modernisation Regulation

42–067   *[Add at the end of the paragraph: page* [1259]]
The Commission has published a *Notice on the co-operation between the Commission and the courts of the EU Member States in the application of Articles 81 and 82 EC.*[191a]

[191a] OJ 2004 C 101/54

Causes of action in English law

42–071   *[Add to note 199, at the end: page* [1260]]
However, the Court of Appeal reversed the judgment of the High Court, and Crehan was awarded damages for the harm he had suffered: [2004] EWCA Civ 637; [2004] E.C.C. 28.

Role of national competition authorities

42–072   *[Page* [1260]]
The Commission has published a *Notice on Co-operation within the Network of Competition Authorities*, OJ 2004 C 101/43.

(g) *Enforcement at the Community Level*

Commission investigations and adverse decisions

[*Line 12, after "... written and oral rights of defence": page* [1261]]
The Commission has adopted this implementing regulation, Regulation
773/2004, OJ 2004 L 123/18.

42–074

3. United Kingdom Competition Law

(a) *Introduction*

Reform of the law

[*Add, at the end of the paragraph: page* [1262]]
A number of statutory instruments have been adopted to amend the Competition Act in order to make it compatible with the principles of the EC modernisation package. See in particular the Competition Act 1998 and Other Enactments (Amendment) Regulations 2004[213a]; The Competition Act 1998 (Land Agreements Exclusion and Revocation) Order 2004[213b]; the Competition Act 1998 (Determination of Turnover for Penalties)(Amendment) Order 2004[213c]; and the Competition Act 1998 (Appealable Decisions and Revocation of Notification of Excluded Agreements) Regulations 2004.[213d] A further statutory instrument has been adopted containing the rules of the Office of Fair Trading: see the Competition Act 1998 (Office of Fair Trading's Rules) Order 2004.[213e]

42–077

[213a] SI 2004/1261.
[213b] SI 2004/1260.
[213c] SI 2004/1259.
[213d] SI 2004/1078.
[213e] SI 2004/2751.

Guidelines

[*Page* [1264]]
The Guidelines referred to in the text have been replaced by a fresh set, written in the light of the EC Modernisation Regulation and the consequent changes to the Competition Act 1998: they are available on the website of the OFT, *http://www.oft.gov.uk.*

42–082

(b) *The Chapter I Prohibitions: Agreements*

Effect on trade within the United Kingdom

[*Add, at the end of sub-paragraph (ii): page* [1266]]
The Commission has published *Guidelines on the effect on trade concept in Articles 81 and 82 of the Treaty.*[225a] It has also published a *Notice on cooperation within the network of competition authorities.*[225b]

42–087

[225a] OJ 2004 C 101/81.
[225b] OJ 2004 C 101/3.

[Add at the end of sub-paragraph (iv)]
The system of notifying agreements for individual exemption has been abolished by the Competition Act 1998 and Other Enactments (Amendment) Regulations 2004.[227a]

[227a] SI 2004/1261.

Agreements, decisions and concerted practices

42–089 *[Page [1266]]*
The OFT's decision in *Hasbro UK Ltd* was upheld on appeal to the Competition Appeal Tribunal, Case Nos. 1014/1/1/03 and 1015/1/1/03 *Argos Ltd and Littlewoods Ltd v OFT* [2004] CAT 24; [2005] Comp.A.R. 588; see similarly Case Nos. 1021/1/1/03 and 1022/1/1/03 *JJB Sports plc v Office of Fair Trading* [2004] CAT 17; [2005] Comp.A.R. 29.

Relevant differences between the Chapter I prohibition and EC law

42–091 *[Page 1267]]*
The exclusion of vertical agreements from the Chap. I prohibition will be repealed with effect from May 1, 2005 as a result of the Competition Act 1998 (Land Agreements Exclusion and Revocation) Order 2004 (SI 2004/1260).

[Add at the end of sub-paragraph (ii) on page [1267]]
This is no longer the case since the adoption of the OFT's new Guideline *Agreements and concerted practices* OFT 401, December 2004.

Appreciability

42–092 *[Page [1268]]*
Since the adoption of the OFT's new Guideline *Agreements and concerted practices* OFT 401, December 2004, the OFT now applies the same standards on appreciability as the European Commission: see in particular paras 2.15–2.21 of the Guideline.

Schedule 2: competition scrutiny under other enactments

42–101 *[Add at the end of the paragraph: page [1272]]*
Some amendments to Sch.2 are effected by para.49 of the Competition Act 1998 and Other Enactments (Amendment) Regulations 2004.[262a]

[262a] SI 2004/1261.

Schedule 3: "general exclusions"

42–102 *[Add, at the end of the paragraph: page [1272]]*
Some amendments to Sch.3 are effected by para.49 of the Competition Act 1998 and Other Enactments (Amendment) Regulations 2004.[262b]

[262b] SI 2004/1261.

Schedule 3, para.2: s.21(2) agreements

[*Page* [1272]]
Schedule 3, para.2 is repealed with effect from May 1, 2007 by the Competition Act 1998 and Other Enactments (Amendment) Regulations 2004.[264a]

42–104

[264a] SI 2004/1261.

Schedule 3, para.4: services of general economic interest

[*Note 268: page* [1273]]
See now OFT Guideline 421 *Services of general economic interest* OFT 421, December 2004.

42–106

Repeal of the exclusion order for vertical agreements

[*Page* [1275]]
The exclusion of vertical agreements from the Chap. I prohibition will be repealed with effect from May 1, 2005 as a result of the Competition Act 1998 (Land Agreements Exclusion and Revocation) Order 2004 (SI 2004/1260). The OFT has adopted a new Guideline *Vertical agreements* OFT 419, December 2004 explaining the application of the Competition Act 1998 to vertical agreements.

42–115

Sections 4 and 5: individual exemption

[*Page* [1277]]
The system of notifying agreements for individual exemption has been abolished by the Competition Act 1998 and Other Enactments (Amendment) Regulations 2004 (SI 2004/1261).

42–118

Sections 12–16: notification

[*Page* [1278]]
The system of notifying agreements for individual exemption has been abolished by the Competition Act 1998 and Other Enactments (Amendment) Regulations 2004 (SI 2004/1261).

42–122

(c) *The Chapter II Prohibition: Abuse of a Dominant Position*

Abuse of a dominant position

[*Page* [1280]]
Note the new Guidelines issued by the OFT in December 2004, in particular *Abuse of dominant position* OFT 402; *Market definition* OFT 403; and *Assessment of market power* OFT 415.

42–128

Section 20–24: notification

42–132   *[Page* [1281]]
The system of notifying conduct to the OFT has been abolished by the Competition Act 1998 and Other Enactments (Amendment) Regulations 2004.[310a]

[310a] SI 2004/1261.

(e) *Investigation and Enforcement*

Power to investigate

42–137   *[Note 327: page* [1283]]
See now *Powers of investigation* OFT 404, December 2004.

Penalties

42–139   *[Add to text after note 338: page* [1284]]
The maximum penalty is now calculated by reference to worldwide turnover rather than UK turnover as a result of the Competition Act 1998 (Determination of Turnover for Penalties) (Amendment) Order 2004.[338a]

[338a] SI 2004/1259.

[Note 340: page [1283]]
See now *OFT's Guidance as the appropriate amount of a penalty* OFT 423, December 2004.

Cartel offence

42–141   *[Note 349, page* [1284]]
See now *Powers for investigating criminal cartels* OFT 515, January 2004.

(g) *The Competition Appeal Tribunal*

The Competition Appeal Tribunal

42–145   *[Add to line 9, after "... apply from June 20, 2003": page* [1286]]
The Competition Appeal Tribunal (Amendment and Communications Act Appeal) Rules 2004[358a] amend the Competition Appeal Tribunal Rules 2003.

[358a] SI 2004/2068.

CHAPTER 43

SALE OF GOODS

2. FORMATION OF THE CONTRACT

(a) *Contract of Sale*

Transactions outside the Act

43–013 [*Add to note 59: page* [1297]]
The Trading Stamps Act 1964 has been repealed by the Regulatory Reform (Trading Stamps) Order 2005 (SI 2005/871).

43–015 [*Add to note 73: page* [1299]]
The Consumer Credit Bill (at present before Parliament) will remove the financial limit: see above, para.38–012A.

Conditional sale agreements

43–016 [*Add to note 66: page* [1200]]
The Consumer Credit Bill (at present before Parliament) will remove the financial limit: see above, para.38–012A.

Credit-sale agreements

43–017 [*Add to note 82: page* [1299]]
The Consumer Credit Bill (at present before Parliament) will remove the financial limit: see above, para.38–012A.

3. TERMS OF THE CONTRACT

(a) *Conditions, Warranties, Misrepresentations and Puffs*

Misrepresentations external to the contract

[*Add to note 176: page* [1311]]
For a recent example see *Thompson v Christie Manson & Woods Ltd* [2004] EWHC 1101 (QB) (attribution of vase by auctioneer without warning of non-finality of attributions). The decision was reversed [2005] EWCA Civ 555; [2005] P.N.L.R. 38.

43–046

Effect of breach of condition

[*Add to note 210: page* [1313]]
See discussion of the view that the Act confers no right of second tender in two Scottish cases, *JH Ritchie Ltd v Lloyd Ltd* 2005 S.L.T. 64 and *Lamarra v Capital Bank plc* 2005 S.L.T. (Sh Ct) 21. However, it should be borne in mind that in Scots law the right to reject is not based on the concept of condition.

43–053

(b) *Implied Terms*

(iii) *Implied Terms about Quality and Fitness for Purpose*

Satisfactory quality

[*Add to note 346: page* [1330]]
Bramhill v Edwards [2004] EWCA Civ 403; [2004] 2 Lloyd's Rep. 653 (American mobile home slightly wider than UK regulations permitted; not of unsatisfactory quality, objective test considered). See a note by Twigg-Flesner (2005) 121 L.Q.R. 205.

43–086

Reliance may be rebutted

[*Add to note 382: page* [1334]]
The *Britvic* case is discussed by Sealy [2003] C.L.J. 260.

43–096

Reasonably fit for purpose

[*Add to note 392: page* [1335]]
It has been held that the seller of a software package may be liable if he does not make clear, at least in general terms, that not all packages are compatible: *Brocket v DGS Retail Ltd* [2004] C.L. Jan. 322.

43–097

(v) *Exclusion of Terms Implied by Sections 13, 14 and 15*

Dealing as consumer

[*Add to note 431: page* [1339]]
The *R & B* case was followed in *Feldaroll Foundry plc v Hermes Leasing (London) Ltd* [2004] EWCA Civ 747 (Lamborghini for managing director of

43–106

finance company: company dealt as consumer). But see Twigg-Flesner (2005) 121 L.Q.R. 41.

4. CONSUMER PROTECTION

(a) *Additional Remedies of the Buyer in Consumer Cases*

Enforcement

43–124   *[Add to note 516: page* [1349]]
See Harris (2003) 119 L.Q.R. 541.

Rescission

43–127   *[Add to note 521: page* [1350]]
See a note on rescission under the Regulations by Hogg in [2003] S.L.T. 277.

(b) *Cancellation Rights*

43–135—   *[Pages* [1353]–[1355]]
43–137   The cancellation rights referred to in paras 43–135—43–137 are discussed by Hellwege [2004] Camb. L.J. 712. See also the cancellation rights conferred by the Supply of Extended Warranties on Domestic Electrical Goods Order 2005 (SI 2005/37).

Consumer credit transactions

43–135   *[Add to note 535: page* [1353]]
The Consumer Credit Bill (see above, para.38–012A) will remove the financial limit.

Consumer Protection (Cancellation of Contracts concluded away from Business Premises) Regulations 1987

43–136   *[Add to end of note 540: page* [1353]]
SI 2003/1400.

Consumer Protection (Distance Selling) Regulations 2000

43–137   *[Page* [1354]]
These regulations have been amended by the Consumer Protection (Distance Selling) (Amendment) Regulations 2005 (SI 2005/689). See also the amendments effected by SI 2004/2095, reg.25, SI 2005/55.
The Consumer Credit (Disclosure of Information) Regulations 2004 (SI 2004/1481) (see para.38–070, above) do not apply to distance contracts (as defined in reg.1(2) of those Regulations).

(d) *Consumer Guarantees*

Consumer guarantees

[*Page* [1360]]
See also the Supply of Extended Warranties on Domestic Electrical Goods Order 2005 (SI 2005/37).

43–155

(e) *Other Enactments*

Enterprise Act 2002

[*Add to note 621: page* [1361]]
See SI 2003/1368, SI 2003/1374, SI 2003/1375, SI 2003/1593, SI 2004/935, SI 2004/1517, SI 2004/2095, SI 2005/917.

43–157

Advertisements etc

[*Add to note 627: page* [1361]]
and amended by SI 2005/871.

43–159

[*Add to note 630*]
See SI 2003/3183.

[*Amend the text to note 633: page* [1361]]
The Price Marking Order 1999 has been revoked and replaced by the Price Marking Order 2004 (SI 2004/102).

5. Effects of the Contract

(a) *Transfer of Property as between Seller and Buyer*

Materials not yet incorporated

[*Add to note 706: page* [1371]]
But see *Petromec Inc v Petroleo Brasileiro SA Petrobas* [2004] EWHC 1180 (Comm); [2005] 1 Lloyd's Rep. 219 at [36].

43–187

"Romalpa" clauses: retention of title

[*Page* [1378]]
In *Benford Ltd v Lopecan SL* [2004] EWHC 1897 (Comm); [2004] 2 Lloyd's Rep. 618 the question was raised (but not answered) as to whether a retention of title clause would be effective if there was a defence to a claim for the price of the goods (at [18]).

43–203

Voluntary agreements

43–214   *[Page* [1386]]
Correct the title of this paragraph to read **Voluntary arrangements**

(c) *Transfer of Title*

(i) *Sale by Person not the Owner*

43–229A   *[Add new paragraph after paragraph 229: page* [1392]]
Estoppel by judgment. Where, in an action between two parties brought to determine the ownership of goods, title to the goods is established by judgment, the unsuccessful party will be estopped *per rem judicatam* from claiming the goods and that estoppel will bind also his privies, *i.e.* those claiming title from or through him, but only if the title claimed was acquired after (and not before) the date of the judgment.[900a]

[900a] *Powell v Wiltshire* [2004] EWCA Civ 534; [2005] Q.B. 117.

Sales under special powers or court orders

43–233   *[Add to note 908: page* [1393]]
S.138B of the Supreme Court Act 1981 has been repealed by s.109(3) and Sch.10 of the Courts Act 2003 and replaced by Sch.7, para.10 of that Act.

[Add to note 911: page [1393]]
Police Reform Act 2002, Sch.4, para.10.

[Add to note 912: page [1394]]
Police Reform Act 2002, Sch.4, para.10.

(ii) *Effect on Title of Writs of Execution*

Effect on title of writs of execution

43–260   *[Page* [1403]]
S.138 of the Supreme Court Act 1981 has been repealed by s.109(3) and Sch.10 of the Courts Act 2003 and replaced by the provisions contained in Sch.7 to that Act.

(iii) *Effect of Limitation*

43–261A   *[Insert new paragraph 43–261A: page* [1404]]
Actions for recovery of property obtained through unlawful conduct etc.
By s.27A of the Limitation Act 1980 (inserted by s.288 of the Proceeds of Crime Act 2002) none of the time limits given in the preceding provisions of the 1980 Act apply to any proceedings under Ch.2 of Pt 5 of the 2002 Act (civil recovery by the Director of the Asset Recovery Agency of proceeds of unlawful conduct). The Director has 12 years in which to bring proceedings for a recovery order from the date on which his cause of action accrued. Moreover, if proceedings are

started by the Director for a recovery order in respect of a chattel, s.3(2) of the 1980 Act does not prevent a claimant from asserting on an application under s.281 of the 2002 Act (victims of theft, etc.) that the property belongs to him, or the court making a declaration in his favour under that section. If the court makes such a declaration, his title to the chattel is to be treated as not having been extinguished by s.3(2) of the 1980 Act.

6. Performance of the Contract

(b) Rules Governing Delivery

(ii) Time for Delivery

[Add new paragraph 43–274A: page [1409]]

Variation of delivery time. The buyer may agree to an extension of the time fixed for delivery and such an agreement will constitute an effective variation of the contract of sale provided that sufficient consideration to support the variation moves from the promisee.[1058a]

43–274A

[1058a] *South Caribbean Trading Ltd v Trafigura Beheer BV* [2004] EWHC 2676 (Comm); [2005] 1 Lloyd's Rep. 128.

Waiver of delivery time

[Add to note 1059: page [1409]]

See also *Fleming & Wendeln GmbH & Co v Sanofi SA/AG* [2003] EWHC 561 (QB); [2003] 2 Lloyd's Rep. 473. Contrast *South Caribbean Trading Ltd v Trafigura Beheer BV*, above, at [112] (estoppel cannot be invoked where unconscionable to do so).

43–275

(c) Examination and Acceptance

Lapse of reasonable time

[Add to note 1182: page [1424]]

The emphasis of *Jones v Gallagher* (now reported at [2005] 1 Lloyd's Rep. 377) seems to be that the question is one of fact. See also *Hawkins v C.D. Bramall plc*, HH Judge Dowse, [2004] C.L. June 94 (car rejected after six days but buyer continued to drive it for nine months and 14,000 miles, during which car damaged in collision: held nothing to prevent reliance on original rejection); *A.C. Daniels & Co Ltd v Jungwoo Logic*, Q.B.D. (HH Judge Hicks Q.C., April 14, 2000 (injection mould: valid rejection after 13 months); *Lamorra v Capital Bank plc*, below, n.1187a (Range Rover returned after two months and 6000 miles, but had been rejected soon after delivery). On *Jones v Gallagher* see Bradgate (2004) 120 L.Q.R. 558; and on *Clegg v Olle Andersson* see Reynolds (2003) 119 L.Q.R. 544.

43–310

Attempts at repair

43–311   [*Insert new note 1187a at end of paragraph: page* [1424]]
Two Scottish cases consider the problem of attempts to repair defective goods. In the first, *JH Ritchie Ltd v Lloyd Ltd* 2005 S.L.T. 64, the defect was rectified but the vendor refused to say what the defect had been. The buyer, who purported to reject, was held by a majority of an Extra Division of the Court of Session to have no right to do so as the goods were compliant on final delivery. The dissenting opinion of Lord Marnoch, pointing out that the Act does not envisage the possibility that the defect is not adequately remedied, and that there is nothing in it permitting a second tender, is persuasive. In the second, *Lamarra v Capital Bank plc* 2005 S.L.T. (Sh Ct) 21, a new and very expensive Range Rover acquired suffered from many defects and despite attempts at rectification it was held that it had not at the time of delivery come within the basic definition of satisfactory quality, and that the Act (actually the Supply of Goods (Implied Terms) Act 1973, as the case was one of hire-purchase) conferred no right of second tender.

7. REMEDIES OF THE SELLER

(a) *Rights of Unpaid Seller against the Goods*

(i) *Unpaid Seller's Lien*

Waiver of lien

43–351   [*Add to note 1388 at end: page* [1441]]
cf. Clifford Harris & Co v Solland International Ltd [2005] EWHC 141 (Ch); [2005] 2 All E.R. 334.

8. REMEDIES OF THE BUYER

(a) *Damages for Non-Delivery*

Damages where there is an available market

43–416   [*Add to notes 1821 and 1823: page* [1480]]
On the possible relevance of the buyer's lack of financial resources, see above paras 26–095A—26–095D, 26–097.

Loss of future business

43–430   [*Add to note 1926: page* [1491]]
cf. Jackson v Royal Bank of Scotland [2005] UKHL 3; [2005] 1 W.L.R. 377 (loss of repeat orders caused by breach of obligation to maintain confidence; see Vol.I, para.26–055.)

(c) *Damages for Defective Quality*

(i) *Diminution in Value*

Prima facie rule only

[Add to note 1988; page [1498]]   **43–440**
See also *Louis Dreyfus Trading Ltd v Reliance Trading Ltd* [2004] EWHC 525
(Comm); [2004] 2 Lloyd's Rep. 243.

Buyer performing sub-contract despite seller's breach

[Add to note 1999: page [1499]]   **43–442**
See the *Louis Dreyfus* case, above (parties contemplated sale of the same
goods to the sub-buyer under a specific contract).

(ii) *Losses other than Diminution in Value*

Loss of future business

[Add to note 2045: page [1505]]   **43–452**
cf. also *Jackson v Bank of Scotland* [2005] UKHL 3; [2005] 1 W.L.R. 377 (see
Vol.I, paras 26–055, 26–062A).

Compensation paid to sub-buyers in a series of "string contracts"

This paragraph was cited in the *Louis Dreyfus* case, above, at [24].   **43–460**

[Add to note 2095 at end: page [1510]]   **43–461**
See also the *Louis Dreyfus* case, above.

(d) *Other Remedies of the Buyer*

Specific performance

[Add to note 2124: page [1513]]   **43–466**
See Harris, (2003) 119 L.Q.R. 541.

CHAPTER 44

SURETYSHIP

1. IN GENERAL

Guarantees and indemnities: the significance of the distinction

44–012 *[Add new text at end of paragraph: page* [1528]

Thirdly, certain other rules of law apply to guarantees (where only a secondary liability is undertaken) but not to indemnities (where a primary liability is undertaken), for example, the rule that any material variation of the contract between the debtor and the creditor will in principle discharge a guarantor but not a person undertaking a primary liability.[48a]

[48a] *Holme v Brunskill* (1877) 3 Q.B.D. 495 (on which see Main Work, paras 44–089 *et seq.*); *Marubeni Hong Kong and South China Ltd v The Mongolian Government* [2005] EWCA Civ 395; [2005] 1 W.L.R. 2497.

Guarantees and indemnities: the distinction itself

[Page [1528]

44–013

The first sentence of this paragraph was quoted by the Court of Appeal with apparent approval in *Marubeni Hong Kong and South China Ltd v The Mongolian Government* [2005] EWCA Civ 395; [2005] 1 W.L.R. 2497 at [20].

[Add new text after note 49: page [1528]

In this respect, while the presence or absence of the language of "guarantee" in the document is not conclusive, outside the context of documents issued by banks (on which see Main Work, para.44–014 performance bonds), the absence of language appropriate to provide for the creditor "the additional security of a demand bond" creates a strong presumption in favour of a merely secondary liability.[49a]

[49a] *Marubeni Hong Kong and South China Ltd v The Mongolian Government* [2005] EWCA Civ 395; [2005] 1 W.L.R. 2497 at [30].

Performance guarantees

[Add new text after note 58: page [1529]

44–014

However, it has been held that cases where documents are issued by banks which are "described as, or assumed to be, performance bonds . . . provide no useful analogy for interpreting a document which was not issued by a bank and which contains no overt indication of an intention to create a performance bond or anything analogous to it."[58a]

[58a] *Marubeni Hong Kong and South China Ltd v The Mongolian Government* [2005] EWCA Civ 395; [2005] 1 W.L.R. 2497 at [28] *per* Carnwath L.J.

4. CONSTRUCTION OF THE CONTRACT

Impact of modern approach to construction

[Add to text at end of paragraph: page [1555]]

44–057

On the other hand, in *Vodafone Ltd v GNT Holdings (UK) Ltd*[277a] the High Court applied the "new approach" to construction found in *Investors Compensation Scheme Ltd v West Bromwich Building Society*[277b] to the construction of a guarantee. There a director of a company, company A, had signed on its notepaper a guarantee of the obligations of its subsidiary, company B. The guarantee was expressed to be for the benefit of company C. However, company B had entered an agreement not with C but with company D, which was in the same group of companies as company C. Company C was merely a holding company and no company in the group other than company D had entered such an agreement. In these circumstances, it was held that the guarantee was given by company A in respect of company C's liabilities to *company D*; the circumstances led the judge "to the conclusion that something went wrong with the drafting of the [guarantee] letter. . . . To construe it literally would be a commercial nonsense."[277c] In *Static Control Components (Europe) Ltd v Egan*[277d] the

Court of Appeal agreed that the ordinary principles of contractual construction as set out in *Prenn v Simmonds*[277e] and the *Investors Compensation Scheme* case applied equally to contracts of guarantee, even where there was no ambiguity in the words used by the document.[277f] Moreover, if the court's purpose is the "ascertainment of the meaning of the document by the objective approach described by the House of Lords" in these cases, then "it may be that the concept that a guarantee should be 'strictly construed' now adds nothing."[277g] The Court of Appeal therefore construed a guarantee in respect of "the price of all Trade Goods that you may supply to the trader" as in the context applying to past debts in respect of goods supplied as well as future ones: any other construction would make "no commercial sense" where the guarantee had been preceded by a guarantee for a lesser amount in respect of existing debts and where the purpose of the later guarantee was clearly known by the guarantor to cover existing indebtedness beyond this lesser amount.[277h] By contrast, in *Dumford Trading AG v OAO Atlantrybflot*[277i] a differently constituted Court of Appeal considered that (apart from the doctrines of rectification or misnomer[277j]), where an existing person is named as guarantor in the guarantee document, there is a danger that extrinsic evidence from the surrounding matrix of facts could create an ambiguity otherwise not present.[277k] Where, therefore, company A in a group of companies was identified as guarantor by the document of guarantee, the court should not look at extrinsic evidence (such as the postal address given for this company) so as to construe this unambiguous reference as being to company B, a very similarly-named company in the same group.[277l]

[277a] [2004] All E.R. (D) 194 (Mar.).

[277b] [1998] 1 W.L.R. 896.

[277c] [2004] All E.R. (D) 194 (Mar.) at [74] *per* Christopher Moger Q.C. sitting as a deputy judge of the High Court. *cf. Amalgamated Investment & Property Co Ltd (In Liquidation) v Texas Commerce International Bank Ltd* [1982] Q.B. 84 (guarantee expressed on its terms to cover loan by bank held in the "factual matrix" of the contract also to cover loan by bank's subsidiary).

[277d] [2004] EWCA Civ 392; [2004] 2 Lloyd's Rep. 429.

[277e] [1971] 1 W.L.R. 1381, 1385.

[277f] [2004] EWCA Civ 392 at [13], [28].

[277g] *ibid.*, at [19] *per* Holman J.

[277h] *ibid.*, at [15]–[16], [31]–[32]. This construction could also be supported by the reference in the later guarantee document to a guarantee of the "whole debt": *ibid.*, at [17], [36].

[277i] [2005] EWCA Civ 25; [2005] 1 Lloyd's Rep. 289. It is to be noted that these observations were made in the context of an application for summary judgment under Pt 24 CPR.

[277j] On which see Main Work, paras 5–092—5–113 and 12–075 respectively.

[277k] [2005] EWCA Civ 25 at [36]; [2005] 1 Lloyd's Rep. 289.

[277l] *ibid.*

Conditional guarantees

44–060   *[Add new note 285a at the end of the first sentence*: page [1556]

[285a] It has been held that English law does not recognise any wider relief in equity based on the mere expectation of a guarantor than is afforded by the determination whether or not the guarantee is conditional on some circumstance, for example, the execution of a guarantee by a third person: *Capital Bank Cashflow Finance Ltd v Southall* [2004] EWCA Civ 817; [2004] 2 All E.R. (Comm.) 675 at [16], discussing *Bleyer v NevilleJefferson Advertising Pty Ltd* (NSW, 1987) (unreported).

[Add new text after note 289: page [1556]

While a guarantee may also be held to be conditional on the execution of a second guarantee on identical terms contained in a different document, in this situation the first guarantee document does not on its face point to a conclusion that execution of the second is necessary for the first guarantee's validity and the fact that all the documents formed part of some larger transaction is not by itself sufficient.[289a]

[289a] *Capital Bank Cashflow Finance Ltd v Southall* [2004] EWCA Civ 817; [2004] 2 All E.R. (Comm.) 675 at [17].

6. DISCHARGE OF SURETY

(b) *Discharge of Surety through Discharge of Principal Debtor*

Discharge of debtor through debtor's breach of contract

[*Add text at end of paragraph: page* [1570]]   **44–085**
For example, in *Manx Electricity Authority v J P Morgan Chase Bank*[404a] the Court of Appeal held that where the main contract is breached by the principal debtor, a guarantor under a performance guarantee remained liable under it to the creditor even where the contract guaranteed had subsequently ceased to exist. "A repudiatory breach [by the debtor] will in the normal course of events lead to the termination of the repudiated contract (although of course it may not do so). It would be extraordinary if a performance guarantee was intended to case to operate in exactly the situation in which its beneficiary most needs it—when the contract has failed because the principal has repudiated it."[404b]

[404a] [2003] EWCA Civ 1324; 2003 WL 22187638.
[404b] *ibid.*, at [37] *per* Rix L.J. See similarly at [47] *per* Chadwick L.J.

Discharge of debtor by operation of law

[*note 415: page* [1572]]   **44–088**
Hindcastle Ltd v Barbara Attenborough Associates Ltd [1997] A.C. 10 was applied in *Scottish Widows plc v Tripipatkal* [2003] EWHC 1874 (Ch); [2003] B.P.I.R. 1413.

(c) *Discharge of Surety through Variation of Contract between Debtor and Creditor*

Variation of contract between creditor and debtor

[*Add to text of note 418 after reference to Howard de Walden Estates Ltd v Pasta*   **44–089**
Place Ltd: page [1572]]
Marubeni Hong Kong and South China Ltd v Government of Mongolia [2004] EWHC 471 (Comm); [2004] 2 Lloyd's Rep. 198 at [58]–[60]; affd. [2005] EWCA Civ 395; [2005] 1 W.L.R. 2497.

(d) *Discharge of Surety on Other Grounds*

Altering the terms of guarantee

44–099   [*Add to second sentence after "held to be whether" in line 5: page* [1576]]
"there is an alteration which affects the very nature and character of the instrument" or

[*Note 457: page* [1576]]
Amend reference to *Raiffeisen Zentralbank Osterreich AG v Crosseas Shipping Ltd* to: [2000] 1 W.L.R. 1135, 1146–1148 *per* Potter L.J.

[*Add at end of text of note 457: page* [1576]]
cf. Bank of Scotland v Henry Butcher & Co [2003] EWCA Civ 67; [2003] 2 All E.R. (Comm.) 557 at [72]–[74] where an alteration by some co-guarantors was held to be plainly beneficial to the others who were not as a result discharged.